PATHWAYS
to COMPETENCE
for YOUNG CHILDREN

A Parenting
Program

PATHWAYS to COMPETENCE for YOUNG CHILDREN

A Parenting Program

by

Sarah Landy, Ph.D.
University of Toronto
and Hincks-Dellcrest Institute
Ontario, Canada

and

Elizabeth Thompson, Ph.D.
University of Toronto
and The Hospital for Sick Children
Ontario, Canada

·P A U L·H·
BROOKES
PUBLISHING C⁰.®

Baltimore • London • Sydney

Paul H. Brookes Publishing Co.
Post Office Box 10624
Baltimore, Maryland 21285-0624

www.brookespublishing.com

Typeset by Integrated Publishing Solutions, Grand Rapids, Michigan.
Manufactured in the United States of America by
Versa Press, East Peoria, Illinois.

The cover photo of Ryan and Tina Schuler is used courtesy of Dr. Harry Hahne. The illustration of the tree used in Figure 7.1, Handout 1.3, and the Supplemental Materials is used courtesy of Michelle Fortnum. Illustrations for the overheads of parenting roles used in Figure 7.1 and in the Supplemental Materials are courtesy of Ana Debem. Illustrations for Handouts 3.5a and b are courtesy of Joanne Galantino.

Library of Congress Cataloging-in-Publication Data

Landy, Sarah.
    Pathways to competence for young children : a parenting program / Sarah Landy and Elizabeth Thompson.
        p.   cm.
    Includes bibliographical references.
    ISBN-13: 978-1-55766-862-2 (pbk.)
    ISBN-10: 1-55766-862-0 (pbk.)
    ISBN-13: 978-1-55766-896-7 (CD-ROM)
    ISBN-10: 1-55766-896-5 (CD-ROM)
        1. Parenting—Study and teaching.   2. Child development—Study and teaching.   I. Thompson, Elizabeth, 1955–   II. Title.
    HQ755.7L34 2006
    305.231—dc22
                                                                                        2006012488

British Library Cataloguing in Publication data are available from the British Library.

CONTENTS

CD-ROM CONTENTS

About the Authors
About this CD-ROM
Order Form

Handouts by Step

Step 9   Encouraging Concentration, Planning, and Problem Solving

Step 10   Encouraging Social Competence, Empathy, and Caring Behavior

ABOUT THE AUTHORS

Sarah Landy, Ph.D., C. Psych., Assistant Professor, University of Toronto; Hincks-Dellcrest Institute, 114 Maitland Street, Toronto, Ontario, Canada

Sarah Landy is a developmental-clinical psychologist who has worked for more than 20 years in early intervention. She has a doctorate from the University of Saskatchewan and completed postdoctoral fellowships with noted early childhood experts Dr. T. Berry Brazelton at the Child Development Unit, Harvard University, and Dr. Stanley Greenspan at the University of Washington. Dr. Landy has worked as a clinician, home visitor, early intervention program developer, clinical and program director, researcher, and teacher. Her research interests include young children with aggression and behavior problems, very high risk traumatized parents, assessment of children with autism spectrum disorder and severe difficulties with emotion regulation, and evaluation of community-based early intervention programs. She is on faculty at the University of Toronto and also teaches in the Certificate in Infant Mental Health program at York University. She also consults and provides training at a number of programs and organizations including the Invest in Kids Foundation, Toronto Department of Public Health, Parents for Better Beginnings, and many Community Action Program for Children programs. She has written more than 50 articles and chapters and two books for Paul H. Brookes Publishing Co., *Pathways to Competence: Enhancing the Emotional and Social Development of Young Children* (2002) and *Early Intervention with Multi-Risk Families: An Integrative Approach* (co-authored with Rosanne Menna, 2006). Dr. Landy has received the Canadian Psychological Foundation award for contribution to knowledge, the YWCA Women of Distinction award, and the Canadian Psychological Association award for distinguished contribution to the community.

Elizabeth Thompson, Ph.D., Lecturer and Psychologist, University of Toronto and The Hospital for Sick Children, 555 University Avenue, Toronto, Ontario, Canada

Elizabeth Thompson is a psychologist and medical educator who has worked with families and children for more than 25 years. She received her doctorate in child psychology from the University of Toronto. Dr. Thompson has researched, taught, and practiced in early intervention in several Canadian provinces. She is on faculty at the University of Toronto and has taught at a number of universities both in Canada and in the United States. She also teaches in the department of developmental pediatrics at The Hospital for Sick Children in Toronto, where she instructs medical students, pediatric residents, and pediatricians in developmental pediatrics. Dr. Thompson conducts research in medical education and early intervention and has written articles and presented at numerous professional conferences. She has developed early intervention programs with First Nations children in the Canadian Artic and has worked with families in a variety of multicultural settings. Dr. Thompson has also worked as a school psychologist and in mental health agencies where she developed parenting groups for parents with children who have developmental and behavioral difficulties. She lives in Gilbert, Arizona.

FOR THE READER

Pathways to Competence for Young Children: A Parenting Program is a comprehensive yet flexible and practical program designed for parent educators and any other professionals working with children and families (e.g., social workers, psychologists, home visitors, early childhood educators). The curriculum is intended for parents of young children from birth to approximately age 7 who are looking for ways to help their children develop competencies in all areas of their lives: physical, emotional, social, and behavioral. It is also intended to help parents gain confidence and skills needed to be better parents and to understand how their own upbringing and temperaments interact with their children's to form the bonds they share with their children.

This program consists of a manual and a CD-ROM. The manual covers the background of the program, how and why it works, and each of the program Steps in detail. The CD-ROM includes all of the Handouts referenced in each of the Steps and the supplementary materials (also provided in Section III of the manual) that help users advertise and conduct the program. The materials on the CD-ROM are photocopiable and can be used for many different types of groups, multiple times.

Pathways to Competence for Young Children: A Parenting Program is a curriculum for parents based on the book *Pathways to Competence: Encouraging Healthy Social and Emotional Development in Young Children* by Sarah Landy (2002, Paul H. Brookes Publishing Co.). For more information on this work, visit http://www.brookespublishing.com/store /books/landy-577x/index.htm

Although *Pathways to Competence for Young Children* is based on extensive research reviewed for *Pathways to Competence* (2002) as well as newer research since that book's publication, because this is intended to be used as an outline for group sessions, research citations have been limited in the Steps and Handouts themselves to make the program more user-friendly. Please refer to *Pathways to Competence* (2002) for a full listing of references used to support the information and strategies provided in this program.

_EDGMENTS

Many people have contributed ideas for _Pathways to Competence for Young Children: A Parenting Program,_ and they have added to our knowledge of how to help parents encourage their children's development.

First, we would like to thank the many parents who have participated in the parenting groups and who have helped us to understand their joys and challenges in raising their children and fostering their healthy emotional and social development.

Many friends and colleagues have contributed significantly to making the _Pathways to Competence for Young Children Parenting Program_ effective. Their ideas, support, and insightful suggestions and their commitment to helping families have helped us to enrich the program. These individuals include Susan Harris, Barbara Sheppard, Norma Sockett-Dimarco, and Susan Wright. We would like to thank Susan Harris and Susan Wright for their suggestion of the tree metaphor and some of the self-care activities. Their work in supporting mothers who had been victims of family violence provided a wonderful and very successful model.

In the development of an earlier version of the Pathways to Competence for Young Children Parenting Program, which was called Helping Encourage Affect Regulation (HEAR), a number of friends and colleagues at the former Toronto District School Board helped by offering the program in schools as well as providing ideas from their experiences that added to our knowledge about how best to provide the program. Special thanks go to Janet Li, Dr. Debbie Minden, Dr. Edite Ozols, Hannah Palansky, Dr. Dorothy Pullan, Dr. Maya Rethazi, and Pauline Tsui for their feedback on using the program with parents in schools.

Many pediatricians completing fellowships in Developmental and Behavioral Pediatrics at The Hospital for Sick Children, Toronto, Canada, have served as co-leaders of the parent groups. We want to acknowledge Sherri Baine, Janine Flanagan, Dr. Karen Harman, Dr. Caroline Hunt, Dr. Tammy Kagan-Kushner, Dr. Tara Kennedy, Dr. Anne Kuwamura, and Dr. Nikki Stokreff-Jones for their contributions to the program. Their desire to understand children's social and emotional development and their willingness to make it a part of their assessment and intervention in pediatric practice have played valuable roles in the production of these materials. Thanks especially to Dr. Wendy Roberts, whose support as a friend and colleague over the years has meant a great deal and has inspired us to go the extra mile in the service of children.

We would also like to thank Dr. Freda Martyn and Dr. Edite Ozols for their contributions in bringing the program to Latvia and Jamaica, respectively, and supporting its use there. Also, we thank Dana Brynelsen for supporting the use of the program in British Columbia and for all of her wonderful contributions to fostering the optimal development of young children.

We are indebted to the wonderful support of the staff at Paul H. Brookes Publishing Co. Our special thanks go to Senior Acquisitions Editor Jessica Allan, who supported the development of the early version of this book. As always I am very grateful for her patience and understanding as the book was developed. We are also grateful to Senior Book Production Editor Leslie Eckard, who took the book through the process of final production and brought innumerable ideas for improving the final text and making it more understandable for parents and others who will use it.

We would like to thank Mary Damianakis, dear friend, who served as our research assistant in writing this book. Her support in so many ways in preparing the manuscript was invaluable and made the task far less onerous.

Thanks to Ana Debem, Michelle Fortnum, and Joanne Galantino for creating artwork to illustrate the concepts. Also to Ryan and Tina Schuler, good friends, for posing for the cover.

Finally, we would like to thank our families for their love and support, which has meant so much to us. Elizabeth would like to thank Nadine, Bruce, Debra, and Carol and her five wonderful nephews and nieces and a great niece who bring so much pleasure—Nathan, Matthew, Joshua, Benjamin, Billy, and Jessie. Her parents, Dorothy and Clarence, were wonderful models of parents who created an environment of unconditional love and a secure place from which to explore the world.

To my children and grandchildren,
who continue to remind me of the joys of being a parent
and who bring new excitement into my life
—SL

To my husband Harry,
one of God's most precious gifts to me,
whose love brings me great joy every day,
making life a great adventure
—ET

WHAT TO KNOW BEFORE STARTING A PATHWAYS TO COMPETENCE FOR YOUNG CHILDREN PARENTING PROGRAM

CHAPTER 1

INTRODUCTION AND OVERVIEW

Most parents want to do the best job they can in bringing up their children. They want their children to grow up to be happy; to have qualities such as positive self-esteem, empathy, and caring for others; to have good problem-solving skills; to do well in school; and to have courage and determination. Parents identify raising children as one of their most important roles; yet, they are often unsure about how best to parent. Families of all types are facing unprecedented stresses in today's world, and this can make helping children grow up to be successful, emotionally mature adults a challenging task. The evolution from childhood to adulthood is not only affected by parents' interactions with their children but also by children's traits and competencies. Children's temperaments and abilities and their interactions with parents and other people in the community in which they live all play a crucial role in creating the adults that they will become. Still, parents play a crucial role in providing an optimal environment and an emotionally safe and secure place from which their children can explore the world, learn about relationships, and eventually find fulfilling lives through work, satisfying relationships, and meaningful activities. This role is especially important during a child's earliest years.

How much do parents know about raising children? Recent surveys have found that parents at different socioeconomic levels answered approximately 65% of questions about child development and parenting correctly (Oldershaw, 2002; Reich, 2005). Most parents identify enhancing the emotional and social development of children as the most important aspect of child rearing but admit that it is the one they know the least about (Oldershaw, 2002; Yankelovich & DYG, Inc., 2000). Parents know some general principles of parenting, and yet they are still concerned about getting them right with their own children. Every parent wonders whether he or she is doing the right things with his or her child or children, what to expect at different developmental stages, and if a certain behavior is normal or something he or she should be concerned about. This is even more of a challenge if a child has symptoms that affect his or her adjustment in the home or child care, such as excessive separation anxiety or extreme noncompliance and aggression.

Aware of their need for information and support in raising their children, parents want to know about their own particular child or children's development and the best ways to parent so as to give them the best possible start in life. To get answers to their questions, most parents turn to their child's doctor or other professionals, a spouse or partner, family members, friends, books, magazines, television shows, support groups on the Internet, and web sites. Many parents today are finding help and support through parenting groups, as well. Such groups provide parents with comfort in knowing that others are going through similar challenges. They can offer generalized information for parents of young children, or they can be more specific, such as those that offer classes in helping children who have particular challenges. These groups can provide answers to parents' questions and often help them to feel more confident in their parenting role (Oldershaw, 2002). The Pathways to Competence for Young Children Parenting Program has been designed to help parents get answers to parenting challenges and to fulfill the need for information on child development and optimal parenting strategies to use with children to foster their development.

FACTORS IN DEVELOPING A PARENTING GROUP THAT MEETS MULTIPLE NEEDS

Many factors go into developing a successful parenting group. The following suggestions are intended to guide new group leaders as they set up a Pathways to Competence for Young Children Parenting Program group to meet the needs of the families with whom they work.

Target Audience

Parents are the primary audience for the Pathways to Competence for Young Children Parenting Program. Because discussion requires participants to talk about the early life of a child and the child's current behavior in many settings and situations, it is expected that parents are the ones most likely to have access to this kind of information. Grandparents or other family members and caregivers such as foster parents may be an appropriate audience *if* they are the primary caregiver of the child.

Sometimes parents would like to bring child care providers, grandparents, or the child's teacher with them. Some of the information discussed in the group may be of a nature that many parents would consider inappropriate to raise with these people present, so it may not be in the best interests of the class to have such individuals there. In order for parents to feel most comfortable disclosing information about their parenting practices, the leaders and parents should discuss the appropriateness of other caregivers attending the meetings if the issue comes up.

The number of participants in each group typically varies; however, the ideal size is approximately 12. This is discussed in more detail in Chapter 5.

Age of the Child

The materials in this program are written for parents with children ages birth to 7 years. This age group was chosen because research has shown the importance of intervening with infants and young children to optimize brain development, to enhance attachment, and to avoid the establishment of negative parent–child interactional patterns that become increasingly difficult to change later. Also, parents of young children are generally motivated to address children's emotional and behavioral difficulties. Often, however, a family includes children older than this target group. Parents have been able to use some of the information in Pathways to Competence for Young Children Parenting Program groups with their older children. For example, strategies suggested for encouraging appropriate behavior in young children and emotion regulation (e.g., using positive reinforcement and/or star charts and token systems and the steps of emotion coaching) can be successfully used with school-age children.

PROGRAM STEPS

The Pathways to Competence for Young Children Parenting Program is based on enhancing developmental capacities that every child needs for optimal social and emotional development. Section II of this book provides a set of 10 Steps that address important aspects of these capacities that form the structure for the program sessions. The Steps are as follows:

- Step 1: Introducing the Program and Understanding Development and Temperament

- Step 2: Developing Body Control and a Positive Body Image

- Step 3: Developing a Secure Attachment

- Step 4: Encouraging Play and Imagination

- Step 5: Encouraging Language and Communication

- Step 6: Laying a Foundation for Positive Self-Esteem

- Step 7: Encouraging Self-Regulation, Morality, and a Sense of Conscience

- Step 8: Encouraging Emotion Regulation

- Step 9: Encouraging Concentration, Planning, and Problem Solving

- Step 10: Encouraging Social Competence, Empathy, and Caring Behavior

THE USE OF THE PROGRAM IN A VARIETY OF SETTINGS

Parents typically become involved in a Pathways to Competence for Young Children Parenting Program through a number of different avenues ranging from having an interest in learning more about parenting in general to being ordered to take the program by a child protection agency. The Pathways to Competence for Young Children Parenting Program may be used with a variety of parent and child populations and in a number of different settings, including the following:

- **Parent drop-in centers and preschool programs:** Parents often turn to these venues when they want to learn more about early child development and parenting.

- **Elementary schools:** A school psychologist, guidance counselor, teacher, or administrator may refer parents to a parenting program if a child is having chronic behavioral difficulties at school and/or in the home. Pathways to Competence for Young Children Parenting Programs have been offered in schools for parents seeking help for these issues.

- **Community and church programs:** Parents often ask religious and other community leaders for advice on raising their children; therefore, parent support groups and parenting programs are often offered in these settings.

- **Health settings:** Psychologists, social workers, speech-language pathologists (SLPs), physical therapists, and other health professionals may use the materials with clients or refer parents to a group available in the community.

- **Medical settings:** Parents may find out about the program through their family physician, pediatrician, or a local hospital. Developmental pediatricians can support their clinical practice and faculty responsibilities by recommending such programs to parents or by using the materials in their practice.

- **Early intervention programs and children's mental health centers:** Parents of young children with behavioral, emotional, or social difficulties may seek out a parenting program such as Pathways to Competence for Young Children from these centers. The centers may refer parents to such programs when parents have identified relationship problems with their children or when the children have problems with eating or sleeping, for example.

- **Family service agencies:** Family service agencies may refer a parent or parents to a program such as Pathways to Competence for Young Children if they see that a family is in a crisis situation, such as when parents cannot agree on discipline approaches and it is affecting the parents' ability to cope with child rearing.

- **Child protection agencies:** Child protection agencies may refer parents to a parenting group when their young children are in foster care or when they have just had their children returned to them. Parents who have been referred to child protection agencies because of parenting concerns but who have not had their children removed from their family may also attend.

- **Agencies providing counseling sessions or home visits:** The Pathways to Competence for Young Children Parenting Program also can be used in counseling sessions or home visits with individual families.

Use for Children Experiencing Violence

Witnessing violence of any kind in the home or community puts children at extreme risk physically and emotionally, and the stress and trauma children suffer as a result can affect brain organization and development and create long-term behavioral, emotional, and social problems. When children have been exposed to violence, without parental support they tend to be chronically anxious or hypervigilant and readily triggered into remembering the trauma situations. These children need particularly nurturing and containing interactions from their caregivers as well as structure and limits. The parenting skills presented in the Pathways to Competence for Young Children Parenting Program help children to feel safe and secure. These skills give children the support they need to be able to explore the environment in a safe way so that they can learn and feel more relaxed and be less likely to have their memories of the trauma triggered.

Workshop Presentations

Although the program is usually presented in its entirety, individual sessions from the program (Steps) can be used for workshops on particular topics of great interest to groups of parents such as those interested in learning more about enhancing self-esteem, encouraging social competence, and the use of play. One group of mothers whose children were in a playgroup enjoyed a workshop on play that used the materials from Step 4, Encouraging Play and Imagination, for example. They gained new insights on how important play was to their child's development, what to expect at each developmental stage in terms of play interests, and ways to play with their child that encourage physical, social, and emotional growth and development.

BACKGROUND OF THE PATHWAYS TO COMPETENCE FOR YOUNG CHILDREN PARENTING PROGRAM

The Pathways to Competence for Young Children Parenting Program is based on the Helping Encourage Affect Regulation (HEAR) parenting program that was developed in 1995. It was originally used for parents with young children with behavioral problems including chronic noncompliance, aggression and tantrums, argumentativeness and stubbornness, and frequent loss of control. These challenges generate a high level of parent–child conflict, which the HEAR group addressed by providing parents with a developmental approach to understanding their children's difficulties and with strategies to use with them to reduce their children's symptoms.

The National Health Research and Development Program (NHRDP) provided a grant in late 1995 to evaluate the program, and a report documenting the success of the program was published in 1998. The report described a number of important improvements in children and parents and in parent–child interactions that resulted from participation in the groups, including an increase in parenting knowledge, a reduction in maternal depression, and an increase in their sense of parenting competence. Children's aggression was also reduced and parents reported an increase in satisfaction in their parenting (see also Landy & Menna, 2006).

USE OF THIS PROGRAM WITH *PATHWAYS TO COMPETENCE: ENCOURAGING HEALTHY SOCIAL AND EMOTIONAL DEVELOPMENT IN YOUNG CHILDREN*

Following the success of early versions of this program, a book was published for professionals in the field of prevention and early intervention called *Pathways to Competence: Encouraging Healthy Social and Emotional Development in Young Children* (Landy, 2002). This work was the result of 5 years of extensive research of the literature in the fields of early child development and parenting. It has been used as a textbook in university courses and to train professionals in agencies. Its greatest use, however, is as a resource for a variety of disciplines including physicians, psychologists, psychiatrists, social workers, nurses, early child educators, child care workers, and community home visitors. The book also includes additional group activities, homework suggestions, tests that could be used for evaluation, and questions for professionals to be used during training courses. It is strongly recommended that this Pathways to Competence for Young Children Parenting Program be used in combination with *Pathways to Competence* (2002) because it is an invaluable resource for the group leader for answering questions that arise from parents and to identify resources beyond those included in the manual. Throughout this book, especially in Section II, Pathways to Competence for Young Children Parenting Program Steps, group leaders are referred to specific pages in what is henceforth called *Pathways to Competence* (2002) for additional information and group exercises that correspond to each Step. These products are designed to work together to give parents all the valuable information and useful tools they will need to be effective caregivers. Copies of either product can be purchased at http://www.brookespublishing.com.

CHAPTER 2

UNDERLYING
THEORETICAL CONSTRUCTS

The first 6 years of a child's life are the most critical in terms of developing the capacities for optimal social, physical, and emotional functioning. Evidence of the importance of the first 6 years of life has arisen primarily out of recent research on the developing brain (Dawson, 1994; Gunnar, 1998; Schore, 1994). Also, early childhood experts are increasingly aware of the significance of the problems that occur for many children in the early years that can continue to have an impact throughout life. In fact, it has been found that a significant percentage of children who have severe difficulties in the early years and who do not receive intervention will continue to have ongoing problems in later years (Campbell, 1995; Rubin, Burgess, Kim, Dwyer, & Hastings, 2003; Tremblay, 2002; Weiss & Hechtman, 1993).

Various risks in the child or the environment can contribute to severe adjustment difficulties: In fact, a number of studies in various parts of the world have found that 15%–25% of children between the ages of 4 and 16 years suffer from one or more serious adjustment difficulties (Costello, 1989; Lahey, Miller, Gordon, & Riley, 1999; Landy & deV. Peters, 1992; Offord, Boyle, Racine, Fleming, et al., 1992; Rutter, 1989).

The widely reported success of certain early intervention programs such as the Perry Preschool Project (Berrueta-Clement, Schweinhart, Barrett, Epstein, & Weikart, 1984) and the Prenatal and Early Infancy Project (Olds, Henderson, Tatelbaum, & Chamberlin, 1988) has also added to the enthusiasm for the possibilities of intervening early and has contributed to the belief in the importance of prevention and early intervention programs. This realization has resulted in the development of a number of approaches to prevention and early intervention that are child and/or parent focused and that use individual and group approaches.

THE CRITICAL CAPACITIES OF EARLY CHILDHOOD

During a child's first 6 years of life, achieving certain capacities or milestones of emotional and social development has been shown to be critical in forming a sound foundation for later development (Landy, 2002). These nine capacities can be viewed as the foundation of a house on which later development builds. If any of them is compromised, later development and behavior can be affected. These capacities (see Figure 2.1) include

1. Body control and a positive body image

2. Secure attachment

3. Play and imagination

4. Language and communication

5. Positive self-esteem

6. Self-regulation, morality, and a sense of conscience

7. Emotion regulation

8. Concentration, planning, and problem solving

9. Social competence, empathy, and caring behavior

As mentioned in Chapter 1, these capacities form the framework for the Pathways to Competence for Young Children Parenting Program. Section II of this book provides parents with an understanding of their importance and strategies to use to assist their children to develop them.

PARENTING INTERACTIONS AND DEVELOPMENTAL OUTCOMES

Children's development is the result of the complex interplay or the "symphonic causality" between nature and nurture or biology and environment (Boyce, 2001). However, even when there are genetic or biological vulnerabilities within a young child, the interactions that the child has with his or her caregiver can dramatically influence the child's developmental outcomes and his or her capacity for resilience or adaptation. The child feels more secure when caregivers are sensitive to his or her cues, accept and show positive feelings toward him or her, and are accessible and focus attention on the child when he or she needs it. Also, when the parent takes the child's needs into account yet accepts the child's need to be separate and independent, the child is more likely to develop the capacities described previously.

THE EFFECT OF RISK ON OUTCOMES

Poverty has been shown to produce deleterious effects on parents and children. For example, the Ontario Child Health Study (OCHS) found poverty to be one of the most significant variables contributing to psychological disorders (Boyle et al., 1987; Offord et al., 1987; Rae-Grant, Thomas, Offord, & Boyle, 1989). Research has also found that the number of risk factors contributes significantly to child outcomes and does so in a multiplicative fashion, with two risk factors contributing fourfold and four

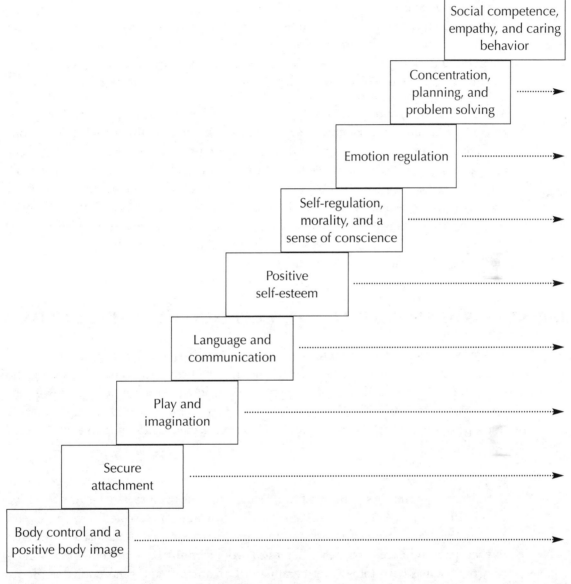

Figure 2.1. The developmental capacities in a child. Development of a capacity, once established, continues to be strengthened and modified as the child grows up. (From *Pathways to competence: Encouraging healthy social and emotional development in young children* [p. 568]; adapted by permission.)

risk factors sixteenfold. For young children, proximal factors (i.e., those closest to the child) such as parenting interactions contribute more than more distal (i.e., those more far removed) factors such as community characteristics. The effects of distal factors are felt more by parents and, consequently, they affect parents' interactions with their children but do not affect the children as directly as proximal factors. For example, a study conducted by Landy and Tam (1997) using data from the National Longitudinal Survey of Children and Youth (NLSCY) found that children who lived in low-income, high-risk areas did well when they were exposed to parenting practices that were positive and when parents were nurturing and provided clear, age-appropriate limits. In fact, children living in high-risk situations who received positive parenting had higher scores on developmental measures than did children who lived in more favorable and higher socioeconomic circumstances who were exposed to negative parenting practices, particularly when discipline was harsh and punitive.

Multi-risk parents and families frequently have difficulties raising their children, and their children are at risk for emotional, social, and behavioral difficulties. Populations in which children are exposed to multiple risks include, but are not limited to, teenage parents, parents with depression, parents with unresolved loss and trauma or posttraumatic stress disorder (PTSD), parents who abuse substances, and families in which there is violence including spousal abuse and child abuse. The Pathways to Competence for Young Children Parenting Program groups have been used with most of these parent populations and with parents whose children have behavior disorders including excessive noncompliance and aggression.

PARENT CHARACTERISTICS THAT INFLUENCE PARENT–CHILD INTERACTIONS

When we consider the characteristics of these multi-risk parenting groups, it becomes clear that *within* each of them there are significant differences including the parents' past history and their ability to parent. Consequently, in order to design interventions for them, it is important to consider some of the characteristics that underlie or contribute to how parents interact with their children. Some of these are discussed next.

Some parents are very **resistant** to receiving services, whereas others are eager to try out different approaches to intervention. More resistant parents may be very sensitive to rejection and have a great deal of difficulty learning to trust and forming a relationship with the interventionist. Often, these parents have been abused or rejected in their past and have adopted strategies to avoid commitment and closeness in relationships. It has been found that parents with dismissive and preoccupied adult attachment patterns do better with very different intervention strategies. On the one hand, preoccupied parents are typically more interested in talking about their experiences of being parented than those parents who are more dismissive. Dismissive parents, on the other hand, enjoy learning about how to parent by being given information and suggestions on what to do (Bakersman-Kranenburg, Juffer, & van IJzendoorn, 1998). Consequently, in the Pathways to Competence groups, strategies are used that both give information and encourage parents who wish to do so to discuss their own experiences of being parented.

Parents with **unresolved loss and trauma** have an increased sensitivity to certain stimuli associated with the original trauma and may also be in a physiological state of chronic overarousal. These stimuli cause involuntary intrusions of the traumatic memories, which can lead to re-traumatization and even more arousal. For some parents, memories of trauma and loss that are unprocessed and become dissociated remain at an unconscious level, available to be triggered by even subtle reminders of the traumatizing event. The wide-ranging effects of trauma can make parenting extremely difficult for people who have experienced it, particularly if the trauma occurred during early childhood (Crittenden, Lang, Claussen, & Partridge, 2000). In the Pathways to Competence for Young Children Parenting Program groups, strategies to encourage self-care and ways to help parents to problem solve are used throughout to help parents deal with various triggers and with symptoms of overarousal.

The capacity for **self-reflectivity,** as defined by Fonagy, Steele, Steele, Moran, and Higgitt (1991), is the "internal observer of mental life." People with high self-reflectivity do not simply feel angry or rejected; they know they have these feelings and reflect on why and in which circumstances they have them. People with high self-reflectivity also understand the mental states of others, including their children, and why they behave in certain ways. For a parent, self-reflectivity, as described by Slade, is the "capacity to keep the baby in mind" (2002), and is believed to allow the parent to interpret the intentions and feelings that underlie his or her child's behavior and to act appropriately in response. Many studies have demonstrated a significant concordance between parents' quality of attachment to their parents and their children's attachment classifications. This relationship has been shown in some studies to be affected by a mother's capacity for self-reflectivity that, in turn, influences her capacity to "keep her baby in mind" and thus, her sensitivity in interactions (Slade et al., 2001). Encouraging parents to be more self-reflective and understanding of their child is an emphasis that is reflected throughout the Pathways to Competence for Young Children Parenting Program.

The transition to parenthood brings a number of new challenges, which in turn result in a self-evaluation of **parenting competence.** Parental sense of competence can, therefore, be defined as the belief that parents develop about their ability to understand, care for, and enhance the development of their child. In turn, it has been found that high self-confidence or sense of mastery is linked with provision of better home environments for children (Rogers, Parcel, & Meaghan, 1991) and greater maternal responsiveness (Hubbs-Tait, Osofsky, Hann, & McDonald, 1994). Conversely, low self-confidence is related to poor mother–infant interactions (Johnston, 1996; McPhee, Fritz, & Miller-Heyl, 1996; Teti & Gelfand, 1991; Wootton, Frick, Shelton, & Silverthorn, 1997). Parents' confidence is enhanced when positive parenting strategies are affirmed and new ones that the parents find useful are introduced.

Emotion regulation refers to the process by which people control and self-regulate their internal response to feelings as well as their outward expression. The importance of emotion regulation to adult functioning and parenting cannot be emphasized enough. One of the most frequent concerns of parents is that they could lose control when they become angry or frustrated at their infant's or young child's challenging behaviors and may scream at or even hit the child. All parents experience feelings of anger and frustration and are concerned about their reactions, but when parents have difficulties with emotion regulation, their reactions may be extreme and can compromise children's development, particularly children's capacity to eventually manage their own emotions. In Step 8, parents are taught ways to manage their own emotions and those of their children.

Parents' **attributions** and expectations of their children are important influences on their own behavior and their child's development. Attribution processes are subject to errors or biases, and these biases are important for understanding dysfunctional parent–child relationships (Hewstone, 1989). When attributions of the child are negative or the child's behavior is interpreted as directed against the parent, they can encourage negative emotional states in the parent and may lead to extremely punitive interactions (Bugental & Johnston, 2000). Negative attributions have been linked to children with withdrawn behavior and aggression and behavior problems (Rubin & Mills, 1990). The Pathways groups emphasize changing parents' attributions of their children and themselves and enhancing children's self-esteem as a consequence.

THE IMPORTANCE OF SOCIAL SUPPORT

A number of studies have linked parenting skills to whether parents have adequate social networks. Specifically, larger, supportive social networks have been associated with various aspects of more nurturing, sensitive, and responsive parenting, whereas lack of social supports has been linked to lower levels of warmth and more punitive discipline (Ceballo & McLloyd, 2002; Roberts, 1989). Other studies have linked social support to children's attachment classifications and to child developmental outcomes (Crockenberg, 1981; Jacobsen & Frye, 1991). Although relationships between social support and child development have been found, it is not clear how these relationships form. It has been suggested that social support may buffer parents from stressful situations and thus enhance their interactions with their children. Certainly, parenting groups can provide a support network for participants who are in similar situations.

EFFECTIVENESS OF SHORT-TERM INTERVENTIONS INCLUDING PARENTING GROUPS

Although many parents who experience difficulties with their children will need multimodal, long-term treatment, short-term intervention approaches within a longer-term framework of intervention can be very effective in enhancing parent–child interactions and encouraging secure attachment in the child (Bakersman & IJzendoorn, 2002; van IJzendoorn, Juffer, & Duyvesteyn, 1995). Group-based parenting programs have been shown to be successful in improving children's behavior and increasing parents' sense of competence (Barlow & Stewart-Brown, 2000; Thomas et al., 1999). Parenting programs have also been shown to improve parenting skills and to prevent chronic dysfunctional patterns developing when they are provided in the preschool years (Briesmeister & Schaefer, 1988; Kazdin, 2000). In general, parenting groups that incorporate both behavioral methods and relation-based strategies are most effective (Kazdin, 1997, 2000; Webster-Stratton & Hammond, 1997). For example, the Incredible Years Program (Webster-Stratton, 1989) is a comprehensive curriculum designed to promote social competence and to reduce and prevent conduct and aggression in young children. Although it initially consisted of the BASIC program, which emphasizes improving parent–child interactions and children's behavior, Roberts, Webster-Stratton, and Hammond (1997) found that adding the AD-VANCE program, which provides strategies to enhance parents' self-esteem and self-care, personal self-control, and marital and relationship skills provided additional benefits and more lasting change and improvements in outcomes.

A number of pilot projects and the evaluation of the HEAR parenting program have demonstrated the effectiveness of the Pathways to Competence for Young Children Parenting Program in reducing child behavior problems and maternal depression and in enhancing parents' knowledge, confidence, and interactions with their children (see Chapter 4; Landy & Menna, 1998; Landy & Menna, in press).

SUMMARY

The achievement of a number of social and emotional capacities is critical to a child's overall development in the first 6 years of life. Factors in the child, parent, parent–child interaction, and social support systems can either enhance the child's development or place him or her at risk for emotional, social, and behavioral difficulties. Parent groups have been shown to provide social support, enhance parent–child interactions, and encourage secure attachment. The Pathways to Competence for Young Children Parenting Program endeavors to help parents as they strive to encourage healthy social and emotional development in their children.

CHAPTER 3

PROGRAM OBJECTIVES, APPROACHES, AND STRATEGIES

GOAL OF THE PROGRAM

The goal of the Pathways to Competence for Young Children Parenting Program is to support parents and other caregivers to enhance the development and behavior of infants and young children.

OBJECTIVES

Objectives of a Pathways to Competence for Young Children Parenting Program group are to

- Enhance parents' knowledge of early childhood development

- Increase parents' self-reflectivity and empathy for their child

- Increase parents' understanding of the influence of their family of origin experiences, or their own early family life, on their current parenting practices

- Encourage parents to develop positive attributions of their child and to reframe negative attributions

- Enhance parent–child interactions and encourage positive parenting strategies

- Encourage parents to develop secure attachments and to bond with their child

- Encourage parents to develop emotion regulation and positive strategies to encourage emotion regulation in their child

- Provide parents with strategies to manage their child's behavioral or emotional difficulties and reduce any symptoms

- Enhance parents' sense of self-efficacy and their child's self-esteem

- Enhance parents' sense of support

- Give parents positive experiences within the group that will encourage them to seek further counseling or intervention if necessary

- Increase parents' sense of parenting competence

Approaches to Achieving the Objectives

As noted in Chapters 1 and 2, the program is effective for a variety of populations and uses a number of approaches in order to successfully achieve these objectives. The initial focus is on providing an overview of early development and temperament and enhancing parents' knowledge about the importance and development of a number of developmental capacities. Parents are encouraged to continually consider and wonder about what the child is thinking and why the child is behaving in a certain way. They are also supported to understand why they parent as they do in order to enhance **self-reflectivity and empathy** for the child.

Group members provide **support** for one another, which helps parents to feel less isolated and more able to cope with parenting challenges. Meeting with parents who are experiencing similar challenges (e.g., child with a behavior problem, family violence, teen parenthood) can be particularly helpful. Parents' **attributions** of their child are discussed and related to the parents' own experiences with attributions (i.e., the way their own parents described them) when they were growing up. Then, parents learn how to reframe any negative attributions of their child and to understand their child's behavior and the reasons for it.

Parents are encouraged to discuss ways in which a particular developmental issue was dealt with as they were growing up. How did their family communicate? How was problem solving dealt with? How nurturing were their parents? By discussing these issues, parents learn how their current parenting behavior and beliefs are influenced by **their own history.** Such discussions can help parents gain insight into any repetitive patterns of behavior and enable them to begin to change maladaptive intergenerational cycles of poor parenting.

Parents are taught a number of **self-care activities** and strategies to calm down when they become stressed out or triggered by their children's behavior. This can be very helpful for parents with **unresolved loss and trauma.** In addition, individuals are taught approaches to **problem solving** around parenting challenges, which can be helpful when coping with parenting problems during the program and afterward.

Parents' sense of parenting competence is enhanced by **having their positive parenting capacities reinforced.** Changes can also take place as they gain insight into their past, have new experiences in the group of being accepted, and practice using the capacities they need to encourage in their children. Their children's sense of self-esteem can be enhanced as parent–child interactions improve and parents work to establish a secure attachment with them and learn strategies to enhance their child's self-esteem.

Parents are given strategies to help them to overcome any difficulties they may be having with **regulating their own emotions** around their child. As shown in Figure 3.1., linkages exist between the child's developmental capacities and temperament, view of self and others, and experience of being parented and the parent's experience of being parented, his or her view of self and others, and social and parenting

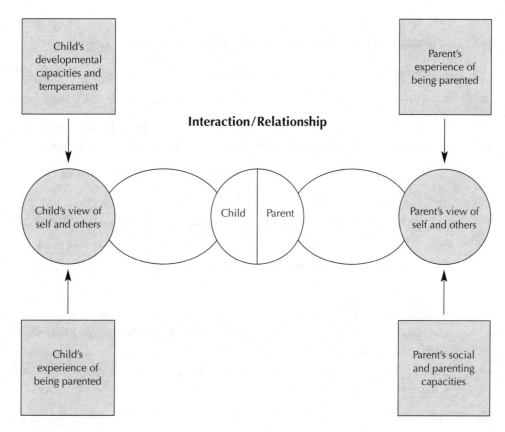

Figure 3.1. Targets of the Pathways to Competence for Young Children Parenting Program. (*Key:* □ = Distal variables, ○ = proximal variables.)

capacities. By focusing on a number of aspects of the parent-child interaction and relationship, the Pathways to Competence for Young Children Parenting Program can lead to a change in one part of the system that can lead to a shift in other parts. For example, changing a parent's attributions of his or her child from very negative to positive can change the parent's interactions with the child, which will shift the child's view of his or her self and of other people to be more positive.

Parents learn new ways to interact with their child in order to help him or her to **overcome any behavior or emotional problems** he or she may have, such as noncompliance and aggression or separation anxiety. Parents learn how to interact with their children in ways that can enhance their children's capacity for emotion regulation.

Group Strategies for Achieving the Objectives

The program employs a number of strategies to enhance these competencies in parents, including

1. Didactic methods, which provide information about typical development of the various competencies and principles of ways parents can encourage their development in their children

2. Role playing around such issues as communication, negotiation and problem solving, and encouraging emotion regulation in children

3. Group discussion of the parents' own situations and and parenting challenges

4. Viewing of video clips of parent–child interactions of the group participants

5. Family of origin activities that help parents to think about how they were parented and how it may be affecting their parenting of their own children

6. Group exercises and activities to encourage the capacitites in their children and in some instances, the capacities in themselves

7. Assigned homework exercises that focus on helping parents to enhance strategies and self-care activities

8. Self-care activities that focus on supporting parents to enhance their self-esteem and sense of competency and suggest ways to nurture themselves

Although parenting behavior is not coached directly, some of the role play, videos, and group exercises provide excellent models of how to respond to a child's behavior, and can increase parents' understanding and empathy for their child. All of these strategies and the structure and format of the program are discussed in more detail in Chapter 7.

CHAPTER 4

EFFECTIVENESS OF THE PROGRAM

The Pathways to Competence for Young Children Parenting Program has been used in a number of types of agencies and other settings in the community, with a variety of groups of parent populations (e.g., parents with children with behavioral difficulties, parents referred by child protection agencies), for workshops, and with individual families. Its effectiveness has been evaluated with some of these parenting populations, and this chapter presents the results.

EVALUATING THE EFFECTIVENESS OF THE PROGRAM WITH CHILDREN WITH BEHAVIORAL DIFFICULTIES

As mentioned in Chapter 1, the Pathways to Competence for Young Children Parenting Program was first conducted as the Helping Encourage Affect Regulation (HEAR) program, and was evaluated with parents who had young children with behavioral difficulties. The children had a variety of behavioral symptoms including chronic noncompliance, extreme tantrums and aggressiveness, argumentativeness and stubbornness, and frequent loss of control. These are behaviors that generate a high level of parent–child conflict, greatly hinder the child's capacity to function with peers, and often lead to referral for professional help during the preschool years. Also, research has shown that a large proportion of children with problems in the early years will continue to have problems into adolescence without early intervention (Campbell, 1995; Fonagy, Target, Cottrell, Phillips, & Kurtz, 2000; Meltzer, Gatward, Corbin, Goodman, & Ford, 2003).

The evaluation was designed to determine the effectiveness of the HEAR Parenting Program in 1) reducing children's problematic behavioral symptoms; 2) improving parenting strategies; 3) enhancing parents' sense of parenting competence and satisfaction in the parenting role; 4) increasing parenting knowledge; and 5) increasing parents' sense of social support (Landy & Menna, in press).

Participants and Setting

For the evaluation, the sample consisted of 35 mothers and their young children. Mothers of children between the ages of 3 and 6 years who showed aggressive behaviors were recruited through advertisements in newspapers and several parenting magazines and from a number of parent resource centers, drop-in centers, and child care centers. Physicians and mental health professionals made referrals, as well. Children of potential participants were initially screened for levels of aggression by administering items of the aggressive subscale of the Child Behavior Checklist (CBCL; Achenbach & Edelbrock, 1983) over the telephone. Those parents whose children 1) showed a high level of aggression or 2) had scores at the 90th percentile or higher (mean score 97th percentile) (i.e., were considered clinically aggressive) were selected for the study. Children with serious developmental delays and mothers and children with any medical condition or physical disability that would interfere with the parent–child interaction procedure were excluded from the study.

Groups and Setting

Of the parents who volunteered to participate, 20 were randomly assigned to a HEAR group (Group 1) and 15 to a waiting list control group (Group 2) of individuals who were put on a waiting list for the HEAR program but who did not attend the initial parenting group. The HEAR program was provided at a children's mental health center. All assessments of children and mothers were also carried out at the center.

Research Design and Procedure

Two assessments using parent questionnaires—a pretest and a posttest—were completed for this project. Research assistants who were blind to or not aware of the purpose of the study or the group assignment of the participants carried out the testing.

Once parents agreed to participate, they were contacted to arrange times for their pretest assessments. The groups met once a week for 2 hours per week for 15 weeks. The groups were conducted by two therapists (both female). The group leader had many years of clinical expertise as well as experience in providing this parenting group. The other group leader was a student who was familiar with the parents and who understood the purpose and methodology of the groups. Mothers and children were reassessed after the completion of the group. The mean number of sessions attended by group participants was 10.69 (SD = 4.90).

Outcome Measures

The following variables were assessed:

- Degree of behavioral difficulties in the children

- Parental confidence

- Parenting knowledge

- Parent–child relationship characteristics

- Demographic variables describing the family background

The tests and measures are described next.

Background Information

Demographic information such as marital and socioeconomic status and the child's position in the family were obtained using a background questionnaire designed for the study.

The Child's Behavior, Cognitive, Emotional, and Social Development

The *Battelle Developmental Inventory* (BDI) (Newberg, Stock, Wnek, Guidubaldi, & Svinicki, 1988) was used to derive a Developmental Quotient (DQ). The BDI is a standardized, individually administered assessment battery of key developmental skills in children from birth to 8 years. Items are grouped around five domains: 1) personal-social, 2) adaptive, 3) motor, 4) communication, and 5) cognitive. BDI test–retest reliability is very high for each domain, varying from .68 to .98. The BDI has very high correlations with the Wechsler Intelligence Scale for Children–Revised (WISC-R), the Stanford-Binet Intelligence Scale (4th ed.; Thorndike, Hagen, & Sattler, 1986), and the Peabody Picture Vocabulary Test (Newberg et al., 1988). Two subscales, communication and cognitive, were also used to assess the sample.

The *Eyberg Child Behavior Inventory* (ECBI; Eyberg & Colvin, 1994) and the *Child Behavior Checklist* (CBCL; Achenbach & Edelbrock, 1991) were used to assess child behavior and any symptoms the children had that reached clinical significance. These measures are described in detail in Chapter 8.

Mother's Psychological Characteristics

Maternal confidence was assessed using the *Early Childhood Care Questionnaire* (ECCQ) (Gross & Rocissano, 1988). (See Chapter 8 for a description of the test.)

The *Knowledge of Child Development Inventory* (MacPhee, 1981) was used to measure mothers' knowledge of child development and parenting of children from 3 to 6 years of age. It is described in Chapter 8.

The *Beck Depression Inventory* (BDI; Beck, 1978) was used to measure maternal depression. Mothers were asked to rate 21 symptoms on a 5-point scale. This is an established measure with good reliability and validity.

Parent–Child Relationship

The *Parent–Child Relationship Inventory* (PCRI; Gerard, 1994), a 78-item questionnaire, was used to measure parents' attitudes toward parenting and their children. The measure is described in Chapter 8.

Sample Description

Background information on variables was analyzed with *t*-tests, and Chi-squares or Fisher's Exact Test. A total of 35 mother–child dyads participated in the study, including 20 in the HEAR intervention and 15 in a waiting list control group. The groups were similar with respect to child age, gender, birth order, and child functioning in communication and cognitive domains. The average age for the children in the study was 4 years, 6 months. The sample was composed of many more boys (80%) than girls (20%). Children were in the average range on the communication and cognitive domains of the *Battelle Developmental Inventory*. The groups did not differ on aggression or delinquency/destructive CBCL subscale scores. The sample had a mean aggression score on the CBCL at the 97th percentile or in the clinical range. For maternal characteristics, the groups were similar in age, education level, family income, and marital status. As a group, the sample tended to be middle-class and to have completed high school. All spoke English. Overall, mothers were in their thirties and their partners were slightly older. In each group, approximately 69% were married or in common-law relationships and approximately 30% were single.

Analyses

A series of analyses of covariance (ANCOVAs), with planned comparisons (*t* statistics) were used to examine the effects of intervention for each dependent variable using pretreatment measures as covariates. Independent *t*-test analyses revealed nonequivalent pre-test scores for parenting knowledge. As a result, ANCOVAs on gain scores were used to examine the effects of intervention on parenting knowledge scores. Table 4.1 summarizes the means and standard deviations for all dependent variable at pre- and post-assessment. Table 4.2 contains *F* values and *t* statistics for group effects.

Results

As outlined above, the ANCOVA results showed that mothers in both groups reported significant differences on the two measures of child behavior problems; however, the planned comparison analysis of the results on the ECBI for intensity of behavior problems reported by the mothers indicated a trend ($p = .09$) toward the HEAR group reporting fewer behavioral problems compared with control group mothers. On the CBCL aggression scale, mothers in the HEAR group reported fewer behavior problems than did mothers in the control group.

The ANCOVA results revealed significant differences on the parenting outcome measures. Compared with the mothers in the control group, the HEAR mothers reported more satisfaction and effectiveness in the parenting role, greater social support, increased involvement and knowledge about their child, and more effectiveness in setting limits for the child and feeling in control as parents.

Table 4.1. Outcome variables at preintervention and postintervention

Measure	Helping Encourage Affect Regulation (HEAR) (Group 1)		Control (Group 2)	
	Pre	Post	Pre	Post
Child Behavior Checklist (CBCL)[a]				
Aggression				
M	23.30	16.60	24.40	21.60
SD	4.90	6.70	5.7	4.60
Parenting Confidence				
M	131.90	142.10	136.30	129.40
SD	24.00	25.00	20.4	23.50
Parenting Knowledge				
M	.72	.76	.77	.76
SD	.06	.04	.05	.09
Parent–Child Relationship Inventory (PCRI)				
Support				
M	43.20	52.90	40.00	43.0
SD	5.66	8.40	8.50	9.2
Satisfaction				
M	35.9	38.09	35.0	35.22
SD	6.17	5.79	6.20	6.14
Involvement				
M	25.89	27.73	25.25	22.11
SD	5.70	5.18	3.05	2.42
Communication				
M	28.89	36.64	25.42	33.56
SD	6.97	4.86	6.69	6.60
Limit Setting				
M	42.17	50.73	40.17	43.33
SD	4.43	8.29	4.06	2.06
Autonomy				
M	51.67	45.20	51.67	49.0
SD	8.86	8.65	7.92	7.79
Role				
M	42.67	39.40	43.25	37.89
SD	6.41	2.97	6.41	8.74
Eyberg Child Behavior Inventory[b]				
Intensity				
M	156.70	136.70	157.70	154.20
SD	23.60	28.70	19.20	14.60

[a]Achenbach & Edelbrock, 1983
[b]Eyberg & Colvin, 1994; Eyberg & Pincus, 1999

An ANCOVA conducted on the gain scores of the Parenting Knowledge Scale showed significant posttest improvements for the HEAR group ($F [1,31] = 6.17$, $p = .02$) compared with the control group. Univariate analysis indicated that at the end of the group, mothers in the HEAR group reported greater knowledge about child development and parenting compared with mothers in the control group. Scores for the control group mothers dropped from pre- and post-assessments.

The findings from this study demonstrated that the HEAR parenting program (now called the Pathways to Competence for Young Children Parenting Program) was ef-

Table 4.2.   *F* Values and *t* Statistics

Measure	ANCOVA *F*	*Df*	Pathways group versus control group *t*
Child Behavior Checklist (CBCL)[a]			
Aggression	15.50**	1,31	−2.62*
Eyberg Child Behavior Inventory[b]			
Parenting Confidence	29.23***	1,31	2.16*
Intensity	11.08**	1,30	−1.76+
Parent–Child Relationship Inventory (PCRI)[c]			
Support	6.59*	1,26	2.91*
Satisfaction	7.60*	1,26	.38
Involvement	14.25**	1,26	3.37**
Communication	1.33	1,26	1.38
Limit Setting	4.50*	1,26	2.21*
Autonomy	.31	1,26	−1.12
Role	1.90	1,26	.55

[a]Achenbanh & Edelbrock, 1983
[b]Eyberg & Colvin, 1994
[c] Gerard, 1994
*$p < .05$, **$p < .01$, ***$p < .001$, +$p < .10$

fective in reducing aggression and behavior problems in a sample of young children. It also enhanced the parent-child relationship and parents' parenting knowledge and sense of parenting competence.

Parents Referred to Child Protection Agencies

The Pathways to Competence for Young Children Parenting Program has also been used with parents who have been referred to various child protection services or agencies because they were experiencing severe parenting problems. In one pilot study, a number of pre- and posttests showed significant improvements in parenting behaviors. Improvements were found on the Emotional Availability Scales (Biringen, Robinson, & Emde, 1993) in the variables of Maternal Sensitivity, Maternal Intrusiveness, and Child Involvement; reduction in child aggressive behavior and delinquent behavior on the CBCL; and improvements in Clarity of Cues and Structuring on a clean-up task. (See Chapter 8 for a description of these measures.) The program has also been provided in parent resource centers, child care centers, and drop-in centers. Satisfaction with the program was high: 85% of parents reported that they found it very useful and 15% reported that they found it useful. All parents (100%) noted that they gained a new perspective and increased understanding of their children. Many of the parents (83%) also noted that they found the group particularly useful because of the variety of topics covered in the group; it dealt not only with discipline but also with a number of other important issues. Of the participants, 90% felt that the course should be universally available to parents with young children. Teachers in the parent resource center and child care centers that the children attended reported improvements in the children's behavior—particularly a drop in aggression (Landy, Menna, & Sockett-DiMarco, 1997).

Mothers Who Were Victims of Spousal Violence

The Pathways to Competence for Young Children Parenting Program has also been used with mothers with children from 6 months to 7 years who had been abused by their spouses. A total of 12 mothers participated in the group. Pretests were completed before the program and after the program's completion. Statistically significant improvements were found on almost all measures after mothers finished the program. Results on the Toronto Alexithymia Scale (TAS; Bagby, Parker, & Taylor, 1994) (see Chapter 8) showed a significant improvement, indicating that the mothers who had attended the program were better able to talk about and understand their own emotions after attending the group (see Table 4.3). Interactional measures and the mothers' levels of self-esteem were improved. Depression and parenting stress were reduced, and mothers reported that they experienced less parent–child interactional dysfunction. All of the mothers expressed satisfaction with the group and would have liked it to continue.

In order to assess if changes in the mothers were maintained 6 months after the program had concluded, further testing using a paper and pencil test was completed. These results are shown in Table 4.4, which shows only one significant change—improvement in the mothers' level of self-esteem. Other changes were not significant, indicating that

Table 4.3. Pre- and posttest means and the significance of the changes for groups 1 and 2 combined

Measures	Pretest means	Posttest means	t tests	Significance
Center for Epidemiological Studies Depression Scale (CES-D)[a]	25.11	18.67	2.87	.02*
Emotional Availability Scales[b]				
Maternal Sensitivity	5.50	7.63	−6.07	.001**
Maternal Intrusiveness/structuring	4.50	5.50	−3.7	.007**
Maternal Hostility	1.75	1.25	−7.6	.47
Child Involvement	5.13	6.75	−3.53	.01*
Child Responsivity	4.75	6.75	−4.7	.002**
Parenting Stress Index–Short Form (PSI)[c]				
Personal Distress	40.00	46.11	−.627	.57
Parent–Child Dysfunctional Interaction	47.5	54.25	−2.25	.05*
Difficult Child	38.66	44.67	−2.10	.05*
Rosenberg Self-Esteem Scale[d]	33.38	39.50	−4.34	.003**
Social Support Inventory[e]	17.00	19.22	−1.49	1.47
Toronto Alexithymia Scale (TAS)[f]	48.22	41.22	2.07	.05*
Total Score on PSI	127.88	144.11	−2.99	.01**

[a] Myers & Weissman, 1980
[b] Biringen, Robinson, & Emde, 1993
[c] Abiden, 1986
[d] Rosenberg, 1979
[e] Cutrona & Russell, 1987
[f] Bagby, Parker, & Taylor, 1994
*p<.05, **p<.01

Table 4.4. Post- and Post-posttest means and the significance of the changes for Groups 1 and 2

Measures	Posttest means	Post-posttest means	t tests	Significance
Center for Epidemiological Studies Depression Scale (CES-D)[a]	18.60	15.20	.44	.68
Parenting Stress Index–Short Form[b]				
Personal Distress	48.20	226.20	.87	.43
Parent–Child Dysfunctional Interaction	52.60	52.00	.22	.34
Difficult Child	44.60	43.80	.21	.84
Rosenberg Self-Esteem Scale[c]	41.25	45.75	−4.32	.02**
Social Support Inventory[d]	18.40	19.00	−.86	.43
Toronto Alexithymia Scale[e]	44.60	45.00	−1.20	.91
Total	145.40	142.00	.67	.54

[a]Myers & Weissman, 1980
[b]Abidin, 1986
[c]Rosenberg, 1989
[d]Cutrona & Russell, 1987
[e]Bagby, Parker, & Taylor, 1994
**p<.01

the positive changes made by the mothers were maintained. Note that although the changes were not significant, the mothers continued to show slight improvements 6 months later in their levels of depression, personal distress, and parenting stress. This indicates that the changes found were enduring and that the parenting group continued to be a positive influence on these mothers and their children.

The Pathways to Competence for Young Children Parenting Program shows significant promise as a parenting group for women who have experienced violence. It could be used preventatively to enhance the sense of competence of women who have grown up in violent situations and to enhance their parenting interactions with their children and consequently, the developmental outcomes of their children (Landy & Harris, 2004).

PATHWAYS TO COMPETENCE FOR YOUNG CHILDREN PARENTING PROGRAM COMPARED WITH ANOTHER PARENTING PROGRAM

The Pathways to Competence for Young Children Parenting Program was compared with the Systematic Training for Effective Parenting (STEP) program when the groups were given for parents of children with behavioral problems. Although both groups showed improvement on a number of variables, the Pathways to Competence program participants were more likely to maintain improvement 12 months later and continued to improve on a number of variables. The Pathways to Competence for Young Children Parenting Program group had only one parent who dropped out compared with five who dropped out of STEP, and the Pathways group had far better attendance and acceptance of the group.

In conclusion, the Pathways to Competence for Young Children Parenting Program has been used with a number of parents of young children from a variety of backgrounds and situations and has been both well-received and successful in improving a number of variables. Chapter 8 describes a number of measures that can be used to evaluate the groups.

CHAPTER 5

SETTING UP A
PATHWAYS TO COMPETENCE
FOR YOUNG CHILDREN GROUP

The Pathways to Competence for Young Children Parenting Program is intentionally designed to be flexible to meet a variety of needs and populations. It is assumed that group leaders will spend some time going over the Steps, printing out the handouts from the accompanying CD-ROM and making copies as needed for the participants, and gathering materials as needed before starting the program. However, it is also assumed that each group leader or set of leaders will tailor the program somewhat to suit his or her needs and the concerns of the particular group of participants.

FACTORS IN DEVELOPING A PROGRAM THAT MEETS MULTIPLE NEEDS

Many factors go into delivering a successful parenting program. The following suggestions are intended to guide new leaders as they develop a program to meet the needs of the families with whom they work.

Sponsoring Agency

Schools, social service agencies, children's mental health agencies, early intervention programs, children's hospitals, and other community agencies have utilized the course for their clients. When entering into a relationship with a sponsoring agency, it is important to establish the requirements of your agency regarding confidentiality, record keeping, and evaluation of the course's effectiveness. Parents need to believe that the group is a safe place in which to express their questions and concerns; often, concerns that the sponsoring agency may intervene or learn more about a parent or family than the parent wants revealed may limit the information that parents will share. The sponsoring agency generally provides a location to meet and may help with refreshments, handouts, child care, and recruitment.

Number of Group Participants

Groups who have used the Pathways to Competence for Young Children Parenting Program have ranged in size from 6 to 20 participants, although an ideal size is approximately 12. Experience has shown that in groups of 12, each parent has a chance to contribute to the discussions, and the parents have the chance to learn from others. Larger size groups may feel overwhelming for some parents and discourage them from talking.

Location

Pathways to Competence for Young Children groups have been held in a variety of locations, including mental health centers, churches, and schools, depending on the sponsoring agency and the logistics of setting up a group. The important factors in selecting a location, other than those dictated by the sponsoring agency, include convenience to parents, access to transportation, and cost considerations such as easy access to materials and limited or no fees for rental of space.

Number of Weeks

The program, which includes 10 sessions or Steps, as they are called, is designed to occur once a week for 20 weeks, with each topic to be discussed for 2 weeks consecutively. This is because, optimally, developing each topic and allowing participants to understand and interact with the information as well as to practice using the suggestions requires at least 2 weeks per topic. However, the course is flexible and can be offered for fewer weeks. For example, some programs have been held over 15 weeks, which allows certain topics requiring more discussion to be covered in 2 weeks, whereas the other topics can be completed in 1 week. The sessions covering the development of attachment (Step 3), language and communication (Step 5), self-regulation and morality (Step 7), and emotion regulation (Step 8) are topics parents may want more time to explore. Although the program has been presented in 10 weeks, this generally is not enough time to cover all of the topics within each Step, and thus, some would need to be eliminated. However, in providing groups, dropping any of the Steps is not recommended; it is important to cover all of the Steps in the program because all have been shown by research to play a crucial role in forming the building blocks of children's social and emotional development. The materials in this program, however, have been used to cover specific topics in workshops of just one or two sessions. Some of the topics that parents may be interested to cover in workshops include attachment, self-esteem, and discipline.

RECRUITMENT AND ATTENDANCE

A variety of methods can be used to recruit and retain group members. In order to recruit successfully, group leaders first need to decide who the target audience will be for the particular group they are planning. The Pathways to Competence for Young Children Parenting Program was initially designed to help parents with children who were aggressive and noncompliant, although it has been helpful to many other parents.

Spreading the Word

Hosting organizations and/or group leaders may want to use the sample advertisement provided in Section III: Supplemental Materials. Some sponsoring agencies have their own requirements for recruitment advertisements or brochures. Check with them before beginning.

Many agencies have identified specific individuals suitable for the group from their current client population. Therapists may initially approach their clients to determine if a group leader can speak with them. The group leaders then call or meet with each parent to describe the program in more detail and determine if the family meets the criteria that have been established for the group.

Some organizations (e.g., schools) follow a different approach and advertise the group more widely by distributing pamphlets to all of the families served by their organization. For example, a school may distribute pamphlets to parents of children in the lower elementary grades (i.e., kindergarten through grade 2). Both parents and teachers may recommend children who are aggressive and/or noncompliant. A review of referrals and interviews with parents and teachers will help to determine which parents are best suited to the group.

Attendance and Meeting Time

Regular attendance at all of the sessions in a series is encouraged. Parents should agree to attend all sessions unless there are extenuating circumstances, such as illness or weather. Pathways to Competence for Young Children Parenting Program topics were chosen based on the factors that have been known to contribute to positive outcomes for children, and some of the topics or skills are not necessarily the ones that parents initially feel will be the most useful to them. These types of topics cannot be taught or learned sporadically or quickly; they take time and repetition to understand and apply consistently. Also, group cohesiveness builds over the weeks as parents come to think of the group as a safe place to share their concerns; thus, this cohesiveness can only be established if group members do not come and go.

Both parents should be encouraged to attend, if possible and when appropriate, although group leaders need to be sensitive to the fact that many individuals are single parents or are estranged from their spouse or partner. If both parents do join a group but it is impossible for both parents to attend all sessions, the mother and father or partners may take turns when needed and share the information with each other, and both parents can implement the homework activities between sessions.

In any case, child care should be provided to make attendance possible. Preferably, the sessions should be held in the evening to accommodate work schedules and to allow both parents access to the program.

Although interview screening and verbal commitment generally result in consistent attendance, occasionally parents miss sessions. Telephone numbers of participants should be obtained at the first meeting and group leaders should call members after a missed session to inquire whether leaders can facilitate attendance at the next group meeting or answer concerns or questions. Problem solving around impediments to attendance, showing genuine interest and a desire to understand, and help with participants' parenting questions are important for encouraging attendance.

Practical Tips for Encouraging Participation

Most participants are eager to discuss their children with peers and professionals in an informal interactive setting; however, in some situations it is hard to be able to attend a weekly group for 10–20 weeks, especially in terms of getting children cared for and preparing dinner for other family members. Child care; a comfortable, informal setting with attention to incentives such as refreshments and some gifts and handouts; and a balance of information, problem solving, and peer/professional support are the strongest motivators for attendance.

Child Care

Providing child care can be a crucial factor to encourage parent participation. Attendance at a Pathways group can be difficult for parents who have no one to care for their children. It also means that evening sessions will need to be offered to accommodate work schedules. In many cases it is difficult for the families to arrange for child care at home, so it is useful to provide child care during the sessions, whether through the help of the sponsoring agency or by some other means. A variety of arrangements may be made, such as holding the sessions in a facility with a separate room that is supervised by child care providers and providing academic tutoring for the school-age children.

Parents are encouraged to help children adjust to the new setting. This room can be equipped with age-appropriate, fun, and educational toys, school supplies in case tutoring is offered, and perhaps a television and videos or DVDs. Snacks or dinner can also be provided to the children. Parents should feel free to check on their children throughout the evening at breaks or as necessary to help parents feel more comfortable about not being able to see them.

Refreshments

Both before the session and during a break, coffee, tea, and snacks should be made available if dinner is not offered. Frequently, these informal breaks allow participants to ask questions of the leaders and each other that they have not had the opportunity to raise during the session. A relaxed, informal style should encourage parents to share their concerns and ideas about their children.

Intangible Motivators

Some other motivators are less tangible, such as being reassuring to parents who might be anxious that they will not catch on quickly or will be judged. Be sure to respect each parent's learning style and make it clear to parents that at no time during a group are parents required to talk about a painful issue. A number of strategies can be used to encourage resistant parents to join the program, including providing a variety of incentives such as child care, tokens or tickets for transportation to the meetings, refreshments or even dinner, small gifts from a sponsoring agency (e.g., sachets of bubble bath or free tickets to a local sporting event to put in their self-care boxes), and a folder of handouts with useful information.

SPECIAL CONSIDERATIONS FOR GROUP LEADERS

The Pathways to Competence for Young Children Parenting Program gives parents support and specific knowledge about parenting that sometimes requires special skills and background for group leaders. For example, the ways in which attachment, temperament, and self-esteem were handled in the parents' own family of origin are common areas of discussion. Discussing these intergenerational issues requires professional skills and insight to help parents to understand and begin to resolve these issues. Leaders may also be called on to help parents to deal with current difficulties concerning their child and family and life circumstances. There also needs to be an awareness of when referral for further professional counseling would be valuable; therefore, it is important that group leaders have some experience leading parenting groups. In many instances, experience in working with multi-risk families would be important, although if the group is more preventative in its goals, this may not be an issue. Leaders should have knowledge of early child development and parenting. One good source for such information is the book *Pathways to Competence: Enhancing the Social and Emotional Development of Young Children* (Landy, 2002). In fact, the Steps in this program are intentionally tied to the information found in *Pathways to Competence* (2002). Throughout each Step, leaders are encouraged to learn more or use additional exercises to be found in this book, and thus it is strongly recommended that leaders have access to a copy. (See www.brookespublishing.com for purchasing information.)

In our experience, we have found that the Pathways to Competence for Young Children Parenting Program works best when led by co-leaders who take turns leading, observing, and supporting individuals in the group. Recognizing each parent's needs while presenting information and leading discussions can be difficult. This program has been conducted successfully with student interns and other trainees who have served as co-leaders. The trainees are then able to offer the program on their own as they gain practical experience under supervision.

It is recommended that one of the group leaders have a graduate degree in a discipline related to child development, early intervention, and/or parenting as well as extensive clinical experience. The co-leader may have cultural affiliation with the members of the group and/or experience working with the particular parent population (e.g., parents who are immigrants and/or English language learners, women living in violent situations, teenage parents, parents with unresolved loss and trauma, parents referred from child protection agencies). In addition, at least one of the group leaders needs experience with the types of issues relevant to a particular group (e.g., childhood aggression, attention-deficit hyperactivity disorder [ADHD]).

Chapter 6 goes into more detail about group processes and rules. Chapter 7 walks group leaders through a typical Step.

CHAPTER 6

GROUP RULES AND PROCESSES

One of the first and most important tasks to complete during the first session is to establish rules for the group and to discuss them with participants. These rules must be agreed on by the participants to ensure a safe place for parents to discuss their feelings and reveal personal information. Group leaders may wish to develop their own rules for their group; however, the following are examples of rules that have been developed and used successfully in Pathways to Competence for Young Children Parenting Program groups.

1. Anything that goes on within the group will remain **confidential** and is not to be discussed or shared with anyone outside the group.

2. Every group member will have an opportunity to **speak and be listened to.** In order to allow every group member time to participate, the group leader may have to keep responses short.

3. **Regular attendance** is important. Participants should not miss more than two sessions.

4. In some instances the leader will go around and ask each of the group members to share experiences so that everyone feels included, but **it is not required that group members speak** if they do not want to.

5. Enhancing **self-esteem** is an important objective of the program, so no one will be allowed to offend, reject, or hurt anyone else within the group (see Handout 1.1 for Step 1 for the group rules).

It is important to discuss the first rule in detail and to stress its importance. Often, groups are formed with people from the same neighborhood or the same social circles (e.g., children in the same school). The families' personal information should not become the subject of neighborhood discussion. Should this become an issue, private discussion with the individuals should help resolve the problem. The other rules relate to interactions within the group. Most parents in groups are very supportive of each other and the process is often helpful to reinforce their sense of parenting competence. As a consequence, a great deal of the effectiveness of the group process comes from parents sharing strategies and ideas.

Sometimes parents may like to bring people who are not the primary caregivers of the child with them, such as child care providers, grandparents, or the child's teacher. Some of the information discussed in the group may be of a nature that many parents would consider inappropriate to raise with these people present, or it may not be in the best interests of the class to have such individuals there. In order for parents to feel most comfortable disclosing information that would help them understand their parenting practices, the leaders and parents should discuss the appropriateness of other family members attending the meetings if the issue comes up.

THE MULTICULTURAL GROUP

Many parenting programs are provided in community agencies with parents from a variety of cultural groups. It is important that parents either have enough of a grasp of the English language to understand the concepts described in the groups or that an interpreter is provided. Preferably, one of the group leaders would be from the same cultural group as most of the parents attending, because communication is built on more than just language. In order to reach out to people and to engage them in the program, one must be sensitive to cultural differences in child-rearing practices and accommodate differences in views. This does not mean condoning differences in parenting approaches that violate basic understandings of child development and parenting, however, such as harsh discipline or feeding practices that can jeopardize the health of the infant or young child.

Group leaders should also recognize the *level* of language skills the members of the group possess, such as reading level or familiarity with certain jargon. The manual describes research results or other concepts with language that may be difficult for participants to fully understand. Also, because group members may have different educational and life experiences, the information must be provided at a level that all group participants will understand. Simply memorizing the "scripts" of the Steps and repeating them will not be sufficient, and it will be important to give the information in a way that is most meaningful and readily understood for the particular group of parents assembled.

Although certain participants may need interpreters for particular areas of discussion, continuous interpretation throughout each Step might make it difficult for other participants. The parenting group is more likely to be successful if a participant only needs some translation to understand the more complex terms and ideas but can participate in most of the discussions without it, although this should be at the discretion and best judgment of group leaders and dependent on the situation and will require sensitivity toward people's feelings and needs.

THE GROUP PROCESS

During the group process, emphasis should be placed not only on the objectives outlined in Chapter 3 but also on giving parents hope, promoting a sense of common purpose, and making sure the instructional content of the sessions is discussed. It is crucial that group leaders ensure that every group member is able to participate in the discussion so that he or she feels as if his or her needs are being met. Making sure this happens can be challenging because parents differ in the ways they like to receive information, their willingness to talk, and their response to other group members. Group leaders will at times need to adapt the material in order to work effectively and professionally with a variety of different personalities and situations. Some suggestions of ways to work most effectively with certain personality types or situations common to group members are described next. Keep in mind that it may be more effective to deal with these issues individually rather than during group meetings.

DEALING WITH CHALLENGING TYPES OF PEOPLE

Sometimes certain group members may create an environment that is not conducive to frank and open discussion. Should these issues arise, group leaders will need to intervene to redirect the discussion and to establish a level of comfort among the participants. The following types of individuals are often encountered in groups, and some strategies for addressing the issues that arise when they are present in a group are described next.

The Group Member Who Dominates the Discussion

Sometimes, one parent, out of eagerness or a very outgoing personality, may dominate discussions that come up. It is important to recognize his or her contribution, but if the problem is chronic you may need to interrupt the individual and ask the group if anyone would like to comment on what is being discussed. Avoid having to single out the parent, but instead, remind the group of the rule to keep comments short in order to allow other participants to speak.

The Parent Who Is Reluctant to Talk in the Group

Some participants may be reluctant to talk and may defer to other group members constantly. To encourage participation from all members, specific questions can be addressed to these individuals. Also, when topics are posed to the whole group, it is important to notice any subject that a parent does seem to like to talk about and to try to include it in other discussions. Sometimes posing a question to the group so that everyone gets an opportunity to respond helps everyone to feel included. Make sure to be very positive about any comments that a reluctant parent does make. Remember to respect the group rule that no one is obligated to speak, however.

The Group that Does Not Support or Ridicules a Participant

It is crucial to stop this situation immediately and to remind participants of the rules that were established in the beginning regarding treating everyone with respect. One way to help this situation is to model acceptance of the particular participant by acknowledging his or her contribution; but if the ridicule or lack of support continues, it may be important to meet with the parent individually and to give him or her some strategies to help prevent this situation from getting worse. If the parent frequently gives inaccurate information or talks very negatively about his or her child, for example, the group leaders could support the effort the parent is making in the group but could point out the particular issue that seems to be unacceptable to other group members. It is important to discuss with the group what might be underlying the group member's beliefs, and to work with the individual in question to bring some new insight that might move him or her beyond the ideas that are detrimental to his or her parenting and to the child. Obviously, the approach will vary according to the issue that has arisen.

The Group Member Who Tries to Assume the Role of an Assistant

Some groups have a participant who wants to assist the group leaders and give advice that may not be consistent with the other information that is being conveyed. If the advice that the participant is giving could be harmful to children (e.g., "If a baby cries, just ignore the crying and eventually it will stop"), the group leaders need to be very sensitive to the parent while pointing out that there are other ways of dealing with the problem. Group leaders could offer something like "That is what some believe, but what research has shown (or what we have learned from doing the group) is that infants form a stronger attachment if they feel secure about their parents attending to them." Giving the parent some responsibility such as watching the time or handing out things may be helpful.

The Parent Who Knows Everything

Sometimes a parent will seem to have objectives that fit with those of the other group members but will repeatedly say that he or she already does everything with the child that is being suggested by the group leaders. The group leader may need to come back to the parent's reason for coming and to ask what areas of discussion would be interesting and useful. Helping to refocus the parent on his or her reasons for coming to the group may need to be done outside the group session.

The Parent for Whom Nothing Works

A parent may keep complaining about his or her child's behavior and yet seem to be unwilling to try any of the strategies during homework or in the group. If the complaints are continual and are bothering other parents, the group leaders should ask the parent to talk specifically about his or her efforts to try to change things and to support him or her in identifying what seems to be getting in the way. Some parents experience a sense of helplessness and need a great deal of praise for any success. At other times, it may be useful to point out that the child has been exhibiting certain behaviors and strategies for a long time, and change always takes a long time.

The "Yes, but . . . ." Parent

This parent agrees that the suggested strategies should work but says that he or she tried them but they did not work out. This type of individual typically gives various reasons for why the strategies did not and cannot work for his or her child. This type of parent may need help in problem solving about ways to make the strategy work. Indicating that many parents find the ideas useful and suggesting ways they can be adapted to the parent's own situation is often the key to helping this type of participant.

The Rambling and Theorizing Parent

Some parents spend a great deal of time rambling on about a topic or theorizing in a way that is very difficult for the other parents, who may even contemplate dropping out of the group as a result. When this happens, it may be necessary to paraphrase what the parent said more succinctly or to bring the topic back to something more practical. Suggesting books and articles that talk about the topic can be helpful as a way to bring the discussion back.

The Aggressive Parent

Some parents become upset that they or their child is being victimized in some way or say that "Things shouldn't be this way." For example, they may argue quite vehemently that child protection services should not be involved, that their husband causes the child's problems, or that their child should behave differently. Parents like this can be helped by having their pain acknowledged while being encouraged and supported to try to find new ways to deal with the issues or symptoms. Often, the aggressive stance can be hiding a feeling of deep shame, and some support for feelings and the positive efforts the individual is making can help the person to go beyond these feelings, especially if members of the group can support the person's efforts.

The Disagreeing Couple

When both parents from a family attend the group, it may become clear that they do not agree about how to raise their child(ren). The group leaders should emphasize to the whole group the need for couples to find solutions together. Group leaders also may need to interrupt any blaming of each other that is going on between the couple. Occasionally, parents may have to be asked to continue their discussion outside of the session. Group leaders may offer to hold a couple of discussions out of the group with the parents to help them to resolve their conflict.

Chapter 7 describes what is included in a typical session in order to familiarize group leaders with the program in more depth.

CHAPTER 7

OVERALL PLAN FOR THE GROUP

As described in early chapters, the competencies covered in the Pathways to Competence for Young Children Parenting Program that parents are supported to develop in their children include body control and a positive body image (Step 2); secure attachment to caregivers (Step 3); play and imagination (Step 4); language and communication (Step 5); self-esteem (Step 6); self-regulation, morality, and a sense of conscience (Step 7); emotion regulation (Step 8); concentration, planning, and problem solving (Step 9); and social competence, empathy, and caring behavior (Step 10). Although each step of the program will provide information on a different competency, a common or similar structure for the group should be followed each week. Within this structure, which is used in the Steps that make up Section II of this book, the program uses a variety of strategies to meet its objectives, including group discussion, group activities, video clips, role playing, and didactic approaches.

What follows are guidelines for conducting the group sessions. Although all of the ideas raised in the program guidelines need to be covered, group leaders should adapt their presentation style to fit the needs of the participants and the comfort level of the leaders.

CONDUCTING A PATHWAYS TO COMPETENCE FOR YOUNG CHILDREN PARENTING PROGRAM GROUP

This chapter provides group leaders with the information they need to conduct the 10 Steps that make up the Pathways to Competence for Young Children Parenting Program and outlines the schedule that should be followed for each session. The pre-group session and how to conduct the initial session are covered first.

The Pre-Group Session and Pretesting of Participants

Usually, before the first group session begins, group leaders or program administrators will meet with parents—and in some cases their children as well—in order to screen them for suitability for the group. This screening can be carried out over the telephone using a questionnaire(s) if appropriate.

The parents should be considered in terms of their goals and how they fit with the objectives selected for the group. In addition, group leaders will want to assess parents' eligibility according to the criteria for the group and watch for any signs of psychopathology that might preclude an individual's attendance at the group. Types of psychopathology that would be difficult to accommodate in the group include a severe character disorder, chronic and severe substance abuse, and/or schizophrenia. Leaders may want to meet the children and also to observe parent–child interactions if it is important to include this information in pretesting or if video clips of the interaction are going to be filmed.

This type of pre-group session also allows parents an opportunity to ask questions about the group. In addition, the parents' need for child care can be discussed and any incentives that will be offered can be described. The group leaders may obtain some ideas about how the members of the group may interact so as to be aware of any possible challenges that may occur. If pretests are going to be used, they should be completed during this session or the questionnaires can be given out to be completed at home.

Preparing the Manuals and Binders for the Groups

Group leaders should familiarize themselves with the program thoroughly so that they can prepare for each session. They should gather materials, set up the room optimally, establish pacing of the Steps or sections, and decide ahead of time who will present each section of the group session or Step when there will be more than one group leader. It is recommended that handouts be printed out from the CD-ROM that accompanies this manual and photocopied before each session so that parents can complete group exercises and follow the handouts during the session. Some group leaders may choose to prepare parent binders before the commencement of the group.

Use of Video Clips or Vignettes

In preplanning, group leaders may also want to videotape an interaction (e.g., playing, feeding, teaching, limit setting) between each parent and his or her child. These could then be used as pretests of the interaction for evaluation purposes. Also, with the parents' permission, these video clips could be edited and relevant clips could be shown in the group sessions to illustrate *positive* interactions and some of the principles of parenting outlined in the program Steps. This can be a powerful way to help the parents to enhance their sense of parenting competence and to teach the principles of parenting. This may not be appropriate for all group leaders to use because of the extra time needed to find suitable vignettes from the videos and to make sure something positive is shown from each interaction. Also, some programs may not have suitable equipment to do the filming. Although it can be a powerful tool for providing parenting information, videotaping is not considered to be an essential component of the program.

THE FORMAT FOR THE GROUPS

Although the information provided in each week of the group will vary, the format will be similar for all 10 Steps of the program. This format is described later in this chapter.

Group Session Structure

A typical group session would last 2 hours; however, certain topics take longer than others, and what cannot be covered in one session may be held over to the following session. Although it may be possible to cover a complete Step in one session, this is not always the case, so *Step* and *session* cannot always be used interchangeably. What follows is the format of a typical Step:

Homework Review

Setting the Stage

Discussion of Key Terms

Understanding the Capacity

    Development of the Capacity

    Importance of the Capacity

    Research About the Capacity

Parenting Principles Related to the Capacity

Other Discussion Topics

The Tree: Metaphor for Development

Homework (for the next group meeting)

Each of these is described in more detail next. Note that Step 1 begins with an additional introductory component.

Introduction

At the beginning of the group, parents will be given the opportunity to introduce themselves and to bring up any issues they have concerning their child or other topics relevant to the group such as issues about their child's behavior or any concerns about emotional or social issues. Group rules and logistics should be established at this time. It is very important to keep this introduction short so it does not use up time needed for the other parts of the group meeting.

Homework Review

Each week, the parents will be assigned homework. Although parents are busy and may not feel that homework is necessary or desired, we believe that practice with feedback is an important factor leading to permanent change in parenting behavior. At the beginning of each meeting (except for the first one), it is important to review the homework from the previous week. Briefly review the key ideas and entertain questions. Give group members the opportunity to help problem solve the issues that each parent raises. Be sensitive to those group members who perhaps found the assigned tasks difficult to carry out because they were busy or felt uncomfortable doing either of the suggested activities.

Consistently encourage self-reflectivity and empathy for the child during these discussions. For example, a homework assignment may have been to ask parents to reframe some "don'ts" into "do's" (e.g., "Don't talk like that!" to "Can you say that to me in a quieter voice?"), after which the parents would be asked to comment on how they thought this made the child feel and anything they noticed about how they acted. Group leaders will want to ask probing questions to find out the following: Did the parents experience more understanding of their child? How did they feel doing the activity? During discussion of self-care activities, ask parents to comment on how helpful they were in reducing stress and enhancing their sense of well-being. Also examine what they felt was important for them about the self-care activity.

Setting the Stage

Each Step contains suggestions on how to introduce the new topic. It is vital to draw the group's attention about the importance of the competency and to engage them in a discussion of the topic at the start of the session. This will set the stage for their involvement in both receiving the information and problem solving the issues for their family and child. Remember, this is often the time when parents are asking themselves, "Do I really want to be here?" and "Am I going to learn anything in the next few hours that will make this a worthwhile use of my time?"

Discussion of Key Terms

Group leaders need to clearly define the terms and skills that will be talked about during each session. Remember, most parents do not know what attachment is or how expressive language differs from receptive language. Finding interesting ways to explain the key words will help capture the group's interest. Making visual or auditory props available and having the parents describe examples from their own children will help pinpoint the kinds of behavior the discussion will be centered around. For example, most group participants will have heard about self-esteem, but further refinement of their understanding will be helpful.

Understanding the Capacity

Development of the Capacity

During this part of the Step or session, group leaders will describe how a particular competency develops in early life. Handouts will be presented that contain tables listing key features at each stage of development (see Handouts 1.4, 2.2, 3.4, on the accompanying CD-ROM for examples). Parents will spend time reviewing the tables and discussing where their child might fit in the developmental sequence and what skills may be emerging as their child develops. These discussions and tables help parents to understand that children are not born with all of the skills they need to have for a certain capacity. For example, it is important for parents to understand when to expect a child to say words and to follow through with requests; otherwise, they may be too demanding too early before a child is really capable of performing one of these skills. Parents will also learn the importance of having age-appropriate expectations. When they realize that a particular "difficult" behavior is age appropriate, this can help parents to see the behavior in a more positive light and change any negative attributions they may have of their child. Also, if a parent realizes that his or her child is delayed in acquiring a developmental skill, reviewing typical development of the capacity may help.

Importance of the Capacity

This section helps parents to understand the importance of the capacity for their child and how this capacity may have an impact on their child's life. It includes questions that parents often wonder about, such as "What about sending my child to child care; will my child still have a secure attachment?" "Why is it important for my child to have opportunities for creative and fantasy play?" "My child has an imaginary friend—is that okay?" "Is it really important for my child to have good self-esteem? She's only 4!?"

Research About the Capacity

The text *Pathways to Competence* (2002) contains extensive reviews of the literature about each of the capacities discussed. The leaders of a group should read the material pertaining to the topic and select some of the information that they think their group would find particularly relevant. A brief description, in terms that are comprehensible for the group, helps them understand what is currently known about different aspects of the capacity. Presenting any information in a way that the parents will find interesting and that will answer their questions is important. Parents often ask questions about topics that have not been presented. Be prepared as group leaders to add details in areas that are of particular interest. A good knowledge of *Pathways to Competence* (2002) is helpful, but be ready to say "I don't know, but I'll look it up and have an answer for you next time."

Parenting Principles Related to the Capacity

Each Step includes a list of principles that parents can follow in order to encourage the development of the capacity in their child. The principles were developed based on a distillation of the current research findings for each capacity. They specify general approaches to developing the capacity in young children. The handouts for each Step include a list of these parenting principles for each capacity that the group can review and discuss. Having parents discuss their understanding of each principle and how they could implement the concept with their child is important.

This part of the parenting group also includes lots of practical parenting ideas. Suggestions are given both in this manual and in *Pathways to Competence* (2002). This is often the part where suggestions are found for the homework part of the program. Some techniques can be practiced during the group session with participants taking different roles. These practice sessions set the stage for trying the skills at home. Parents love the new ideas they get from this practice—and if a safe, secure environment has been established—the active participation can be fun and helpful to parents.

Other Discussion Topics

For each Step, group leaders can introduce other important topics that are raised by parents about the developmental capacity being discussed. For example, under Emotion Regulation some parents may want to discuss sibling rivalry and under Concentration, Planning, and Problem Solving they may want to find out more about attention-deficit/hyperactivity disorder (ADHD). Under each Step, the more important topics are identified but the group leader is referred to *Pathways to Competence* (2002) for others. Topics for discussion should be selected on the basis of the topics that the group is most interested in.

The Tree: Metaphor for Development

Group leaders will also want to introduce the concept of a tree as a metaphor for development in the first session. Specifically, for the purposes of this program, the roots symbolize the developmental competencies, the branches symbolize parenting strategies, and the leaves or fruit symbolize what the participants want for their children. The roles of parenting can also be represented on the tree and can be referred to as various strategies for parenting are examined.

This metaphor will be used throughout the program in each Step. (See Figure 7.1 and Section III, Supplemental Materials, for a sample of the tree and label cards that can be made into overheads or other presentation materials for various uses.) These trees can be created by group leaders or purchased in most local teacher supply stores in the bulletin board sections. Internet sites selling teacher supplies may also be a good source.

In Step 1, the group participants will be asked to record characteristics and positive attributes they desire for their children on pieces of paper shaped like leaves or fruits and to place them on the tree. Pictures representing the different roles (e.g., Nurturer, Playmate, Limit Setter, Teacher) will also be placed on the branches of the tree during

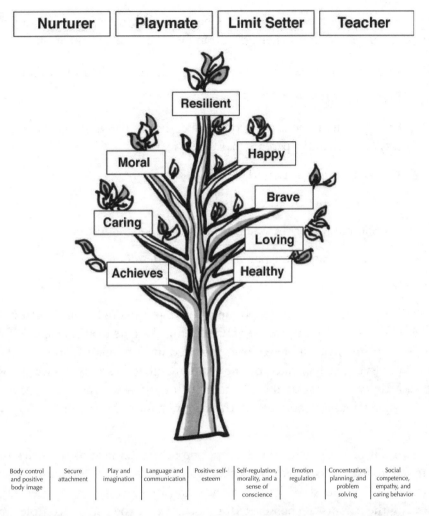

Figure 7.1. The model of the tree, with the roots symbolizing developmental competencies, the branches symbolizing parenting strategies, and the leaves or fruit symbolizing what the participants want for their children. (Illustration courtesy of Michelle Fortnum.)

Step 1. At the beginning of each Step, then, the leader will place the competency being discussed (e.g., self-esteem, emotion regulation) on the roots of the tree. During each subsequent Step, the parenting principles for developing that competency will be written on cards by the parents. Parents will then discuss what roles they would play when using the principle or parenting strategy with their child (e.g., *showing unconditional love* would be placed under Nurturer and *following the child's lead in play* under Playmate). At the conclusion of each Step, have parents place each principle under the parenting role that the group decides is most important. Some of the principles could fit under more than one role, so the discussion and choice of a role to put it under provides an opportunity to discuss each principle further.

Homework

Each week it is important to assign homework for the parents. Allowing parents the opportunity to practice skills with the chance for feedback from leaders and peers the next week will ensure a greater likelihood that parents will implement new methods of parenting after the group is over. Changing their ways of interacting with children requires parents to implement the strategies they learn in the group.

Provide parents with two homework assignments based on two different areas:

1. Parenting Activity

    Give parents a choice of a couple of activities based on the topic covered in the session. Generally, parents may select from

    - An activity to try with a child

    - A behavioral strategy to implement

    - Something for the parent to observe about a child

    - Reflections on the parents' own families of origin

2. Self-Care Activity

    Self-care activities are important to help parents to lessen the stress in their lives and to enhance their sense of well-being. Parents may choose a self-care activity from among a list of activities provided in Handout 1.22 on the CD-ROM, and others can be generated by the group members. Parents should choose a self-care activity that is related to the topic being discussed that week. Many homework suggestions are contained in this program or in the text of *Pathways to Competence* (2002).

If two sessions are used for one Step, one of the homework activities should be assigned for each of the weeks. In other words, the first assignment could be given the first week and the second assignment could be given the next week rather than allowing the parents to choose. It is important that the parents complete a homework assignment each week in order to keep them practicing.

Group Strategies

Each Step will follow a similar format, but the format can also be varied according to the experience of the group leaders and the composition of the group. Although the format of the group sessions will be similar, the amount of information provided and discussion allowed will vary significantly depending on the number of sessions (one or two) that will be spent discussing a particular capacity (Step). Group participants may also vary in their readiness to delve into certain topics; for example, in some situations, parents may want to talk about their own experiences growing up; some may want to discuss these experiences earlier in the session than other groups. Other groups may prefer to start the group activities earlier than suggested. The group sessions, including the first session, should follow the order described in the next sections. However, in our experience, we have found that although it is important to conduct the first group following this suggested order, in subsequent sessions the plan could be varied in order to keep the interest and involvement of group members high. During each of the Steps, a variety of strategies can be used to convey the information and achieve the objectives of the group. If time is limited, the group leaders should choose at least one from each of the following types of strategies, identified with icons so that the approaches can be readily identified when looking through the text of the Steps.

Homework

The homework icon appears both at the beginning of the session and at the end. The first icon appears for the Homework Review section and then closes the session for the homework assignment to be worked on between sessions.

Handouts

As the Step progresses, group leaders will refer the participants to particular handouts that are included on the CD-ROM that accompanies this manual. These handouts are identified by this icon. Handouts are labeled with a number that refers to the particular Step (e.g., 1.1, 1.2, 3.1, 3.2). For ease of use before starting the program, it is recommended that prior to the entire group starting or prior to each step, group leaders print and photocopy enough handouts for each of the participants and ask that the participants keep them in a binder. Binders could be brought in by the participants or purchased in advance by the sponsoring agency.

Group Discussion

At any point in the program, when parents ask questions or when time for discussion is allocated, group leaders pose questions to the group to stimulate group discussion of the topics in each Step. These discussions encourage reflection on the topics, and group members can share their knowledge, understanding, and any experiences related to the issue. When appropriate, group leaders could carefully record parents' ideas as accurately and completely as possible on an overhead projector or flip chart or easel. Group leaders need to be careful not to record any ideas that could be harmful to children (e.g., "Beating a child"); instead, reasons should be given for not acting in a certain way.

View Video Clip

If the parent and child have been videotaped interacting together before the beginning of the group, preselected video clips showing each parent in a positive exchange with their child can be shown at appropriate times in the group sessions to illustrate various parenting principles.

Family of Origin

A key factor predicting how people will parent is how they were parented. Thus, each session provides activities to help parents think about their own parents' ways of parenting them and how the competence being discussed was handled in their family while they were growing up. These activities are not put under one section of a Step but are integrated across a number of areas that are considered most suitable. These strategies often play a pivotal role in changing parents' thinking and behavior. The manual poses several questions for parents to answer that will help them think about how their family of origin functioned and how their own parents dealt with the capacity. The "light'" comes on when they see their own behavior mirrored in the behavior of their parents. Some parents may also discuss how their own difficult experiences have made them try not to repeat that model of parenting with their own children. Group leaders should listen carefully to make sure that a parent is not overcompensating for his or her parents' behavior and gently point it out, if that is the case. For example, a father may be reluctant to set appropriate limits for his child because he experienced one of his parents as being too strict, harsh, or even abusive.

Group Activities

Group activities are interspersed to help with learning throughout each of the Steps in this manual. Additional group activities are included in *Pathways to Competence* (2002) and could be used if more activities are needed because groups require more time to learn about a particular developmental capacity. These activities include questionnaires and exercises that will help parents to understand themselves, their parenting style, how their behavior is influencing their child, and how to help their child develop the different competencies. Group leaders should choose the activities that will work best for the parents in their groups. The choice of what activities to use will vary according to the parents who will be attending, the particular issues they are dealing with, the number of weeks assigned to each capacity, and how comfortable the group leaders feel with a certain activity.

Role Playing

Opportunities for role plays are provided in each of the Steps and can be carried out by the two leaders together, one parent and a group leader, or two parents. On the one hand, role playing positive interactions allows parents to practice the appropriate ways to respond to their child, which is an excellent reinforcement for learning new strategies to use at home. On the other hand, role playing negative interactions in some of the Steps can help parents to see the possible effects their parenting can have on their children.

Self-Care Activity

As part of the homework, group leaders suggest a self-care activity each week to discuss at the beginning of the group next week. Some suggestions of self-care activities are provided in Handout 1.22 in the Step 1 handouts. In addition, group leaders could provide parents with small self-care items during each session that parents could collect in a self-care box. Some examples might be a sample size of bubble bath or body lotion, their list of positive qualities from Step 6, or a sample of hot chocolate or a tea bag. Local merchants may be willing to donate these to the program. The parents would then take them home following the last group meeting. Be imaginative in creating these ideas. They need not be expensive; some could be made from inexpensive materials, or an inspiring or hopeful poem could be photocopied for each group member. Also, group leaders could provide a healthy snack or a participant may wish to bake some cookies to share with others. The recipe could then be given to the parents for their self-care box.

CHAPTER 8

MEASURES FOR EVALUATING A PATHWAYS TO COMPETENCE GROUP

Because funding often is limited to programs that are backed by research, many agencies that provide parenting groups are looking for programs that are evidence based. These agencies seek programs in which interventions have been evaluated for effectiveness with the children and parents they serve. This chapter looks at how to conduct an effective evaluation of a Pathways to Competence for Young Children Parenting Program group.

DECIDING ON GOALS AND OBJECTIVES

In planning an evaluation of the effectiveness of a Pathways to Competence for Young Children Parenting Program group with the particular population served by the agency, it is first important to decide on the program's goals and objectives. The overall goal is likely to be improvements in child development. Objectives could include changes within a child (e.g., reduction in symptoms, enhancement of attachment to caregivers); improvement in the parent–child interaction (e.g., increased sensitivity, reduction in intrusiveness); changes within a parent (e.g., improved sense of parenting competence, reduced depression, resolution of trauma); and parent satisfaction with the group. See Chapter 3 for a list of possible objectives that are addressed by the group.

In an effective evaluation of a Pathways to Competence for Young Children Parenting Program group, a baseline of these areas or variables needs to be collected in order to be able to show any improvements after the program's completion. Thus, pretests should be administered during a pre-group session. Suggestions for assessment tools are listed next in the Methodology section. Group leaders who would like to do a pre- and posttest evaluation of the group can use any of the recommended measures that are suitable for their group population and the goals and objectives they have chosen for the group.

DETERMINING METHODOLOGY

For many community agencies, arranging a control or comparison group and carrying out analysis of data will not be possible. However, it is sometimes possible to arrange a partnership with a staff member at a local university who may be interested in conducting the evaluation. If staff members are interested in carrying out an evaluation, however, having pre- and posttests of some measures and parent satisfaction questionnaires can be useful tools to show to managers to demonstrate the usefulness of the group. In our experience, the most common and simplest methodology for evaluation has been to have a control group made up of parents on a waiting list because this avoids the ethical dilemma of denying services and also allows parents and children who received the intervention to be compared on various measures with a group of children and parents who have not yet participated in the program. The waiting list group can then attend the program after the posttest data have been collected for both sets of parents—those who have and have not participated in the program.

Measures for Evaluating Success in Meeting Group Objectives

Several measures are available that can be used to determine outcomes such as child behavior change, parenting knowledge, and parent attributions of the child. Group leaders may also informally discuss how they found working with the program, although this is seldom part of the evaluation. Parental assessment of the program may be used as part of the evaluation, however (see Section III: Supplemental Materials for a sample parent satisfaction form).

Child Behavior Change

The following assessment tools can be used to determine changes in children's behavior, parenting knowledge, and other program outcomes.

Child Behavior Checklist

The Child Behavior Checklist (CBCL; Achenbach & Edelbrock, 1983) is a widely used, standardized measure that can identify children who display clinically elevated levels of behavior problems and excessive aggression. The assessment has two versions: one for 2- to 3-year-olds and one for children ages 4 years and older. The scale yields overall externalizing, internalizing, and total problems scores, as well as scores related to individual behavioral syndromes (i.e., clusters of symptoms that go together). With regard to validity, all scales of the CBCL for both age groups have been shown to discriminate significantly between referred and non-referred samples. The CBCL correlates highly with other parent checklists such as the Conners, Quay-Peterson and Richman instruments. Test–retest reliability is .88 for 4- to 18-year-olds and .87 for 2- to 3-year-olds.

Eyberg Child Behavior Inventory

The Eyberg Child Behavior Inventory (ECBI; Eyberg & Pincus, 1999) is a short (i.e., brief) rating scale designed to record parent reports of childhood behavioral problems, particularly oppositional behavior and conduct disorders. The inventory results in two scores on completion: an intensity score, reflecting the sum of ratings across all items, and a problem score, made up of the number of items endorsed as a problem by the parent. Over a period of 21 days, test–retest reliability has been reported as 0.86 for the intensity score and 0.88 for the problem score. The validity of the scale has been primarily established by demonstration of adequate discrimination between children with typical behavior and conduct problems as well as children who have been neglected and other clinic-referred children. Scores have been found to relate significantly to direct observational measures of noncompliance and negative parent–child interactions. The ECBI has been shown to be sensitive to intervention effects from parent training in child behavior management skills.

Likert Scale

Behavioral goals for children can be chosen by the parents and rated on a Likert scale before and after the group. For example, a parent might decide on certain behavioral goals such as sitting at the table for dinner or getting ready to go to child care without a fuss, that he or she would rate before and after the program on a scale of 1 to 5.

Parenting Knowledge

Knowledge of Child Development Inventory

Knowledge of Child Development Inventory (MacPhee, 1981) is a 58-item questionnaire that tests parents' knowledge of child development and parenting of children from birth to 6 years. Two versions are offered, one for children from birth to 3 years and one for children from 3 to 6 years. Higher scores indicate a better understanding of child development and parenting. MacPhee (1981) reported a test–retest reliability of .92 for the total score over a 2-week interval and a Cronbach's alpha of .82 for parents' score.

Parents' Self-Reflectivity and Capacity for Empathy for the Child

The Working Model of the Child Interview*

The Working Model of the Child Interview (Zeanah, Benoit, & Barton, 1993) is used to assess parents' attributions of their relationship with their child. Parents are interviewed in order to gather information regarding their perceptions, feelings, and interpretations of their child and the parent–child relationship. The interview is scored for qualitative and content features of the representations. Four scales are used to characterize the qualitative features of the caregiver's representation of his or her child: 1) richness of perception, 2) openness to change, 3) intensity of involvement, and 4) coherence.

---

*Assessments designated with an asterisk require training to score them. Others can be used by carefully following the scoring procedure.

Three categories are used to classify the parents' perception of the relationship: 1) balanced, 2) disengaged, and 3) distorted. The categories reflect organized child and adult attachment patterns but not disorganized attachment in the child or unresolved loss and trauma in the parent. The interview can also be checked for instances in which the parent shows understanding of his or her child's perspective and empathy for his or her child (e.g., "He cried a lot when he was a baby, but he seemed to be in pain and had difficulty dealing with it. I found that holding him and keeping things calm helped him the most." As opposed to "He cried all the time; he was spoiled and difficult from the beginning, and there was nothing to do about it so I just let him cry.") The measure requires training to administer and score.

The Toronto Alexithymia Scale

The Toronto Alexithymia Scale (Bagby, Parker, & Taylor, 1994) is a 20-item scale that assesses the construct of alexithymia, which is a reduced ability to accurately identify subjective feelings as well as reflect and communicate emotional experiences and distress. Such a characteristic makes it difficult for an individual to modulate emotional experiences and to receive relevant interpersonal support. It also significantly reduces the person's capacity to understand the thoughts and feelings of others, and for parents, it reduces their ability to understand the feelings their child.

The scale has demonstrated internal consistency of .76 as well as convergent and discriminant validity based on its pattern of correlation with self-report measures of traits theoretically related and unrelated to alexithymia. Cut-off scores have been set at more than 61 out of a possible 100 denoting alexithymia and less than 51 denoting non-alexithymia. Intermediate scores range between 52 and 60. High scores denoting alexithymia have been found with parents with unresolved loss and trauma (Martyn, 2002; Martyn & Dundas, 1997).

Parent Attributions

Parent Attibution Scale

The Parent Attribution Scale (Bugental & Cruzcosa, 1985) is used to assess parents' attributions of their child and how they perceive the balance of power (whether they ascribe high power to themselves and little to the child or low power to themselves and high power to the child). This is important because a parent who assigns high power to the child and not to him- or herself typically has attributions of the child that are based on blaming and tends to see the child as threatening. This parent, then, would also be more likely to abuse his or her child (e.g., Dix & Grusec, 1985). The assessment asks parents to assign importance ratings to a series of factors as causes of hypothetical caregiving success and failure. The items are evenly split between adult variables (e.g., parenting ability, parental circumstances) and child variables (e.g., child's disposition, child's physical environment). Causes are assessed as either internal (e.g., ability or effort) or external (e.g., luck, other people), and they are either stable (e.g., ability, determined by other people) or unstable (e.g., effort, luck). The dimensions obtained are 1) adult versus child control, 2) "good" versus "bad" causes, and 3) controllable versus uncontrollable. Parents who make strong attributions to uncontrollable variables (i.e., take low credit) for caregiving success and to controllable variables for the child (i.e., assign high blame or responsibility) for caregiving behavior are likely to be easily triggered by child behavior (Bugental, 1992). Consequently, Pathways to Competence groups will be more successful if they can encourage parents to rate themselves as having more control over their children and to assign less blame to the children by the end of the group.

Parent Locus of Control Scale

The Parent Locus of Control Scale (PLOC; Campis, Lyman & Prentice-Dunn, 1986) is a 47-item questionnaire that assesses the degree to which parents feel that they can influence or control their child's behavior. Adequate internal consistency and concurrent validity have been reported (Lefcourt, 1991). The measure has been found to discriminate between parents who report management problems with their children and those who do not (Campis et al., 1986).

Parenting Strategies/Discipline

Home Observational Measure of the Environment*

The Home Observational Measure of the Environment (HOME; Bradley, Casey, & Caldwell, 1997) evaluates constructs such as maternal responsiveness, involvement and acceptance of the child, organization of the infant's physical environment, and opportunities for a variety of stimulation. The measure has two versions, one for infants from birth to 3 years old and one for preschoolers from 3 to 6 years old. It has been used with a number of groups from different cultures, and information is collected in the home by observation and interview. Interrater reliability ranges from .75 to .95, and HOME scores correlate substantially with children's scores on cognitive tests. For example, the HOME correlated at 3 years with the Stanford Binet Intelligence Scale (4th ed.) (Thorndike, Hagen, & Sattler, 1986) (r = .59) and at 3 years with the Illinois Test of Psycholinguistic Abilities (Kirk, McCarthy, & Kirk, 1968) score, .57 for African American children, and .74 for Caucasian children (Bradley & Caldwell, 1976).

The Parenting Scale

The Parenting Scale (PS; Arnold, O'Leary, Wolff, & Acker, 1993) is a 30-item self-report questionnaire that provides an assessment of dysfunctional discipline practices in parents of young children. The questionnaire consists of three subscales: 1) laxness (lacking discipline or not following through), 2) overreactivity (getting very upset

---

*Assessments designated with an asterisk require training to score them. Others can be used by carefully following the scoring procedure.

with the child and becoming very punitive), and 3) verbosity (talking too much instead of setting limits). The overreactivity subscale measures harsh, aggressive, and authoritarian discipline behaviors. The scale has been found to discriminate between mothers and fathers who were clinic- and nonclinic referred (Arnold, O'Leary, & Edwards, 1997). Good internal consistency and test–retest reliability (over 2 weeks) have also been found (Arnold et al., 1993).

Parent Emotional Well-Being

Center for Epidemiological Studies Depression Scale

Center for Epidemiological Studies Depression Scale (CES-D; Myers & Weissman, 1980) is a self-report measure of depressive symptomatology. Its two major uses are screening populations for the incidence of depression and serving as a short measure for outcome research. The scale has 20 items that assess the frequency and duration of symptoms associated with depression experienced in the preceding week. Scores range between 0 and 60. Scores of 16–20 indicate mild depression; 21–30, moderate depression; and 31 or higher, severe depression. Test–retest reliabilities range between .48 and .50 after 3 months. Strong discriminant validity has been found in a number of studies. Concurrent and construct validity has been shown, as well, with correlations of .8 with longer tests of depression and other clinical measures.

The Rosenberg Self-Esteem Scale

The Rosenberg Self-Esteem Scale (Rosenberg, 1965) consists of 10 items that assess global positive and negative attitudes toward the self. Items fall in a range between feeling that one has several good qualities to believing that one is a complete failure. Subjects rate the questions on a 5-point Likert scale from (1 = *not at all accurate* to 5 = *completely accurate*), which represents the extent to which each statement is felt or experienced. A total is computed by summing the ratings on all of the items. The possible scores on self-acceptance and self-worth range from 1 = *low self-esteem* to 5 = *high self-esteem.* High self-esteem signifies that the individual respects him- or herself and feels worthy of love. Low self-esteem reflects both lack of self-respect and feelings of inadequacy. The scale was standardized on a sample of 5,024 college students with an internal consistency of .77. Concurrent validity has been established by a demonstrated high relationship between low scores on the measure and depressed affect. Test–retest reliability of .61 over 7 months has been found. It is a strong predictor of unwed pregnancy, drug use, and depression.

Parenting Stress Index–Short Form

Parenting Stress Index–Short Form (Abiden, 1986) considers three factors that are added together to give a total parenting stress score: Parental Distress (items signal parental distress coming from a variety of aspects of their experience), Parent–Child Dysfunctional Interaction (items indicate the degree to which parents derive satisfaction from interaction with their children and how much their children meet their expectations), and Difficult Child (items here are related to the child's temperament).

The form includes 12 items scored between 1 and 5 in each of the sub-scales to a total of 60 (total score out of 180), with high scores indicating less stress. Test–retest reliabilities are high and vary from .84 for the total score and .78 for the difficult child scale. Concurrent validity has been established by comparing the short form with the long form of the scale that is well validated. The correlation between scores on the two forms of the scale was .94 (Abiden, 1986).

Early Childhood Care Questionnaire

The Early Childhood Care Questionnaire (ECCQ; Gross & Rocissano, 1988) measures maternal confidence, defined as the mother's perception of her effectiveness in managing a series of tasks or situations relevant to raising her child. The questionnaire consists of 37 items in which each mother rates her confidence in her ability to perform parenting tasks specific to her child. It can be used with mothers with toddlers between 1 and 3 years. The items are summed to obtain a total score. Higher scores indicate greater maternal confidence. Gross and Rocissano (1988) estimated Cronbach's alpha reliability from .91 to .95 and demonstrated a test–retest reliability of .87 over a 4-week interval.

Parent Sense of Competence Scale

The Parent Sense of Competence Scale (PSOC) (Gibaud-Wallston & Wandersman, 1978) is a 16-item questionnaire that measures parenting self-esteem and two aspects of parents' self-reported competence: feelings of satisfaction and efficacy in the parenting role. Satisfactory test–retest reliability (ranging between .46 and .82) and a significant inverse relationship between the PSOC and the CBCL have been reported (Johnston & Mash, 1989).

Social Support

Social Support Inventory

The Social Support Inventory (Cutrona & Russell, 1987) assesses the mother's subjective experience of reliable alliances, social integration, opportunity for nurturance, and sense of support from family and friends. The inventory assesses 6 items on a 4-point scale, with a score of 24 indicating a strong sense of support. Test–retest reliability is .92 and the test correlates with other social support measures and measures of the individual's personal characteristics.

Parent–Child/Interaction/Relationship

Parent–Child Relationship Inventory

The Parent–Child Relationship Inventory (PCRI) (Gerard, 1994) is a self-report instrument that yields a quantified description of the parent–child relationship while giving an overall picture of the subjective quality of the relationship. The inventory has six subscales: 1) Limit-Setting, 2) Communication, 3) Support, 4) Involvement,

5) Autonomy, and 6) Role Orientation. Tests of internal consistency of all PCRI sub-scales have yielded Cronbach's alpha values of between .70 and .88.

Emotional Availability Scales—Infancy and Early Childhood Version*

The Emotional Availability Scales—Infancy and Early Childhood Version (EAS; Biringen et al., 1993) include five dimensions that are viewed as relationship variables. Each dimension has detailed behavioral dimensions for coding. A minimum of 15 minutes of interaction is recommended in order to obtain high reliability and validity. The Maternal Sensitivity Scale assesses how warm and positive a mother is with her child, her responsivity and acceptance of her child's actions and verbalizations, how well she can resolve conflict, how flexible and creative she is, and how well she can time her actions to those of her child's. The scale ranges from 1 = *highly insensitive* to 9 = *highly sensitive.* The Maternal Structuring and Intrusiveness Scale rates a mother's ability to set limits and to structure her child's play appropriately. The scale ranges from 1 to 5, in which 1 denotes that the mother is either *very passive* or *very intrusive* and 5 denotes that the mother is *actively involved in the play while letting the child lead.* The Maternal Hostility Scale assesses covert or overt hostility toward a child. The highest score is given to a mother who is markedly hostile physically, verbally, and/or facially. *Covert hostility* is rated as 2 or 3, whereas *no hostility observed* is rated as 1. The Child Responsiveness to Mother Scale is described as the child's sensitivity scale. This scale assesses the child's willingness to engage with the mother in play, as well as the amount of pleasure the child is displaying in his or her interactions with the mother. Scores range from 1 = *unresponsive child* to the optimal score of 7 = *highly responsive child.* Finally, the Child Involvement with the Mother Scale rates how the child engages the mother in play and attends to her. A child who scores a 1 is considered an *uninvolving child* according to this assessment, who does not pay attention to the mother at all, or if responding, does not elaborate or initiate exchanges with the mother. The optimal rating, 7, is given to the *highly involving child,* whose interactions show a clear balance between playing autonomously and seeking to involve the mother. The scales have been found to show consistency or reliability over time and to correlate with other interactional measures and assessment of maternal risk (Biringen et al., 1993; Oyen, 1996; Oyen, Landy, & Hilburn-Cobb, 2000; Rethazi, 1997). This test requires training to administer and score.

Nursing Child Assessment Satellite Training Teaching and Feeding Scales*

Nursing Child Assessment Satellite Training (NCAST) Teaching and Feeding Scales (Zeanah, Larrieu, Heller, & Valliere, 2000) assess a set of observable behaviors in children from birth to 3 years of age during a feeding or teaching situation. These scales can be used to assess whether parents or children are having problems in their interaction and communication patterns. They are divided into six subscales of 75 items. Four scales describe the parent's behavior and responsibility for the interaction: 1) sensitivity to cues, 2) response to distress, 3) social–emotional growth promoting, and 4) cognitive growth fostering. Two subscales describe the child's behavior and responsibility for the interaction: Clarity of Cues and Responsiveness to Caregiver. Test–retest reliability is high for parent scales over time but the child scores are not as stable. The scales' validity has been established by the findings that scores are lower for mothers who are abusive and neglectful, for teenage mothers, and for mothers of infants who are considered to have nonorganic failure to thrive. Total parent scores with children as young as 3 months show a significant correlation with subsequent measures of children's cognitive abilities. The NCAST Teaching and Feeding Scales require training to administer and score.

Attendance and Dose Effect

In order to be able to assess whether those parents who regularly attended the Pathways to Competence group meetings had better outcomes than those whose attendance was not as good, it is important to keep a record of group attendance each week so it is possible to estimate if there is a dose effect, or evidence that those parents who attend more sessions have better outcomes than those who miss several sessions (see a sample attendance sheet in Section III: Supplemental Materials).

Parent Satisfaction

In assessing parent satisfaction with the Pathways to Competence for Young Children Parenting Program, it is helpful to ask parents to rate specific aspects of the group and to rank them in order of how helpful they were (see Parent Satisfaction Form in Section III: Supplemental Materials).

CONCLUSION

This section has provided background information and strategies for recruiting and retaining members, setting up a program, and evaluating a program's success. Section II provides the actual Steps on which the program sessions are based. After an introductory Step that discusses overall development from birth to 6 years and temperament, the remaining Steps follow the outline of the nine key developmental capacities that form the foundation of a child's social-emotional growth: developing body control and a positive body image; developing a secure attachment; encouraging play and imagination; encouraging language and communication; laying a foundation for positive self-esteem; encouraging self-regulation, morality, and a sense of conscience; encouraging emotion regulation; encouraging concentration, planning, and problem solving; and encouraging social competence, empathy, and caring behavior.

REFERENCES

Abiden, R.R. (1986). *Parent Stress Index: Test manual.* Charlottesville, VA: Pediatric Psychology Press.

Achenbach, T.M. (1991). *Manual for the Child Behavior Checklist/4–18 and 1991 profile.* Burlington, VT: University of Vermont, Department of Psychiatry.

Achenbach, T.M., & Edelbrock, C. (1983). *Manual for the Child Behavior Checklist.* Burlington, VT: University of Vermont Press.

Arnold, D.S., O'Leary, S.G., Wolff, L.S., & Acker, M.M. (1993). The Parenting Scale: A measure of dysfunctional parenting in discipline situations. *Psychological Assessment, 5,* 137–144.

Arnold, E.H., O'Leary, S.G., & Edwards, G.H. (1997). Father involvement and self-reported parenting of children with attention-deficit/hyperactivity disorder. *Journal of Consulting and Clinical Psychology, 65,* 337–342.

Bagby, D., Parker, C., & Taylor, G. (1994). *Alexithymia: An important aspect of unresolved loss and trauma.* New York: Guilford Press.

Bakersman-Kranenburg, M.J., Juffer, F., & van IJzendoorn, M.H. (1998). Interventions with video feed-back and attachment discussions: Does type of maternal insecurity make a difference? *Infant Mental Health Journal, 19,* 202–219.

Bakersman-Kranenburg, M.J., van IJzendoorn, M.H., & Juffer, F. (2003). Less is more: Meta-analyses of sensitivity and attachment interventions in early childhood. *Psychological Bulletin, 129,* 195–215.

Barlow, J., & Stewart-Brown, S. (2000). Behavior problems and groups-based parent intervention programs. *Developmental and Behavioral Pediatrics, 21,* 356–370.

Beck, A.T. (1978). *Depression: Causes and treatment.* Philadelphia: University of Pennsylvania Press.

Berrueta-Clement, J.R., Schweinhart, J., Barett, W.S., Epstein, A., Weikart, D.P. (1984). *Changed lives: The effects of the Perry Preschool Program on youths through age 19.* Ypsilanti, MI: High/Scope Press.

Biringen, Z., Robinson, J.L., & Emde, R.N. (1993). *Manual for scoring the Emotional Availability Scales: Infancy to early childhood version.* Unpublished document, University of Wisconsin.

Boyce, W.T. (2001, May). *Biology and context: Symphonic causation and origins of childhood psychopathology.* Paper presented at the Millennium Dialogue on Early Child Development, University of Toronto.

Boyle, M.H., Offord, D.R., Hofman, H.G., Catlin, G.P., Byles, J.A., Cadman, D.T., Crawford, J.W., Links, P.S., Rae-Grant, N.I., Szatmari, P. (1987). Ontario Child Health Study. *Archives of General Psychiatry, 44,* 826–831.

Bradley, R.H., & Caldwell, B.M. (1976). Early home environment and changes in mental test performance at fifty-four months: A follow-up study. *Developmental Psychology, 47,* 1172–1174.

Bradley, R.H., Casey, P.H., & Caldwell, B.M. (1997). Quality of home environment. In R.T. Gross, D. Spiker, & C.W. Haynes (Eds.), *Helping low birth weight, premature babies: The Infant Health Development Program* (pp. 242–256). Stanford, CA: Stanford University Press.

Briesmeister, J.M., & Schaefer, C.E. (1988). *Handbook of parenting training: Parents as co-therapists for children's behavior problems.* New York: John Wiley & Sons.

Bugental, D., & Cruzcosa, M. (1985). *Causal attributions for caregiving success and failure: A theoretical and methodological analysis.* Unpublished paper, University of California, Santa Barbara.

Bugental, D.B. (1992). Affective and cognitive processes withing threat-oriented family systems. In I.E. Sigel, A.V. McGillicuddy-DeLisi, & J. J. Goodnow (Eds.), Parental belief systems: The psychological consequences for children (2nd ed., pp. 219–248). Mahwah, NJ: Lawrence Erlbaum Assoc.

Bugental, D.B., & Happaney, K. (2002). Parental attributions. In M. Bornstein (Ed.), *Handbook of Parenting, Volume 3*, pp. 539–505.

Bugental, D.B., & Johnston, C. (2000). Parental and child cognitions in the context of the family. *Annual Review of Psychology, 51,* 315–344.

Campbell, S. (1995). Behavior problems in preschool children: A review of recent research. *Journal of Child Psychology and Psychiatry, 36,* 113–149

Campis, L.K., Lyman, R.D., & Prentice-Dunn, S. (1986). The Parental Locus of Control Scale: Development and validation. *Journal of Clinical Child Psychology, 15,* 260–267.

Caspi, A., Henry, B., McGee, R.O., Moffitt, T.E., & Silvan, P.A. (1995). Temperamental origins of child and adolescent behavior problems: From age three to age fifteen. *Child Development, 66,* 55–68.

Ceballo, R., & McLloyd, V.C. (2002). Social support and parenting in poor, dangerous neighbourhoods. *Child Development, 73,* 1310–1321.

Chess, S., & Thomas, A. (1996). *Temperament: Theory and practice.* New York: Brunner/Mazel.

Costello, E.J. (1989). Development in child psychiatric epidemiology. *Journal of the American Academy of Child and Adolescent Psychiatry, 28,* 851–888.

Crittenden, P.M., Lang, C., Claussen, A.H., & Partridge, M.F. (2000). Relations among mothers' dispositional representations of parenting. In P.M. Crittenden & A.H. Clausen (Eds.), *The organization of attachment relationships: Maturation, culture, and context* (pp. 214–233). Cambridge: Cambridge University Press.

Crockenberg, S.B. (1981). Infant irritability, mother responsiveness, and social support influences on security of infant–mother attachment. *Child Development, 52,* 857–865.

Cutrona, C., & Russell, D. (1987). The provision of social relationships and adaptation to stress. *Advances in personal relationships, 1,* 37–67.

Dawson, G. (1994). Frontal electroencephalographic correlates of individual differences in emotion expression in infants: A brain systems perspective on emotion. *Monographs for the Society for Research in Child Development, 59,* 135–151, 250–283.

Dix, T.H., & Grusec, J.A. (1985). Parent attribution processes in the socialization of children. In I.E. Sigel (Ed.), *Parental belief systems: The psychological consequences for children* (pp. 201–233). Mahwah, NJ: Lawrence Erlbaum Associates.

Dodge, K.A., & Frame, C.L. (1982). Social cognitive biases and deficits in aggressive boys. *Child Development, 53,* 620–635.

Elkind, D. (2001). *The hurried child: Growing up too fast too soon* (3rd ed.) New York: Perseus Books.

Eyberg, S., & Colvin, A. (1994). *Restandardization of Eyberg Child Behavior Inventory.* Poster presented at the annual meeting of the American Psychological Association, Los Angeles.

Eyberg, S., & Pincus, D. (1999). *Eyberg Child Behavior Inventory & Sutter-Eyberg Student Behavior Inventory–Revised.* Odessa, FL: Psychological Assessment Resources.

Fonagy, P., Steele, M., Steele, H., Moran, G., & Higgitt, A. (1991). The capacity for understanding mental states: The reflective self in parent and child and its significance for security of attachment. *Infant Mental Health Journal, 12,* 201–218.

Fonagy, P., Target, M., Cottrell, D., Phillips, J., & Kurtz, Z. (2000). *A review of the outcomes of psychiatric disorder in childhood: MCH 17–33. Final report to the National Health Service Executive.*

Gerard, A.B. (1994). *Parent–Child Relationship Inventory (PCRI) manual.* Los Angeles: Western Psychological Services.

Gibaud-Wallston, J., & Wandersman, L.P. (1978, August–September). *Development and utility of the Parenting Sense of Competence Scale.* Paper presented at the 86th Annual Meeting of the American Psychological Association, Toronto, Ontario, Canada.

Gross, D., & Rocissano, L. (1988). Maternal confidence in toddlerhood: Its measurement for research and clinical practice. *Nurse Practitioner, 13,* 19-29.

Guerin, D.W., & Gottfried, A.W. (1994). Temperamental consequences of infant difficultness. *Infant Behavior and Development, 17,* 413–421.

Gunnar, M. (1998). Quality of care and the buffering of stress physiology: Its potential role in protecting the developing human brain. *IMPrint, 21,* 4–7.

Guralnick, M.J. (1997). *The effectiveness of early intervention* (pp. 3, 11–12). Baltimore: Paul H. Brookes Publishing Co.

Hazan, C., & Shaver, P. (1987). Romantic love conceptualized as an attachment process. *Journal of Personal and Social Psychology, 52*(3), 511–24.

Huttunen, M.O., & Nyman, G. (1982). The Middle Childhood Temperament Questionnaire. *Journal of Developmental and Behavioral Pediatrics, 3,* 197–200.

Hubbs-Tait, L., Osofsky, J.D., Hann, D.M., & McDonald, C.A. (1994). Predicting behavior problems and social competence in children of adolescent mothers. *Family Relations: Interdisciplinary Journal of Applied Family Studies, 43,* 439–446.

Jacobsen, S.W., & Frye, K.F. (1991). Effects of maternal social support on attachments: Experimental evidence. *Child Development, 62,* 572–582.

Johnston, C. (1996). Parent characteristics and parent–child interactions in families of nonproblem children and ADHD children with higher and lower levels of oppositional-defiant behavior. *Journal of Abnormal Child Psychology, 24,* 85–104.

Johnston, C., & Mash, E.J. (1989). A measure of parenting satisfaction and efficacy. *Journal of Clinical Child Psychology, 18,* 167–175.

Kazdin, A.E. (1997). Parent management training: Evidence outcomes and issues. *Journal of the American Academy of Child and Adolescent Psychiatry, 36,* 1349–1356.

Kazdin, A.E. (2000). Treatments for aggressive and anti-social children. *Child and Adolescent Psychiatric Clinics of North America, 9,* 841–858.

Kirk, S.A., McCarthy, J.J., & Kirk, W.D. (1968). *Illinois Test of Psycholinguistic Abilities.* Urbana: University of Illinois Press.

Kolb, B. (1989). Brain development, plasticity, and behavior. *American Psychologist, 44,* 1203–1212.

Lahey, B.B., Miller, T.L., Gordon, R.H., & Riley, A.W. (1999). Developmental epidemiology of the disruptive behavior disorders. In H.C. Quay & A.E. Hogan (Eds.), *Handbook of disruptive behavior disorders* (pp. 23–48). New York: Kluwer Academic/Plenum Press.

Landy, S. (2002). *Pathways to competence: Encouraging healthy social and emotional development in young children.* Baltimore: Paul H. Brookes Publishing Co.

Landy, S., & deV. Peters, R. (1992). Towards an understanding of a developmental paradigm for aggressive conduct problems during the preschool years. In R. deV. Peters, R.J. McMahon, & V.L. Quinsey (Eds.), *Aggression and violence throughout the life span* (pp. 1–30). Thousand Oaks, CA: Sage Publications.

Landy, S., & Harris, S. (2004). Presentation at the Violence Prevention Conference. Toronto. Landy, S., & Menna, R. (in press). An evaluation of a group intervention for parents of aggressive young children: Improvements in child functioning, maternal confidence, and parenting knowledge and attitudes. *Early Child Development and Care.*

Landy, S., & Menna, R. (1998). *Effects of the Helping Encourage Affect Regulation (HEAR) parenting program on preschoolers with aggressive behaviour problems.* Ottawa, Ontario: Health Canada.

Landy, S., & Menna, R. (2006). *Early intervention with multi-risk families: An integrative approach.* Baltimore: Paul H. Brookes Publishing Co.

Landy, S., & Menna, R. (in press). An evaluation of a group intervention for parents of aggressive young children: Improvements in child functioning, maternal confidence, and parenting knowledge and attitudes. *Early Child Development and Care.*

Landy, S., Menna, R., & Sockett-DiMarco, N. (1997). A pilot study to evaluate a treatment model for parents of preschoolers with behavioral problems. *Early Child Development and Care, 131,* 45–64.

Landy, S., & Tam, K.K. (1997). Yes, parenting can make a difference in the development of Canadian children. In Statistics Canada, *Growing up in Canada: National longitudinal study of children and youth.* Ottawa, Ontario: HRDC, Statistics Canada, 103–118.

Lefcourt, H.M. (1991). Locus of control. In J.P. Robinson, P.R. Shaver, & L.S. Wrightsman (Eds.), *Measures of personality and social psychological attitudes* (pp.413–419). New York: Academic Press.

MacPhee, D. (1981). *Knowledge of child development inventory.* Unpublished manual and questionnaire. University of North Carolina, Chapel Hill.

MacPhee, D., Fritz, J., & Miller-Heyl, J. (1996). Ethnic variations in personal social networks and parenting. *Child Development, 67,* 3278–3295.

Martyn, D., & Dundas, S. (1997). Schooling the emotions: Results of an experimental emotion regulation group in a sample of high risk parents. Poster presented at the Society for Research in Child Development. Albuquerque, New Mexico.

McKay & Fanning, (1992) Naparstek, B. (1993). *General wellness.* Los Angeles: Time Warner Audio Books.

Meltzer, H., Gatward, R., Corbin, T., Goodman, R., & Ford, T. (2003). *Persistence, onset, risk factors, and outcome of childhood mental health disorders.* London: TSO.

Myers, J.K., & Weissman, M.M. (1980). Use of a self-report scale to detect depression in a community sample. *American Journal of Psychiatry, 37,* 1081–1084.

Newberg, J., Stock, J., Wnek, L., Guidubaldi, J., & Svinicki, J. (1988). *Batelle Developmental Inventory.* Allen, TX: DLM Teaching Resources.

Offord, D.R., Boyle, M.H., Racine, Y.A., Fleming, J.E., Cadman, D.T., Blum, H.M., Byrne, C., Links, P.S., Lipman, E.L., Macmillan, H.L., Rae Grant, N.L., Sanford, M.N., Szatmari, P., Thomas, H., & Woodward, C.A. (1992). Outcome, prognosis, and risk in a longitudinal follow-up study. *Journal of the American Academy of Child and Adolescent Psychiatry, 31,* 916–923.

Oldershaw, L. (2002). *A national survey of parents of young children.* Toronto: Invest in Kids Foundation.

Olds, D.L., Henderson, C.R., Tatelbaum, R., & Chamberlin, R. (1988). Improving the life course development of socially disadvantaged mothers: A randomized trial of nurse home visiting. *American Journal of Public Health, 78,* 1430–1445.

Oyen, A-S. (1996). *Maternal attachment and emotional availability in an at-risk sample.* Unpublished Ph.D. dissertation. York University, Toronto, Canada.

Oyen, A-S., Landy, S., & Hilburn-Cobb, C. (2000). Maternal attachment and sensitivity in an at-risk sample. *Attachment and Human Development, 2,* 203–217.

Rae-Grant, N., Thomas, H., Offord, D., & Boyle, M. (1989). Risk, protective factors and the presence of behavioral and emotional disorders in children and adolescents. *Journal of the American Academy of Children and Adolescent Psychiatry, 28,* 262–268.

Reich, S. (2005). What do mothers know? Maternal knowledge of child development. *Infant Mental Health Journal, 26,* 143–156.

Rethazi, M. (1997). *Maternal working models of the child and emotional availability in a sample of aggressive preschoolers.* Unpublished doctoral dissertation, University of Toronto, Canada.

Roberts, W.L. (1989). Parents' stressful life events and social networks: Relations with parenting and children's competence. *Canadian Journal of Behavioral Science, 21,* 132–146.

Rogers, S.J., Parcel, T.L., & Meaghan, E.G. (1991). The effects of maternal working conditions and mastery on child behavior problems: Studying the intergenerational transmission of social control. *Journal of Health and Social Behavior, 32,* 145–164.

Rosenberg, M. (1989). *Society and the adolescent self-image* (rev. ed.). Middletown, CT: Wesleyan University Press.

Rosenberg, R. (1979). *Conceiving the self.* New York: Basic Books.

Rubin, K.H., Burgess, K.B., Kim, B., Dwyer, K.M., & Hastings, P.D. (2003). Predicting preschoolers' externalizing behaviors from toddler temperament, conflict, and maternal negativity. *Developmental Psychology, 39,* 164–176.

Rubin, K.H., & Mills, R.S. (1990). Maternal beliefs about adaptive and maladaptive social behaviors in normal aggressive, and withdrawn preschoolers. *Journal of Abnormal Child Psychology, 18,* 419–435.

Rutter, M. (1989). Pathways from childhood to adult life. *Journal of Child Psychology and Psychiatry, 36,* 23–51.

Schore, A.N. (1994). *Affect regulation and the origin of the self.* Mahwah, NJ: Lawrence Erlbaum Associates.

Slade, A. (2002). Keeping the baby in mind: A critical factor in perinatal mental health. *Zero to Three, 22,* 11–16.

Slade, A., Grienenberger, J., Bernbach, E., Levy, D., & Locker, A. (April, 2001). *Maternal reflective functioning and attachment: Considering the transmission gap.* Paper presented at the biennial meeting of the Society of Research on Child Development, Minneapolis, MN.

Teti, D., & Gelfand, D. (1991). Behavioral competence among mothers of infants in the first year: The mediational role of self-efficacy. *Child Development, 62,* 918–929.

Thomas, H., Camiletti, Y., Cava, M., Feldman, L., Underwood, J., & Wade, K. (1999). *Effectiveness of parenting groups with professional involvement in improving parent and child outcomes.* PHRED Program, Public Health Branch, Ontario Ministry of Health.

Thorndike, R.L., Hagen, E.P., & Sattler, J.M. (1986). *Stanford-Binet Intelligence Scale* (4th ed.). Chicago: Riverside.

Tremblay, R.E. (2002). The development of aggressive behavior during childhood. In W.W. Hartup & R.K. Silbereisen (Eds.), *Growing points in developmental science: An introduction* (pp. 241–265). Philadelphia, PA: Psychology Press.

Van IJzendoorn, M.H., Juffer, F., & Duyvesteyn, M.G.C. (1995). Breaking the intergenerational cycle of insecure attachment: A review of the effects of attachment-based interventions on maternal sensitivity and infant security. *Journal of Child Psychology and Psychiatry, 36,* 225–248.

Webster-Stratton, C. (Producer) (1989). *The Incredible Years program* [Videotape]. (Available from Incredible Years, 1411 8th Avenue West, Seattle, WA 98119.)

Webster-Stratton, C., & Hammond, M. (1997). Treating children with early onset conduct problems: A comparison of child and parent training interventions. *Journal of Consulting and Clinical Psychology, 65,* 93–109.

Weiss, G., & Hechtman, L.T. (1993). *Hyperactive children grown up* (2nd ed.). New York: Guilford Press.

Wootton, J.M., Frick, P.J., Shelton, K.K., & Silverthorn, P. (1997). Ineffective parenting and childhood conduct problems: The moderating role of callous-unemotional traits. *Consulting and Clinical Psychology, 65,* 301–308.

Yankelovich, D., & DYG, Inc. (2000). *What grown-ups know about child development: A national benchmark study.* Washington, DC: Civitas Corporation, Zero to Three, and Brio Connection.

Zeanah, C., Benoit, D., & Barton, M. (1993). *Working Model of the Child Interview.* Unpublished document. Providence, RI: Brown University.

Zeanah, C.H., Larrieu, J.A., Heller, S.S., & Valliere, J. (2000). Infant–parent relationship assessment. In C.H. Zeanah (Ed.), *Handbook of infant mental health* (pp. 222–235). New York: Guilford Press.

STEPS OF THE PATHWAYS TO COMPETENCE FOR YOUNG CHILDREN PARENTING PROGRAM

STEP 1

Introduction and Understanding Development and Temperament

MATERIALS

Required materials

Handouts 1.1–1.22 (on Pathways to Competence for Young Children CD-ROM accompanying this manual)

Tree picture cards on which to write principles

Velcro or tape to stick cards on the tree

Suggested materials

Pathways to Competence: Encouraging Healthy Social and Emotional Development in Young Children (2002)

Three-ring binders with handouts (one for each group leader and parent)

Overhead projector, blackboard, or flip chart

Pencils and/or pens for the group to use

Markers and erasers for the group leader(s) for discussions

Small file card boxes to use as "self-care" box for parents

Video clips of parent–child interaction if available

INTRODUCTION

The first session is very important for establishing ground rules and setting up the Pathways to Competence for Young Children Parenting Program. Prior to the start of the program, organize and familiarize yourself with this manual and all program materials. Before you present each Step of the program, read over the handouts to make sure you understand them all. Each group leader and participant should have his or her own three-ring binder for handouts and other materials. Often, a sponsoring agency will provide these binders, or if not, you may request that parents bring their own. Instructions for how and when to hand these out are given later in this Step. The handouts are included on the CD-ROM that accompanies this manual.

Set up the room to optimize discussion and a sense of connection between the parents and the group leaders. It is also important to give parents a surface that they can write on in order to make notes on things they want to remember and to complete some of the questionnaires and group activities. For group discussions (indicated throughout each Step), make sure to have something to write on that is visible to all participants, such as a flip chart, overhead projector, or blackboard. You and the other group leaders will probably want to keep your own notes, as well, in a separate notebook.

Group Introductions

This is the time to introduce the group members to one another. Have parents tell the group their names, the name and age of their child, and anything else they would like the group to know about them or their child.

Parents with more than one child may describe any or all of their children. Encourage parents to discuss why they decided to attend the group.

Write down relevant notes such as parents' names and comments on a flip chart, blackboard, or overhead projector. Continue to do so whenever a group discussion takes place, when appropriate.

Some group members may enjoy the opportunity to discuss child or parenting issues with others, especially those groups focusing on particular issues, such as having a child with emotional or behavioral problems. Other parents may be reluctant to speak; however, finding out early in the program that other parents face the same challenges as they do can give parents an incredible sense of relief and can increase a sense of support very early in the group process.

Instead of having each parent introduce him- or herself, you may wish to have parents pair off and find out a few facts about each other and have each parent introduce the other participant to the group as an icebreaker.

Be sure that you and any other group leaders introduce yourselves, as well, and describe your training and experience. You may talk about your own children or other children you have had experience with, such as younger siblings, nieces and nephews, and neighbors' children.

At this point, provide any further explanation about running the group. If you have decided to provide each participant with a binder in which to keep copies of the handouts, homework, and other materials related to the program, this is a good time to hand them out. Encourage each parent to bring the binder to each group session.

Group Rules and Confidentiality

Distribute Handout 1.1: Group Rules.

This is the time to establish rules for the group. One of the most important rules to cover concerns confidentiality—or what goes on in the group stays in the group. This is very important to setting up an environment of trust.

Handout 1.1 covers rules about confidentiality and group process. The following are some ideas behind the rules covered in the handout. You may also include any other rules deemed appropriate or necessary for this particular group by the group leaders:

- Participants should respect the confidentiality of any information that is shared in the group (Rule 1).

- Group leaders will ensure that no one is hurt physically or emotionally during the groups (Rules 2 and 3).

- Participants are asked to try to avoid dominating the discussion because it is important that everyone gets an opportunity to speak and participate (Rule 7).

- Joining in the discussion is optional, and parents are free to refuse to comment about or to discuss a topic that the group is discussing (Rule 8).

- Unless there are extenuating circumstances, participants should try to attend all of the group sessions. Explain that each week builds on the last and that it can be difficult to share personal material if some participants come and go during the program (Rule 9).

Discussion of Group Logistics

If group leaders have decided to make incentives available (e.g., meals, a child's toy to take home, transportation tokens or tickets), explain about these now. Explain child care arrangements if they are available. You may also want to discuss break time and when that will occur. Encourage parents to ask questions so that any concerns or uncertainties can be dealt with. Fun activities for home (homework) will be discussed. Explain to participants that the process of doing homework and reporting how things went during the week allows the group leaders to help participants to work out any problems they may have encountered when interacting with their children and when completing home assignments.

This is also the time to describe the importance of group discussion. Let parents know that although information will be provided in each of the Steps, experience with this program has shown that the best learning comes through discussing and practicing certain parenting principles related to each competence that will be featured in the Pathways program.

If you plan to use video clips or vignettes of the parents interacting with their children to illustrate good parenting practices, check with the parents again about this. Make it clear that the video clips will be examples of **positive** parenting.

SETTING THE STAGE

Parents often need help in getting a discussion started during the first week. Set the stage by asking parents general questions about why they decided to join the program. The following are some suggestions for questions to use, although you may want to develop your own.

- **Why are we here today?** Discuss some of the reasons for holding the group, such as reducing child behavior problems, getting information about child development, and sharing the ideas or parenting strategies that have worked for other parents in the groups.

- **What makes it hard to parent today?** Some topics raised might include two-career families, an increase in poverty, or concern about violence in society. The topics raised by the group may vary somewhat according to the group membership.

Explain how the topics for the group sessions were chosen based on research about child development and best parenting practices. This forms the basis for the various parenting principles and techniques that will be featured throughout this program.

Emphasize that the group is all about supporting parents to enhance the development of their children.

Introducing the Building Blocks of Competence

Distribute Handout 1.2: The Building Blocks of Competence.

Handout 1.2 describes the nine developmental capacities that serve as the topics of Steps in this order: 1) body control and positive body image; 2) secure attachment; 3) play and imagination; 4) language and communication; 5) positive self-esteem; 6) self-regulation, morality, and a sense of conscience; 7) emotion regulation; 8) concentration, planning, and problem solving; and 9) social competence, empathy, and caring behavior. These same capacities are featured in *Pathways to Competence: Encouraging Healthy Social and Emotional Development in Young Children* (Landy, 2002), which is referred to throughout this and other Steps as *Pathways to Competence* (2002).

Go over the list of topics in Handout 1.2 and explain their meaning, if necessary. Ask parents to discuss which topics are of particular interest to them.

Ask parents about where they get their advice on how to parent children and whether this advice is sometimes conflicting. Make the point that differences in parenting beliefs vary from generation to generation but that research has enabled us to have some clear "dos and don'ts" about parenting. Also emphasize that in some areas, parents can be flexible.

Introducing the Tree Metaphor

Distribute Handout 1.3: The Tree.

Explain how the roots of the tree represent the nine evolving developmental capacities of healthy social and emotional growth that are needed by children as they mature. Later in the group meeting the parents will discuss their hopes and wishes for their children and the adults they would like their children to become (e.g., happy, caring, intelligent). The tree in Handout 1.3 is already labeled with several of these characteristics. Labels describing the four parenting roles are placed at the top of the tree. Explain that during each Step of the program, as each capacity is discussed, parents will write the parenting principles on cards and place them at the top of the tree under the roles. These will illustrate parenting strategies and parent–child interactions that can be used with children to help them to develop the developmental capacities. A tree without labels is provided in Section III, Supplemental Materials, or another version of a tree can be drawn or purchased commercially from most local teacher supply stores in the bulletin board section. Explain that this tree metaphor, as it relates to the individual capacity being considered, will be discussed toward the end of each Step.

If you plan to give out self-care boxes, as described in Chapter 7 of Section I, do so now. Explain to the participants that they will be given something each week during class to put in the box that represents a way to honor themselves, and that they will be taking the box home at the end of the program. If you are not using such a box, make sure to have the participants choose a self-care activity from Handout 1.22 at the end of each session anyway for a homework activity.

UNDERSTANDING DEVELOPMENT

Discussion of Key Terms Related to Development

Each session will include some terminology that parents may not understand, or even if they are familiar with the words, they may not know how those words relate to the capacity being discussed. This is why it is important to discuss certain key words. For this Step, the following terms will be important for parents to understand: *Development, developmental milestones,* and *developmental pace.*

Development

Development is about the child "unfolding gradually." Although development takes place slowly, a number of qualitative shifts or reorganizations occur over time that can lay the foundation for the child's social and emotional development. For example, it is obvious how learning to walk changes a child's view of the world, but a number of shifts or reorganizations occur in the child's emotional and social development that also are as important to development. These include developing a secure attachment, learning to pretend play, learning to communicate, learning to manage emotions, understanding another person's perspective, and being able to care about others.

Ask participants what they think are the major areas in which children develop (e.g., speech).

If parents do not list all of the major areas, add them yourself.

Distribute Handout 1.4: Major Areas of Development.

Children develop in these major areas:

- **Gross motor:** These are skills children can do using their large muscle groups, such as rolling over, sitting up, crawling, walking, running, or riding a bike.

- **Fine motor:** These are skills children can do with their small muscle groups, such as picking up and holding small objects, building with blocks, targeting small objects, banging things together, and doing puzzles.

- **Cognitive:** This is about what children understand about their world, including concepts such as object permanence (i.e., objects are still there even if out of sight), concepts such as *large* and *small,* classification, and problem solving.

- **Language and communication:** This area includes skills in receptive language (i.e., what the child understands) and expressive language (i.e., what the child can say). Gestures and nonverbal communication are also considered here.

- **Self-help:** Skills included here are independent feeding, dressing, and toileting.

- **Emotional:** This area includes typical emotions (e.g., happiness, sadness, anger) and the child's control of them.

- **Social:** The area of social development includes children's attachment or relationship to their parents, how well they can play with other children, and if they show the capacity for sharing and caring for others.

Other important developmental areas to be considered, including auditory and visual processing, sensory integration, memory, and motor planning, are discussed later in this Step. Although all of these areas affect one another and are important, this Step emphasizes the areas of social and emotional development.

Developmental Milestones

Distribute Handout 1.5: Milestones of Development.

Ask parents to look closely at the parts of Handout 1.5 detailing development for their child's age level. Help parents to discover the skills their child may have just acquired or may be acquiring soon. Ask the parents what they are doing to encourage their child's development in these areas.

Using Handout 1.5, point out the major emotional and social milestones of each age and highlight certain interesting facts related to them:

- Attachment (i.e., the bond between a child and a parent) is in place by approximately 7–8 months of age.

- Two-year-old children only follow parents' requests about 45% of the time.

- Tantrums are common when children are between 1 and 3 years of age, but should begin to subside after age 3.

- Fights over possession of toys are common in children between the ages of 1 and 2, but children can usually begin to play cooperatively from 2 years of age.

- Children do not develop a conscience or feel guilty if they disobey rules until they are about 5 years of age.

Ask parents how they think development unfolds or takes place. Explain that nature or biology (i.e., what is inherent in the child) and nurture or environment (i.e., how parents and others interact with the child) are both important influences on development. It is important to point out that various things must be in place in order for development to proceed. For a new skill to happen, such as toileting or walking, the following are crucial:

- Developmental readiness (e.g., muscle groups have enough control)

- The child's inherent drive to learn new skills—a motivation to try them out (e.g., wants to be a "big boy," is cruising around furniture and wants to stand up all of the time)

- Involved, loving caregivers who show interest in their child's learning of a new skill; they encourage their child's learning and keep alive the child's motivation to keep trying to succeed

Distribute Handout 1.6a: Analyzing the Influences on Learning a New Skill or Behavior (Sample).

Handout 1.6a has been completed for the skill of *walking.* Review with parents the acquisition of this skill as it relates to the aspects just discussed.

Distribute Handout 1.6b: Analyzing the Influences on Learning a New Skill or Behavior (Blank).

The following exercise helps to reinforce the importance of the contribution of both nature and nurture in children's development.

Have the parents complete Handout 1.6b by choosing a skill (e.g., toilet training, learning words, managing tantrums) and filling in the blanks.

Developmental Pace

Children develop at their own pace and are often more advanced in one particular area or another. For example, one child may be advanced in walking and other gross motor activities but is slower to learn language. Another child, sometimes in the same family, may be quite content to sit in one place but advances more rapidly in terms of learning words and communicating. Although these differences are usually overcome, development should be monitored and assessment and consultation sought in certain situations. Generally, by about 3 years of age, children's growth evens out across the developmental areas. However, when concerning signs are noticed, follow-up may be necessary.

***Distribute Handout 1.7: When to Be
Concerned About Your Child's Development.***

If any of the red flags listed here and in Handout 1.7 are present, they require further investigation, assessment, and sometimes intervention.

Signs to be concerned about include the following:

- The child is significantly delayed in all areas of development.

- The child shows significant delays in any of the major areas of development by 2 years of age.

- The child has few or no words by 2 years of age.

- The child is not walking by 18 months of age.

- The child's muscle tone is atypical (e.g., floppy or rigid).

- The child shows lack of responsiveness to others or when his or her name is called or exhibits very repetitive or obsessive behavior.

- The child is extremely active or has difficulty attending to instructions and/or concentrating on an activity.

- The child is excessively aggressive and/or noncompliant.

- The child is very withdrawn, anxious, or fearful around other children.

- The child has significant difficulty relating to other children.

- The child's development or behavior regresses with no obvious reason, is extreme, and the child is unable to recover from this regression.

Encourage parents to refer back to Handout 1.5 on developmental milestones and to identify any areas of concern they may have about their child.

Importance of Development

If young children achieve the nine capacities described in the Pathways to Competence for Young Children Parenting Program in a timely fashion, a foundation for resilience and coping throughout their lifetime will be established. These capacities appear at different ages and then strengthen until they are fully developed. Once they are established in the early years, other developmental achievements or qualitative shifts become more readily attained later. It is important for a child to have all of the capacities because if one is missing or is poorly developed, this seriously affects the others. Although intellectual development is important, emotional intelligence also makes an enormous difference in coping and having a successful life, for example. Having these skills is critical to developing satisfying relationships and careers.

Developmental Qualities Important to Parents

In addition to the nine capacities listed previously, parents have in mind certain qualities or characteristics that they would like to see their children develop.

Distribute Handout 1.8: Characteristics that I Want My Child to Have.

Ask parents to list qualities (e.g., happy, intelligent) that they would like their child to have as an adult using the top portion of Handout 1.8. Ask parents to read out their list of characteristics. Write down their comments on the flip chart or overhead projector. Organize the qualities that parents list into the following categories, each of which is followed by an example.

- Achievement/competence: *"Finding a satisfactory job or career"*

- Physical and emotional well-being: *"To be healthy and to handle stress," "To be happy and content"*

- Courageous/determined: *"To stand up for what she believes in," "To be brave in difficult situations"*

- Caring/moral: *"To care about other people in society who, for example, live in poverty or have disabilities," "To help people in need," "To have religious faith"*

Each group typically provides their own examples that are different from the ones listed here and places a somewhat different emphasis on each of the categories. Generally, parents are surprised to find how similar their hopes and dreams for their children are to those held by other participants in the group.

Then ask parents to identify one or two characteristics from the list they generated that they want their child to develop, to think about any concerns they may have around their child achieving them, and to consider how they will help their child to develop them.

Have parents write two characteristics on cardboard leaves or fruit that they wish for their child. Place the fruit or leaves on the Tree (see Handout 1.3).

Parents' Important Roles in Children's Development

Distribute Handout 1.9: My Parenting Roles.

Explain that children need the caregivers in their lives to play four critical roles, and explain the importance of these roles.

- **Nurturer:** A child needs parents to be responsive in a nurturing way when he or she is hurt, ill, upset, crying, afraid, or worried about something.

- **Limit Setter:** Children need routines and structure and clear, consistent limits for their behavior.

- **Teacher:** Children need to learn about rules and the reasons for them, the parents' moral beliefs, academic subjects such as letters and numbers, and so forth.

- **Playmate:** A child needs to have fun times with parents, including roughhousing, going to the park, painting a picture, and so forth.

Parents are often more comfortable with some roles than others, and when there are two parents, roles may be divided somewhat between them. However, because all roles are important, one should not be emphasized over another. Relationships between parents and children also are strengthened if both parents are involved in all four roles. In other words, it is not a good idea for one parent to do all of the fun activities and the other parent to do all of the disciplining because of the effect it could have on parent–child (and parent–parent) relationships. Have parents complete Handout 1.9 by dividing the circle into a pie chart with one piece representing each of the parenting roles. Draw a pie chart on the flip chart or overhead projector as an example.

Encourage parents to discuss these roles and how they work in their family. Then, have them add the roles to the top of the Tree. (See the Supplemental Materials in Section III for pictures illustrating each of the parenting roles and Handout 1.3 for where to position the pictures of the roles on the tree.)

Research Related to Development

Perhaps the most significant recent findings about development in the early years have been about brain development; for example, in early development, rapid growth of both the number of brain cells and the connections between them occurs. Although much of this is determined by an individual's genetic makeup, it can also be significantly influenced by early experiences.

Ask parents what they have heard and believe about how early experiences affect brain development. What does this knowledge mean in terms of the parenting needs of children?

Make sure to mention to parents that it is critical to be sensitive to a child's cues as well as to adapt their interactions to their child's needs. As well, it is important to be careful to be neither overstimulating nor understimulating. Point out that calming the upset child and sensitive interactions can relieve the child's stress and enhance the child's developmental outcomes.

Also, ask parents what things they consider stressful for a young child and how they can protect their child from them.

For a more in-depth consideration of these research findings and some other facts from which to choose to discuss with the group, read *Pathways to Competence* (2002), pages 28–35.

UNDERSTANDING TEMPERAMENT

Discussion of Key Terms

Begin by pointing out that any parent who has two or more children or who has seen his or her child interacting with another child who seems to be their child's complete opposite already knows that children can be very different. These individual differences are called *temperament.* Explain that temperament is about *how* a child behaves, not *what* a child does or *why* (the child's motivation). For example, all children react when they are upset, and most have temper tantrums. However, some will be very intense about their feelings, have tantrums more frequently, and be much harder to calm down than others. Some children may be very persistent, staying with tasks until they are completed, whereas other children are more distractible and go from one thing to another. There are several different temperament types and many combinations, and there is no right or wrong or good or bad temperament, although some temperament characteristics can be challenging for parents.

Invite discussion from parents about their child's temperament.

Distribute Handout 1.10: Do You Have a Difficult Child?

Have parents complete the "Do You Have a Difficult Child?" questionnaire and discuss what they learned. Tell parents not to panic or be overly worried if the questionnaire indicated that they have a difficult child. Parents can learn how to bring out the best qualities in all children by adapting the child's environment to enhance the child's temperament qualities. Explain that this will be discussed in more detail later in the session.

Distribute Handout 1.11: Temperament Traits or Behavioral Styles.

Refer parents to Handout 1.11 on the temperament or behavioral styles identified by temperament pioneers Thomas, Chess, and Birch, who observed children over many years in the New York Longitudinal Study (NYLS; Thomas, Chess, & Birch, 1968) on children's temperaments. Go over the explanations or definitions of the following terms with them:

- Activity level

- Rhythmicity/regularity

- Approach or withdrawal/first reactions

- Adaptability

- Threshold of responsiveness

- Intensity of reaction

- Quality of mood

- Distractibility

- Attention span and persistence

Distribute Handout 1.12: Types of Temperament in Children.

According to Thomas, Chess, and Birch, children's temperaments fall into four general behavioral styles or categories: 1) difficult (10%), 2) easy (40%), 3) slow to warm up or shy (5%–15%), or 4) mixed (35%–40%).

As you are discussing Handout 1.12, go through each temperament trait and have parents think about their child on each trait.

Distribute Handout 1.13: Understanding Your Child's Temperament.

Have parents record their ratings of their child's temperaments in Handout 1.13. When completed, use the results to help assess whether their child is *easy, slow to warm up,* or *difficult.*

Development of Temperament

Because most people believe that temperament is attributed to biological inheritance, it may sound strange to talk about the development of temperament. However, individuals do express temperament differently at various ages, so, for example, a baby who is irritable may become the toddler who has a lot of temper tantrums. Although the difficult child temperament pattern was found to be predictive of later behavior problems, it is also clear that many children who are difficult as young infants or children adjust well at a later age. Similarly, shy children can become comfortable with being around other children if they are encouraged to do so at an early age without being pushed too much.

Importance of Temperament

The temperament of a child can have a very significant effect on both the development of the child and the parent–child relationship. The child's temperament may be particularly relevant in the early months if a baby is very irritable and difficult to settle. Later, if a child is slow to warm up, it can influence his or her adjustment to child care or school and could affect the child's ability to concentrate. The influence of temperament is most likely to be on emotional and social development.

Research Related to Temperament

Much of the research on temperament has considered the physiological bases of temperament. Children of different temperaments have been found to have differences in the physiology of their brains and nervous systems. Some evidence points to genetic influences on temperament, as well, with some temperament characteristics present at birth and showing continuity over time. The highest stability has been found for intensity, mood, rhythmicity, and activity level.

In general, it is believed that a child's temperament can affect parenting styles and that positive parenting styles can significantly influence temperament outcomes in children. For a more complete discussion of this research, read *Pathways to Competence* (2002), pages 35–42.

PARENTING PRINCIPLES AND TECHNIQUES RELATED TO DEVELOPMENT AND TEMPERAMENT

Distribute Handout 1.14: Principles for Dealing with Stage-Related and Temperament Issues.

Explain that during each of the Steps, you will be passing out a similar handout that will include principles for encouraging the particular developmental capacity being covered in that Step.

If video clips are going to be used, they should be shown to illustrate one or more of the following principles.

PRINCIPLE 1: Spend time observing your child and relate his or her behavior to what you know about your child's developmental level.

Encourage parents to observe their child during the program and throughout the child's development in order to better understand the meaning behind the different behaviors they have seen. This is important to help them to understand what skills they would want to be encouraging in their child.

Ask parents to discuss some of the things they have observed about their child at different ages or behaviors that relate to their temperament.

PRINCIPLE 2: Set up the environment and your child's schedule to accommodate his or her developmental characteristics.

Encourage parents to try to adapt schedules and the environment to the child's level of emotional and social development. Refer to Handout 1.5 (Milestones of Development). For example, to encourage an infant of 3 months to be responsive and to settle into a sleep-wake-feeding routine, it is important that parents play with their infant when he or she is awake and alert and help the infant to calm down and fall asleep when tired. Discuss the emotional and social developmental changes that occur at the ages outlined in the charts on development (Handout 1.5) and discuss briefly how parents can encourage their children to achieve them.

PRINCIPLE 3: Try to learn about your child's temperament characteristics and any physical characteristics that may be contributing to his or her behavioral style.

Remind the parents about Handout 1.13. In addition to the temperament traits listed there, the child may also have some physical characteristics that contribute to his or her behavior.

Explain and discuss a few of the "hidden" physical characteristics that may contribute to the child's temperament or his behavioral style. These may include

- Hyper- or hyposensitivity, excessive reactivity, or lack of reactivity to touch, sound, sight, smell, and movement

- Motor difficulties, including motor tone, motor planning, and clumsiness

- Auditory and visual processing and sensory integration problems

This is a good time to raise additional hidden physical characteristics and to have parents suggest others that they have noticed in their children.

Sometimes these challenges can go unnoticed or be misinterpreted and can cause difficulties for a child at home and in child care or school.

PRINCIPLE 4: Spend time changing negative labels into positive ones that reflect your child's developmental stage and temperament type.

Have parents think about any labels that their own parents used with them as they were growing up, and the effects that these labels had on them.

Distribute Handout 1.15:
Labels and How They Influence Self-Esteem.

Have parents complete Handout 1.15 and discuss the labels that were used to describe them. Have them think about any negative labels they use with their own children and what language they could use, instead.

PRINCIPLE 5: Identify behaviors that trigger anger and anxiety in yourself and see how you are affected by your own temperament characteristics.

Distribute Handout 1.16:
Understanding Your Own Temperament.

Have parents fill out Handout 1.16 to rate their own temperaments.

Distribute Handout 1.17: My Temperament Characteristics Today.

Ask parents how they may have worked to overcome a temperamental trait they found difficult to deal with (e.g., shyness, hyperactivity) and ones they are still struggling with. Ask them to fill out the chart in Handout 1.17. Have parents discuss anything they discovered about their own temperament and how they have adapted to it or worked to overcome it and any that they are still working on.

Distribute Handout 1.18: My Parents' Temperament Characteristics.

Have parents consider the temperament characteristics of their own parents and write them down in Handout 1.18. Have them discuss how their own traits are the same or different from their parents' traits.

Ask parents some of the following questions: While you were growing up, was your temperament different from your parents' temperaments? How did that work in the family? Did you experience a developmental challenge that your parents criticized or ridiculed you about? Was there a child with a difficult temperament in your family of origin? If so, how did your family deal with that?

Distribute Handout 1.19: You and Your Child's Temperament.

Discuss with the parents whether they noticed any of their own temperament characteristics that were different from their child's.

Have parents discuss behaviors that they find difficult in their children. Introduce the idea of *goodness of fit* or how parents adapt to their child's characteristics. (See *Pathways to Competence*, 2002, pp. 51–52.) Describe some positive and negative examples of goodness of fit between children and caregivers you know.

PRINCIPLE 6: Identify and adopt strategies that can help you adapt to your child's special temperament characteristics.

 Talk about temperament characteristics and encourage parents to discuss their child's temperament. Choose an example that is discussed by the parents and provide parents with some useful strategies.

 ### Distribute Handout 1.20: Dealing with Temperament Characteristics.

Provide parents with the list of strategies in Handout 1.20 to help them to accommodate to various temperament characteristics of their child.

 Using Handout 1.20, choose some strategies that will work with various difficult temperament traits and have the parents role play being the child and parent to illustrate how they might work in different situations (e.g., dropping the shy child off at child care or helping the very active child deal with his high energy level). Invite parents to role play any strategies they have used with their child.

THE TREE: METAPHOR FOR DEVELOPMENT

 At the end of the group, before talking about the homework, ask parents to write the principles for dealing with stage-related and temperament issues on pieces of cardboard and to place them under one of the primary roles of parenting at the top of the tree.

HOMEWORK

 ### Distribute Handout 1.21: Homework and Handout 1.22: Self-Care Activities.

 Describe the homework activities listed on Handout 1.21. If the Step is given over only 1 week, have parents choose one of the activities under Parenting Activities and choose one activity from Handout 1.22. If the Step is given over 2 weeks, parents can do both activities under Parenting Activities and choose a second self-care activity that would be meaningful to them. Point out that the group will discuss how these assignments, including the self-care activities described next, worked out at the group's next meeting.

1. Ask parents to observe their child's behavior during the week and notice characteristics typical of his or her developmental stage.

or

2. Ask parents to watch their child and think about his or her temperament in some of the areas discussed.

Parents may use Handout 1.21 to record their homework assignments that will be discussed during the following week. You may also use activities from *Pathways to Competence* (2002) or make up your own for homework if you prefer.

Self-Care Activity

As mentioned, refer parents to Handout 1.22 for self-care activities from which parents can choose. Have parents generate a list of other activities they find stress reducing. Include suggestions for self-care provided by parents on the handout for self-care. They can also add to this list in subsequent weeks and choose from this expanded list each week.

STEP ② Developing Body Control and a Positive Body Image

MATERIALS

Required materials

Handouts 2.1–2.10 (on Pathways to Competence for Young Children CD-ROM accompanying this manual)

Self-Care Activities Handout 1.22

Suggested materials

Pathways to Competence: Encouraging Healthy Social and Emotional Development in Young Children (2002)

Three-ring binders with handouts for parents

Overhead projector, blackboard, or flip chart

Pencils and/or pens for the group to use

Markers and erasers for the group leader(s) for discussions

Self-care box

HOMEWORK REVIEW

Encourage the participants to report on their observations of the developmental level and temperament characteristics of their child, which they learned about during Step 1. Were there any aspects of their observations that surprised them? Did they complete a self-care activity during the week? What did they choose and was it helpful in reducing stress?

SETTING THE STAGE

Increasingly, the field of medicine is beginning to look at the link between the mind and body and how they can influence each other. Examples include the effect of early experiences on the development of the brain and how stress can affect the immune system. The public is increasingly interested in the use of complementary treatments such as acupuncture, exercise, massage, meditation, prayer, and yoga.

 Ask parents for any examples of this mind–body link that interest them, that they know about, or that they have experience with.

Ask parents to think about and to describe how the "ideal" body is portrayed on television and in the movies. How does this make them feel about themselves? Do they compare themselves to the ideal and try to be that way?

Sometimes, before a child is born, a parent will imagine what the child will look like or be like. How do their children fit with their expectations of how they expected them to look when they were born? Write down the participants' comments on a blackboard, overhead projector, or flip chart, or keep your own notes in a separate notebook if you'd like to refer to them during or after the session.

UNDERSTANDING BODY CONTROL AND BODY IMAGE

Discussion of Key Terms Related to Body Control and Body Image

Talk with the group about the two main aspects of the psychology of the body: 1) the physical and objective aspects of the body and its appearance, and 2) the internal or subjective experience an individual has about bodily characteristics. For this Step, the following terms will be important to understand: *body control, body self,* and *body image.* Body self and body image both refer to a child's sense of a physical self and are important parts of the child's self-concept.

Body Control

Body control has both objective and subjective aspects. Obviously, children who excel in sports or who have advanced motor skills are going to feel more in control of their bodies. A number of obvious or more subtle physiological difficulties as discussed in Step 1 can affect a child's sense of body control, as well (e.g., the child's ability to hold and move a pencil can affect his or her sense of body control).

Body Self

Body self describes a child's physical sense of self and develops from infancy. A sense of self is one aspect of self-concept in which the child first comes to realize his or her separateness from others. The child also gains a sense of body self through sensations from the muscles and joints. Later, a sense of body self has more to do with the child's body control and sense of attractiveness.

Body Image

Body image is the sum of one's feelings and attitudes toward one's own body. It is a mental picture of one's own body and how much one likes it or does not like it. A multidimensional entity, body image is believed to be formed out of body experiences beginning in the early days of life.

What are some of the things that can affect our body image or how we think about our bodies? Write some of the parents' thoughts about this on an overhead projector or flip chart.

Parents will probably note that multiple experiences and factors can affect body image. Make sure that the following are covered in the discussion (if parents do not mention these things, you can suggest them):

• Objective aspects of appearance (e.g., tall, short, brown hair)

• Interpretation of body attractiveness by caregivers and/or peers

• Cultural views of beauty

• Sense of body control the person experiences (e.g., being a good athlete, being skilled at creating things by hand)

Unfortunately, many adults are uncomfortable or dissatisfied with their bodies and would like to change them.

Have parents discuss the new trend toward having plastic surgery, even among teen-agers, to enhance one's appearance.

Distribute Handout 2.1: How Aspects of Body Control Can Affect Body Image.

Discuss different aspects of body control that affect a child's body image. Either conduct a discussion with the whole group or have the parents complete Handout 2.1 and then discuss it.

DEVELOPMENT OF BODY SELF

Distribute Handout 2.2: Development of Body Self.

When discussing Handout 2.2, make reference to the column titled "Body scheme and body image." Pick out some of the developmental characteristics noted in this column that are relevant to the age of the children being discussed in the group. Ask parents if there is anything related to the age of their child and development of body self that surprises them. Here are some examples based on age grouping:

Birth to 1 month

Touching or rocking the baby helps him or her to experience his or her body as separate from the caregivers.

4 to 8 months

The baby likes to look at him- or herself in the mirror, although he or she will not recognize him- or herself yet and may be as apt to look at a nearby person. However, babies are most attracted to the human face and love to look at it, even when it is their own. Looking at faces also helps the baby to realize that Mommy and Daddy look different from each other and from him or her.

13 to 24 months

The child is learning to walk and run. Parents need energy and they need to be alert to safety issues in order to avoid accidents with their now much more mobile toddler.

2 to 4 years

The child is becoming aware of body parts and gender differences. During this stage, the child usually loves to run and jump and do other physical activities.

4 to 6 years

With an increase in motor abilities, the child develops a full sense of body integration and constancy and an understanding that all body parts work together and stay the same over time.

Refer to Chapter 2 in *Pathways to Competence* (2002), if possible, for more details about development of the body self that could be useful for discussion.

Importance of Body Self and a Positive Body Image

Parents may be wondering why body image is so important. For young children, movement and a sense of body control is at the very core of their being. In fact, they express many of their thoughts and feelings through the movement of their bodies. As caregivers support and encourage their children's body development, children experience a sense of achievement and pride in being able to make their bodies work successfully.

Research studies on children who have been very neglected have shown that when, for any reason, parents have difficulty with touching and holding their baby and other caregivers are not available, this can result in psychological and neurological damage to the child.

Research Related to Body Self and Body Image

If possible, refer again to Chapter 2 of *Pathways to Competence* (2002) and then highlight some interesting research findings that would have relevance to the parents in the group. Some research findings that could prove interesting include the following:

- Babies' movements follow the rhythms of their caregivers. For example, during face-to-face interactions, babies will often mirror the facial expressions of their caregiver and will move forward when the caregiver leans toward them.

- Massaging babies can often help to settle them and increases weight gain in low birth weight (LBW) infants. If a parent performs the massage, it can increase the parent's sense of closeness and bonding with his or her baby.

- More than 50% of men and women have negative feelings and thoughts about their body image. Women's major body concerns typically center around weight, and men are concerned with their muscularity.

- The use of soft infant carriers that increase the contact between mothers and their infants has been found to contribute to the child having a secure attachment later.

- Having physical and visual impairments can affect an individual's sense of body self. In addition, less obvious problems such as sensitivities and sensory integration difficulties can also contribute significantly to a poor sense of body self. Sensory integration therapy has sometimes been found to be helpful for some children with these difficulties.

PARENTING PRINCIPLES RELATED TO BODY CONTROL AND BODY IMAGE

***Distribute Handout 2.3: Principles for
Encouraging Body Control and a Positive Body Image.***

If you are using the video clips of parent interactions, choose one that would relate to these principles.

PRINCIPLE 1: Provide your infant or young child with plenty of experiences of touch and physical contact.

Touch has been shown to be important in the development of both human and non-human infants. Many believe that holding and touching an infant early on encourages bonding with the newborn, and touch and massage have been shown to improve weight gain in premature and ill newborns. Also, touching and holding infants can improve their alertness and attention and encourage those responsive interactions so critical in the early months of a baby's life. Research has shown that babies who are put in a Snuggli and carried close to their parents are more likely to be securely attached than those who are put away from the caregiver in a hard infant seat. Without handling and holding, the child may develop a distortion or lack of integration of his or her body image. Touch has also been shown to be important for older children and can speed healing and improve the well-being of those who are sick and of older individuals.

Ask the parents how touch was dealt with in their family of origin. Did their family share lots of hugs, or was affection expressed in other ways? Was touch ever experienced as too intrusive?

PRINCIPLE 2: Encourage your toddler or preschooler to get to know his or her body and body parts.

Awareness of body parts is necessary for adequate motor planning. Also, an infant's knowledge of the world begins with knowledge of his or her body as it moves through space and as it relates to others.

Between 1 and 2 years of age, the child experiences a significant increase in his or her ability to identify body parts. In fact, by 2 years of age, many children can point to and name as many as 11 different body parts.

Distribute Handout 2.4: Action Songs.

A number of songs can be used to help children to learn their body parts and to make the learning fun. The action song "Head and shoulders, knees and toes" and other examples are provided on Handout 2.4.

Look in *Pathways to Competence* (2002) to find other suggestions of songs and games that can be used.

Ask the parents if they can think of other ways to teach the names of body parts that they have used.

Also ask parents if they use the actual names of genitals when talking to their child. For any parents who are uncomfortable about using the proper words for genitals, point out that it is important to encourage children to talk about their private parts using the actual words in case they have concerns about them at any time and need to tell someone. Further discussion of children and sexuality comes later, and strategies for discussing sexuality with children are given in Handouts 2.9 a and b, to be distributed later in this Step.

PRINCIPLE 3: In order to encourage fine motor control, provide interesting toys and fine motor activities that your infant and young child will enjoy.

From a very early age, children need to be provided with a variety of toys that they can use that give them a sense of being able to control their body. These toys need to be adapted to the special characteristics of each child, especially if a child has an obvious physical disability or less obvious challenges or difficulties with motor planning or sensory integration.

Have parents think of and discuss fine motor activities for children at different ages (birth to 1 year, 2 to 3 years, 3 to 4 years, 5 to 7 years).

If leaders are having difficulty with fine motor activity suggestions for different age levels, some of the suggestions in Step 4 on the topic of play may be helpful.

PRINCIPLE 4: Provide activities that allow for the integration of a number of senses.

Some children who have behavior problems and emotional or social difficulties have various types of sensory integrative dysfunction. The problem is usually not with receiving, for example, auditory or visual sensory input such as words or sights, or with hearing sounds or seeing objects, but with making meaning from the input. In other words, the brain does not process sensory input well and does not integrate information from the various sensory systems adequately. This makes learning difficult and results in a child feeling uncomfortable about him- or herself and his or her body. For example, if the child has difficulty understanding a verbal instruction such as "Put the block in the box," he or she will have difficulty executing the movement even though his or her fine motor skills may be intact. Frequently, children who have hypersensitivity to certain types of stimulation have difficulty with sensory integration functioning. Children may be hypersensitive (i.e., overreactive) or hyposensitive (i.e., underreactive) in the following sensory systems:

- Auditory (hearing) (e.g., startle at loud noises)

- Visual (seeing) (e.g., get upset if lights are very bright)

- Olfactory (smelling) (e.g., react strongly to strong smells)

- Taste (may refuse some foods)

- Vestibular (gravity and movement)

- Tactile (touch) (may pull back from touch)

- Proprioceptive (muscles and joints)

Children may also have difficulty with processing and making meaning of the information or stimulation they receive from these sensory systems and/or problems with integrating the information (i.e., sensory integration dysfunction or other difficulties).

Ask parents to think about any sensory systems that they or their child might have difficulty with.

In a discussion, have parents suggest some ways to encourage integration of the senses. Make your own list, as well, so that parents can learn from your experience, but wait until they do their list to share your ideas. Your list should include some of the following:

- Trace letters that are made of sandpaper while repeating the name of the letter(s).

- Draw to music and have the child talk about the picture and his or her feelings.

- Use playdough to make objects that are then named.

When children have severe difficulties, they should be referred to a physiotherapist or occupational therapist for assessment and treatment.

PRINCIPLE 5: Join your child in fun motor and movement activities.

Movement activities can be fun for children, and it is important that caregivers participate in them with their children. Rolling over with children, running through the leaves, clapping hands, blowing bubbles, playing catch with a balloon, and dancing are all wonderful movement activities that children like to be involved with. When caregivers join in the activities, it gets children involved and makes them want to play because it serves as a motivator. These activities can be marvelous ways to help children feel in control of their bodies. For children who are very active, these types of exercises may be crucial to help them "let off steam" and calm down.

Distribute Handout 2.5: Strategies for Helping the Very Active Child to Slow Down.

Many parents have children who seem to have difficulty slowing down when it is supposed to be a quiet time or are "on the go" all the time. Discuss the suggestions in Handout 2.5 as a way to help a child to learn how to slow down when it is important to be more focused and to concentrate.

PRINCIPLE 6: Help your child to develop appropriate eating, sleeping, and toileting routines. Avoid creating battlegrounds around them.

As children begin to individuate and become autonomous, many become oppositional in areas in which they have some control. It is very difficult to make children eat, sleep, or go to the toilet, so it is often around these important physical achievements that conflicts between children and caregivers may develop.

Have the group suggest some ways that battles are sometimes created around these issues.

Point out to parents that making a child eat things he or she hates, always rocking the child to sleep without letting the child learn to fall asleep on his or her own, and trying to toilet train too early are examples of how battlegrounds can be established.

Have parents think about how these issues were managed in their families as they were growing up and if they remember or were told about any issues that occurred (e.g., not sleeping well, being a picky eater). Discuss these issues from the past and whether they are having any influence now on how parents deal with these issues with their own children.

Note that parents may vary in terms of what they believe warrants further attention, depending on the group you are working with. If so, allow them the opportunity to discuss their particular concerns once you go over a few of the ones presented in the handouts.

Toilet Training or Teaching

Distribute Handout 2.6: Steps in Toilet Teaching.

When toilet teaching or training (depending on the term you prefer), it is important to ensure that the child is developmentally ready to learn the skill but, at the same time, to recognize that schools and many child cares require children to be toilet trained before they can attend.

Depending on the age of the children in the group, you may wish to ask the group about any difficulties they are having with toilet teaching their child. If the children being discussed in the group are older, you may want to forego this discussion.

Sleeping Problems

Distribute Handouts 2.7a: Tips for Preventing Sleep Problems, b: Methods for Overcoming Sleep Problems, and c: Characteristics of Nightmares and Night Terrors.

The majority of sleeping problems arise because children do not learn to fall asleep on their own. It has been well documented through research that all children wake at some time during the night. Although most children develop ways to fall back to sleep on their own, some children experience difficulty with self-soothing. Therefore, in order to prevent sleeping difficulties, parents need to develop strategies to help their children to fall asleep on their own.

Many community agencies or hospitals have sleep clinics for supporting parents in overcoming sleep problems with their children. However, there are many simple strategies parents can use at night and before naps to help children to fall asleep.

If any of the parents in the group have indicated that their child appears to have some serious sleeping problems, go over the strategies to help overcome them included in Handouts 2.7a, b, and c. Point out that these strategies should not be used until the end of the first year.

Have parents look at the handouts and discuss how the strategies have worked for them or might work if they have not tried them.

Eating Problems

Distribute Handout 2.8: Establishing Good Eating Habits.

Ask parents if they have had any eating problems with their child. Children differ significantly in how regular they are about eating and the types of food they are willing to eat. They tend to go through growth spurts when they may eat voraciously, whereas at other times their appetites are far more modest. Some children object strongly to the texture or taste of certain foods. At such times, parents may worry that their child is malnourished or is not getting an adequate range of foods because he or she is not eating a balanced diet.

Establishing a certain routine for mealtimes is very important. Children should be expected to come to the table and eat with the family; they should be excused when they have been at the table for a reasonable time for their age and become disinterested or act up. Once they leave the table, they should be told that they can only eat a small, healthy snack until the next meal. These routines need to be established calmly and, as much as possible, without fuss. It is important that children are required to eat their meals at the arranged time. If they refuse to eat, parents should follow through with the suggestions just mentioned and not offer unplanned food between meals except for a small healthy snack because it may end up substituting or replacing the meal.

Have parents think of some rules for mealtimes. Make a list on the flip chart, overhead projector, or blackboard.

Ask a parent to role play by taking the part of a child who is refusing to eat or go to sleep. Respond as the parent using some of the strategies in Handouts 2.7 and 2.8.

PRINCIPLE 7: Respond to your child's early sexual curiosity by providing answers to questions, acceptance of interest, and appropriate limits for sexual play.

Ask parents to give an example of how their parents talked to them about sexuality. Ask them to explain how this may influence how they plan to deal with sexuality with their children.

Infants at a very young age like to touch their genitals, and, in the second year of life, their genitals become a source of pride. Toddlers, if given the opportunity, love to run around naked and to show off. As they become a little older, children become very interested in gender differences and may wish they could have some of the attributes of the opposite sex. This means that girls may wish they had penises, whereas boys may want to have breasts and to be able to have a baby. Usually, around age 5 or 6 years of age, children become far more modest and request privacy when they bathe or dress.

Have the group list other sexual behaviors often shown by preschoolers and young children.

Your final list should include the following:

- Interest in toileting and wanting to peek at other children in the bathroom

- Swearing and using sexual words

- Touching themselves or masturbating in various forms

- Showing their own nudity

- Handling each other's bodies while playing doctor or house

- Joining with another child in "sex" play with dolls

- Using toileting words such as "poop" or "butt" and making jokes about them

In general, caregivers should avoid being shocked by these behaviors and expressing a sense of shame by tone of voice and attitude. Indicate firmly which behaviors are acceptable and which are not (e.g., touching each other's genitals, looking at other children in the bathroom, using rude words). Help to socialize the child without destroying his or her pleasure or creating shame. Also, answering questions about sexuality in accepting ways can set the stage for ongoing communication later.

Distribute Handouts 2.9a: Dealing with Sexual Behavior and Questions About Sexuality and b: Some Suggested Answers to Common Questions About Sexuality.

Have parents look at the handouts and see if they have any questions or comments.

PRINCIPLE 8: Express delight in your child's body and his or her control of it. Adapt to your child's physical self.

A child's body image develops out of positive experiences with controlling his or her body and being able to make it do what he or she wants it to do. Constantly emphasizing a child's physical appearance either positively or negatively may give a message that these attributes are more important than others.

Here are some encouraging remarks that parents can say to children that can make them feel good about their bodies and physical appearance:

"What a bright smile you have."

"How shiny your hair looks in the sun."

"I liked the way you kept trying when you built that tower."

"Wow—you really jumped high today!"

If your child does have areas of physical challenge, it is so important that you provide the supports necessary for the child to feel some success.

In a society that idealizes perfect-looking people, we all fall far short. Unless a person is under 25, has a toned body, has perfect skin, and looks good in front of a camera, he or she is not likely to model in any magazine. Although girls tend to be more obsessed with their looks, boys also fall prey to stereotyped views of good looks perpetuated by the media.

Ask parents to spend a few minutes thinking about friends, relatives, or public figures they admire. Then, ask the parents to list the characteristics they like about these individuals.

Have parents discuss the likeable characteristics they just listed. Interestingly, discussion of the characteristics that people admire typically relates to personal characteristics such as strength, kindness, fun, commitment, and helpfulness. Physical attributes and attractiveness are seldom mentioned.

Point out that in personal relationships and the workplace, personality characteristics are more important than physical appearance. Have parents think about a boss or a colleague whom they enjoyed working with and think about the characteristics of that person.

PRINCIPLE 9: Respond to body language and validate the reality of the experience being expressed.

Children may show their fears by facial expressions or behaviors because they have difficulty expressing fears verbally. Responding empathetically to a child's body language can help the child to feel secure and confirm the ability and integrity of the child's body—that it is accepted and understood.

Have the parents recall the time before their child could talk. What kinds of body language did the child use to tell them his or her wants and needs, feelings, and likes and dislikes?

What kind of body language does the child use now?

Ask parents how they respond to their child's body language.

Suggest that sometimes they may be able to read their child's body language and use the signs to help the child calm down before he or she gets too upset, or to provide a frightened child with more support.

OTHER DISCUSSION TOPICS

Mind–Body Link and Guided Imagery

This is an excellent place to introduce the importance of using various ways to relieve stress and get relief from worrying. Point out that calming the autonomic nervous system in these ways can optimize physical and mental health and even enhance the immune system. Describe the meaning of guided imagery, breathing techniques, and relaxation exercises.

If possible, use a recording that parents can listen to in order to go through guided imagery or relaxation techniques. Explain that these exercises could be used as a self-care activity. Suggestions of possible audio recordings that could be used include Cash's (1990) *Body-image Therapy: A Program for Self-directed Change,* Kabat-Zinn's (1995) *Mindfulness Meditation: Cultivating the Wisdom of your Body and Mind,* and Naparstek's (1993) *General Wellness.*

THE TREE

At the end of the group, before talking about next week's homework, ask parents to write the principles from Handout 2.3 on pieces of cardboard and stick them on the Tree under one of the primary roles of parenting at the top of the Tree.

HOMEWORK

Distribute Handout 2.10: Homework.

Describe the homework activities. If the Step is given over only 1 week, have parents choose one of the activities and do one self-care activity that is nurturing to their bodies. If the Step is given over 2 weeks, they can do both parenting activities and repeat the self-care activity or do another one that would be meaningful to them related to self-care of the body. Point out that the group will discuss them next week.

1. Parents could take their child on an outing that involves physical activity such as walking, climbing, swimming, or riding a bike.

   or

2.   Ask parents to comment and acknowledge to their child that they have noticed their child's body language (e.g., "You smile a lot when you play with your friends"; "You seem tired; you're starting to yawn") and record what happened.

Self-Care Activity

See Handout 1.22, which includes several self-care activities from which parents can choose. This week, as mentioned, it is especially appropriate to choose an activity that nurtures the body such as a special bath, a long walk, or a massage (either from a professional or a friend).

STEP ③

Developing a Secure Attachment

MATERIALS

Required materials

Handouts 3.1–3.11 (on Pathways to Competence for Young Children CD-ROM accompanying this manual)

Self-Care Activities Handout 1.22

Suggested materials

Pathways to Competence: Encouraging Healthy Social and Emotional Development in Young Children (2002)

Three-ring binders with handouts for parents

Overhead projector, blackboard, or flip chart

Crayons, markers, pencils and/or pens for participants

Paper for each participant on which to draw a picture

Markers and erasers for the group leader(s) for discussions

Self-care boxes

HOMEWORK REVIEW

Encourage the participants to report on their experiences with either joining their child in a physical activity or commenting on or acknowledging their child's body language. Also, make sure that parents are invited to comment on their choice of a self-care activity and how they felt about it and if they think that it helped to ease some of their stress.

SETTING THE STAGE

Our society often seems obsessed with understanding love, and yet we see increasing evidence indicating that relationships that were supposed to last forever frequently come to an end—often dramatically. Perhaps most obvious are the lives of the rich and famous. It is hard to escape the images of certain public figures who once seemed so happy but who broke up in a very public way (you may want to suggest current celebrity figures that are in the news because of having troubled relationships). Relationships that seem enchanted and full of romance and sparkle often come to ugly ends. Apart from these public figures, statistics show that about half of all marriages end in divorce, and the anger that sometimes accompanies the separation can be devastating for those involved. All of this can make individuals cautious about becoming involved in new relationships and investing their love in hopes that these relationships will endure over time. Perhaps because of the fragility of adult relationships, we often perceive the relationships with our children as having the potential for being the most long lasting and rewarding.

If individuals search for one thing that has affected their personalities, they would probably all identify their relationship with their parents as at least one of the most influential. In fact, the early relationship with a primary caregiver, usually one's mother, may in many ways become a model for later relationships that are formed, especially with one's own children.

Distribute Handout 3.1: My Relationship with My Parents and How I Am Today.

Have parents complete Handout 3.1, providing comments about their relationship with their mother and father (examples are provided to give parents an idea of what to write).

Ask parents to discuss the following questions:

How do you think that your relationship with your mother and/or father has affected your personality? How has it affected the way you parent?

Researchers and those who work with parents and infants have been able to demonstrate that the quality of the attachment, or the relationship children have with their parents, affects children's later development—particularly their emotional and social development. They have also been able to show that the style or quality of attachment often passes from generation to generation.

Ask parents to think about how their relationship with their child can affect their child's development. Make sure to mention some of the following if they are not suggested by the participants:

- I can give my child trust in the world by being available to him or her.

- Being close to someone influences how that individual feels about and interacts with other adults and children.

- A good relationship with caregivers allows a child to feel competent in managing his or her world.

- A good or nurturing relationship gives a child good memories that can help him or her to find the positive in the world.

UNDERSTANDING ATTACHMENT

Discussion of Key Terms Related to Attachment

Point out that two terms, *bonding* and *attachment,* have often been used synonymously; however, they actually describe two processes that are different in terms of direction and timing.

Distribute Handout 3.2: Definitions of Bonding and Attachment.

Handout 3.2 illustrates the differences between bonding and attachment. Point out that the term *bonding* was commonly used in the 1970s to describe what was believed to be a "magical" process that happens at birth when the mother feels an immediate surge of love for her baby. Explain that for some mothers and fathers, this love takes longer to develop, especially if the pregnancy or birth experience was difficult.

Ask parents about their experiences after their baby's birth and their feelings about their baby at that time.

Assure parents who may have felt anxious and too tired to feel much for the baby at birth that these are normal feelings. Also explain that many mothers get the "baby blues" and feel down for a few days, usually from the third day postnatally. Also point out that postpartum depression that lasts longer is relatively common and that treatment can be very helpful.

Attachment, which differs from bonding, is the relationship that develops between the child (and later the adult) and their parent. A child develops a secure relationship (attachment) to his or her parents when the child finds the parent to be a safe place from which he or she can explore his or her world. The parents' ability to respond to the child sensitively when the child needs them is crucial to the child forming an attachment to the parents. Attachment develops gradually over the first year and is not established until about 8 months of age when the infant has acquired certain cognitive abilities. The child needs the understanding of cause and effect and object and person permanence, which is the understanding that objects and people still exist when they are out of sight. For example, if a parent has a ball in her lap and then hides it behind his or her back, the baby knows that the ball still exists and may search for it. This understanding enables the child to be aware of the differences between people because he or she can remember familiar people and how they look and recognize that other people are different from them.

Attachment is about two primary aspects of children's relationships to their caregivers: a set of behaviors and a way of thinking and feeling about themselves and others in their world (a representational system).

Distribute Handout 3.3: Defining Attachment: Two Aspects of the Definition.

Point out the behaviors listed in Handout 3.3 that infants and young children use to maintain contact with and get close to their parents. Ask the participants how they remember their experiences with their parents and how these memories affect how they view other people and events. Have parents describe any attachment behaviors they have noticed in their infants or young children. Have parents think about how attachment might look in school-age children and teenagers and write this on the handout.

Explain that a child whose bids for closeness with his or her parent are rejected may come to expect rejection from others, and may feel rejected even when the other person is not rejecting him or her.

Ask parents if they know anyone who seems overly sensitive to rejection. How does this affect his or her relationship with others?

Sometimes attachment problems may arise, and a parent may find it difficult to respond sensitively and/or consistently or to bond with a particular child. These difficulties can be triggered in the parent for a number of different reasons.

Ask parents to suggest some things that could get in the way of forming an attachment to a baby. (Examples will be provided after group discussion.)

A number of issues within a parent can affect attachment and cause problems. Sometimes a mother may become depressed after she gives birth to a child, and this postpartum depression may continue for a year or more after the birth. Such feelings make it very difficult for a mother to find the energy to be interested in or to play with a baby, leading to both mother and baby tending to turn away from each other.

In other instances, painful memories of abuse or rejection can affect how a mother or father adjusts to being a parent. And even more interesting—sometimes a particular child will trigger memories or bad feelings that another child doesn't—just because the child looks or acts like someone with whom the parent had a very difficult relationship or experience, such as an abusive parent or violent husband.

Also, because of events or situations that are going on at the time their baby is born, parents may lack the emotional energy needed for the baby. Some examples may be the death of a close relative or friend, divorce or separation, serious illness, loss of a job, or the stress of living in a high-risk neighborhood. All of these situations can cause intense anxiety in a parent and can lead the parent to withdraw from the baby— getting the attachment off to a poor start.

Development of Attachment

Distribute Handout 3.4: Development of Attachment.

Pick out some developmental milestones relevant to the age of the children being discussed in the group. The following are some examples:

Birth to 6 months

By the time they are approximately 6 weeks old, most babies smile at anyone who smiles and talks to them. Babies also typically engage in two-way "conversations" of babbling back and forth.

7 to 24 months

The period from 7 to 24 months is the age at which attachment is typically established. Babies may be upset in the presence of strangers and show separation anxiety or cry when parents leave them with someone else. They are also typically very happy to see their parents return.

2 to 3 years

By 2 or 3 years of age, young children manage separations better, and caregivers can talk about and negotiate plans with the child (e.g., "Mommy will be going to work today but we will do something together tonight").

3 to 6 years

Between the ages of 3 and 6, physical contact is not as necessary to maintain attachment except when a child is very upset, and a child can be settled by words from a parent or by seeing his or her parents at times. Parents and children are now more able to talk about and to negotiate conflicts and cooperate around plans and understand the other's perspective in different situations.

6 years and older

Although children in adolescence go through a process of separating from their parents and forming new relationships with peers and others in their lives, the role of parents continues to be critical, and young people with secure attachments tend to navigate this stage of development better.

Remind the participants about the relationships they have with their parents, if they are still alive, and how these relationships can continue to be important into adulthood whether they are positive or negative. Although new relationships are formed throughout life, our early attachments to our parents still have an influence on us in many areas of life and particularly on how we parent.

Encourage parents to look at the section of Handout 3.4 that would be relevant to their child and to discuss any other attachment relationships they have noticed that their child has developed (e.g., with a child care provider or grandparent).

Refer to Chapter 3 in *Pathways to Competence* (2002) for more details about development that could be useful for discussion.

Importance of Attachment

As mentioned previously, the quality of attachment children have with their parents can influence how they relate socially with other children and adults in their world, such as child care providers and teachers. It also influences how children manage their negative emotions such as fear, sadness, and anger. The quality of attachment can affect how children process information and their ability to solve problems. Most important, it influences how they see the world and the people in it and how they react.

Securely attached children feel confident that their parents are there for them and can serve as a safe harbor to come to in order to be comforted when their feelings become too intense and uncomfortable.

Distribute Handouts 3.5a and b: Attributions of the World.

Point out that the securely attached child, because he or she feels safe, interprets an ambiguous situation very differently from an insecurely attached child, and that this has a very significant effect on a child's view of the world and behavior. Handouts 3.5a and b illustrates this phenomenon.

Ask parents to discuss how attachment can affect a child's interpretation of situations and how it can lead to cycles of rejection or affirming interactions and experiences. Explain that it is about the view or schemes of the world that the child develops. As can be seen in the handouts, on the one hand, if a child is securely attached, he or she is more likely to respond positively in an ambiguous situation and to remember it as a positive experience. On the other hand, an insecurely attached child, and particularly a child with a disorganized attachment, will be likely to react very negatively, even aggressively, and will set up a negative interaction with other children. He or she will also see the situation in a negative way and perceive rejection from the other children when it was not intended and will remember the situation as negative. In this way, further cycles of interactions in which the child perceives rejection can lead to the child being isolated and to other children withdrawing from him or her.

Description of the Three Main Attachment Classifications

Distribute Handout 3.6: The Love Experience.

Before you begin a discussion of different attachment classifications, distribute Handout 3.6 and have parents complete The Love Experience questionnaire. To make this somewhat less threatening, explain that they could fill it out for themselves or about someone they know.

Using the three descriptions in the questionnaire, explain what classification each one refers to. Explain that, in this example, answer 1 refers to a child who has an ambivalent/resistant attachment or an adult who is preoccupied with relationships and likes to think and talk about emotions. People in this classification often worry about being abandoned or rejected and may be constantly trying to ensure that this does not happen or to repair difficult relationships with their parents. This is characteristic of 23% of the population.

Answer 2 refers to a child who has an avoidant attachment or an adult who is dismissive of emotions and relationships and who does not like to get too close to other people. Approximately 12% of the population falls in this category.

Answer 3 refers to a child who is "secure" or to an "autonomous" adult who finds it relatively easy to be close to others and who does not worry about closeness or being abandoned. As a parent, this person would tend to be positive and to accept his or her child. The individual would allow the child to be as separate and autonomous as would be appropriate for the child's age. Approximately 65% of the population is considered securely attached.

Encourage parents to discuss people they know who fit one of the classifications.

Point out that the various types of attachment are adaptive for the situations people have found themselves in. For example, children in category 3 (securely attached) most likely have been responded to in a sensitive and consistent way by an accessible caregiver. As mentioned, the caregiver is likely to have been positive and accepting and to have allowed the child some independence as he or she got older. Children in categories 1 and 2 (insecurely attached), however, have either had their emotional needs dismissed by caregivers or have received inconsistent responses to them from caregivers.

Have parents close their eyes and imagine that they are babies all alone in their cribs and that they are crying because they are hungry and have soiled diapers. Have them imagine that their parent comes in and picks them up or talks to them. Ask them how that would feel. Have them then imagine how it feels if no one comes in to comfort them.

Parents could be asked to draw how it felt in both situations. Provide paper and markers or crayons if you decide to have parents draw the situations.

Discuss the parents' experiences with them.

IMPORTANT RESEARCH FINDINGS

If possible, read the section in *Pathways to Competence* (2002), pages 170–177, and highlight some interesting findings that would have particular relevance for parents in the group. Some of these findings are provided for you here:

- A number of characteristics of parent–child interactions contribute to the child having a secure attachment to that parent: being sensitive to the child's cues, responding to and calming an upset child, cooperating with rather than constantly intruding and interfering with the child, and showing acceptance of the child.

- Not only does attachment affect behavioral outcomes but it can also have an impact on the child's physiology. For example, children with insecure attachment have been shown to have elevated heart rates and a higher level of stress hormones in situations involving separation from the caregiver or during painful procedures such as inoculations. Also, for children in orphanages who lack warm and sensitive interactions, their stress levels tend to go up throughout the day and they secrete more of the stress hormone cortisol. In contrast, for children who have secure attachment to their parent(s) or secure relationships with child care providers, their stress levels get lower throughout the day. This has tremendous implications for the development and organization of the brain and the immune system.

- Attachment classifications tend to pass from one generation to another. In other words, if a mother's attachment classification with her parents is assessed during pregnancy, in 80%–85% of cases the baby's attachment classification at 12 months will be the same as the mother's.

Have parents discuss some of the reasons why the baby's attachment classification at 12 months might be the same as the mother's during pregnancy.

Point out, however, that the quality of attachment for a child or adult can change in certain situations and discuss with parents what they think these situations may be.

If no one brings it up during the discussion, mention that attachment can change from insecure to secure for a parent and a child. A child can become more secure if a parent becomes more sensitive to his or her child's cues, and an adult can become more secure by having a nurturing relationship that allows him or her to learn to trust that a significant other person will respond to his or her emotional needs. Conversely, attachment can change from secure to insecure if an individual experiences stressful events or difficult relationships later. For children, attachment can change in this direction if a parent becomes more stressed by circumstances in his or her life such as losing a job and becomes less emotionally available to the child.

If not mentioned during the discussion, point out that parents frequently replicate the parenting behavior that they experienced when they were growing up.

Distribute Handout 3.7: Describing Your Own Parents.

Have parents list the adjectives that describe their own parents and incidents from childhood that illustrate those adjectives on Handout 3.7 and share the content with another group member. If parents are struggling to come up with something, provide them with an example or two. For instance, say to them "You might use an adjective such as *loving* and illustrate that with 'She always spent time with me before I went to sleep.' Your adjective might be *distant* and an example might be, 'He was so busy building up his business that I never got to spend any time with him, and this was very difficult for me.'"

Ask some of the participants to share some of the information with the group. Empathize with any parents who share difficult or unhappy memories.

PARENTING PRINCIPLES AND TECHNIQUES

Distribute Handout 3.8: Principles for Encouraging a Secure Attachment.

Keep this handout handy because you will continue to refer to it throughout this Step.

If you are using video clips of the parents' interactions with their children, choose an example of positive behaviors to show to the group that illustrates one of the principles, such as comforting a child who is upset or responding to a child's cues.

PRINCIPLE 1: Comfort your child when he or she is physically hurt, ill, upset, frightened, or lonely.

Explain that it has been found that one of the keys to secure attachment in children is to comfort them when they are hurt, ill, upset, frightened, or lonely. If parents bring up the idea that this can spoil children, point out that in young children this is not the case. With older children it is important to comfort them but also to encourage and support them to not be overwhelmed by difficult emotions and to learn to express them in a positive way. It is also important to foster independence in older children so that they can learn to handle these emotions themselves. Explain that a parent needs to do something with his or her child to help the child to feel better, such as talking to him or her in a calming or reassuring way or suggesting an activity that the child enjoys. In Step 8 the process of "Emotion Coaching" will be outlined, which is invaluable in helping children to gradually learn to self-regulate.

Distribute Handout 3.9: My Family and Nurturing.

Have parents fill out Handout 3.9 and share it with the group.

 Ask participants to discuss what happened when they were young—when they were hurt, upset, ill, or frightened. To whom did they go, and why?

In the feedback and discussion following the exercise, emphasize that children need supportive responses when they are both physically and emotionally upset. When children receive the nurturing they need at the time, they become able to self-regulate more readily later. Make it clear that this kind of responding does not make children more whiny or spoiled, but, rather, builds their sense of trust in other people. If parents bring up stories of rejection, listen and help them to also remember any positive aspects of their relationships with their parents as well.

PRINCIPLE 2: Respond to and notice your child so that he or she learns that you care about him or her.

Encourage participants to give attention to their child, as much as possible, when he or she needs it. Tuning into the child's cues, letting him or her know that you have noticed how he or she is feeling, and sharing special moments of this kind of attunement and understanding of the child's day-to-day emotions can be very helpful. This tuning in can also be accomplished by letting the child take the lead rather than insisting on your way, whenever possible. For example, if the child wants to play house, join in and let the child describe the people and the actions rather than you suggesting what the family members are doing and insisting that the child do it your way. Encourage parents of older children to find an activity they can both enjoy together;

this is very important because these times will be remembered and can form the child's basis of trust in relationships and in the world. Examples of activities include going to the park, reading a story, or having a meal together. It is important that the parent can enjoy the activity too. If the parent really dislikes doing something, it will be difficult for him or her to convey a sense of enjoyment on an ongoing basis that the child will experience as sincere and real.

 Ask group participants to describe activities that they enjoy as a family or with one particular child.

PRINCIPLE 3: Give your child a sense of trust in the world and the people in it.

In today's often dangerous times, it is sometimes difficult to find a balance between encouraging children to explore the world in a trusting way and ensuring that they are safe. Children need to be given some warnings about strangers and other potentially dangerous situations, but, as much as possible, the home and outside environment need to be made safe enough to allow children to explore.

 Encourage parents to discuss any dilemmas that have come up for them about keeping their children safe and giving them trust in the world. How have they dealt with these dilemmas?

Make sure that parents understand that it is crucial to protect their young child from too much exposure to traumatic events that the child would be unable to process properly. For example, they should limit their child's exposure to the media and other sources of detailed information about violence, wars, or natural disasters such as a fire or flood.

PRINCIPLE 4: Help your child to review experiences and reenact frightening situations so that the memories can be integrated into your child's self-narratives.

Research is increasingly showing how important it is for children and adults to develop an understandable life story about their past that integrates any upsetting events. It is important to help children to understand and cope with any traumatic events that they may experience. Even with less dramatic events like a friend leaving town, a trip to the hospital, or the birth of a sibling, parents need to talk to their child about the event or help him or her to use pretend play to play it out. (Strategies to do this are described in Steps 4 and 5.) If the event were more tragic, such as the death of someone close, a divorce, or a manmade or natural disaster, it may be difficult for parents to talk about it if they were involved as well. If this is the case, it is important to seek an intervention with a professional for the child. Play therapy or attachment-based family therapy is often used in these kinds of situations. See Step 4 for an explanation of play therapy. Ignoring the event and not talking about it will not be helpful and may lead to a splitting off of that memory and storing it in a part of the brain that is not under conscious control. This, in turn, can lead to reoccurrence of the memory in the form of nightmares and flashbacks that can become very disabling for the child.

Ask parents if their child has experienced a difficult event and how they or someone else helped the child to understand and process the experience.

My Favorite Place

 To help parents to appreciate the impact of past memories, have them describe or draw a favorite place they have lived or visited. Ask them to show the drawing or describe their favorite place to the group. Ask parents to expand on the importance of their chosen place and to talk about any significant events that happened there. Also ask them to describe what it felt like when they left it. Was there anything they missed? Did they feel sad?

 Suggest that if the place made them feel safe, then it could be used as a positive visualization for a self-care activity when they are feeling sad or lonely.

PRINCIPLE 5: Create and keep alive good, warm, and joyful memories because they, in turn, can keep alive secure attachment relationships. Establish predictable family traditions.

Family traditions vary from culture to culture and can be related to holiday times; religious celebrations; or to festivals around birthdays, christenings, or weddings. They can instill in children a sense of predictability and security.

 Have parents discuss any traditions they maintain that they experienced as children or new ones that they have established for their own family.

 Good memories can also be created in other ways such as keeping a baby book or a photograph album that can help children feel valued and cherished. Have parents describe other ways they keep happy memories alive.

PRINCIPLE 6: When you leave your child, let him or her know where you are going and when you will be back. Provide objects to give security and keep alive memories of you or another absent caregiver.

If handled well, separations can strengthen a secure attachment. However, it is important that caregivers follow some strategies such as establishing a goodbye ritual and letting the child know when they will be back and being there at the specified time if this is not a daily separation such as going to child care. Caregivers should also leave with confidence, without a lot of fuss or emotion once the time comes. Parents may also suggest things that the child might do while the parent is away.

Have parents suggest other ways they help their child to cope with separations.

Distribute Handout 3.10: Tips for Separating from a Child.

Make sure that the child is introduced into child care gradually if he or she seems to be having difficulty separating. The child can take a photograph or other mementos of home to help ease the time away. Security blankets and familiar toys can also be helpful.

Substitute caregivers can also talk about parents during the day and let them know that their parents miss them and are thinking about them. Caregivers should make sure that the child knows when the parent will return, and parents should be careful to return as closely as possible to the time promised.

Have parents role-play what they would do and say if they were leaving their child for the first time at child care or school.

PRINCIPLE 7: Try to be as predictable and as positive as possible in reacting to your child's behavior.

One of the best ways to give children a sense of security is to be as predictable or consistent as possible in reacting to their behavior. This lets them know that their needs will be met. Although it is impossible to be totally predictable all of the time, examples of predictability include the following:

- Setting up a routine for mornings, mealtimes, bedtimes, and so forth

- Giving a child a clear sense of rules and consequences for misbehavior, and following through with them consistently

- Always comforting the child when he or she is hurt or upset

- Developing strategies for self-calming if a parent loses his or her temper frequently or becomes unable to respond predictably

Ask parents to give other suggestions of how they provide a predictable environment for their children. Also ask them to discuss situations or ways they are finding it difficult to provide structure and adhere to predictable routines.

OTHER DISCUSSION TOPICS

Parents may wish to discuss a number of other topics related to attachment. Some of these may include

- Attachment and child care

- Attachment and other caregiver such as fathers and child care providers. Some parents may find it difficult to understand that the child can be attached to more than one caregiver but still care about them as much.

- Security blankets, teddy bears, and other soft objects

- A loss of or change in a caregiver

- Adults and attachment

A few facts could be given about each topic as suggested next. If parents wish to discuss the topics in more detail, see *Pathways to Competence* (2002), pages 183–188, for more information.

Attachment and Child Care

Although the effects of child care on children are generally positive, what is certain is that the quality of the child care influences how well children manage it. Also, children with a secure attachment to a parent seem to adjust more easily to child care. It is important that child care providers respond when a child is upset or hurt and that they interact well with the children. Children whose temperament can be described as slow to warm up may find the transition to child care more challenging, but once they are comfortable with it they will usually adjust just as well as the children who adapt more quickly and easily.

 Ask parents, "What feelings and worries do you have when you leave your child with the child care provider or babysitter?" "What has helped you to overcome your concerns and any fears your child had?"

Fathers and Other Caregivers and Attachment

By 12 months of age, many children will have at least three attachment figures. These attachment figures will probably include a child's mother; father; and possibly a child care provider, grandparent, close friend of the family, or sibling. Whether an attachment relationship is established will depend on how much time the person spends with the child, and the quality of the attachment will depend on how responsive the person is to the child.

Security Blankets, Teddy Bears, and Other Soft Objects

Many children have some attachment to a blanket or other soft object. This attachment is particularly strong in children between the ages of approximately 12 and 48 months. To a child, the object's warmth and softness may represent the child's mother, and its appeal is that—unlike a parent—the child can control its coming and going. As a consequence, the attachment object can reduce the stress of separation (even the separation the child experiences when going to bed) and can provide calming and soothing. This kind of security object can be a real advantage to a child.

Dealing with the Loss of a Caregiver

Most children will go through some predictable stages such as anger, denial, and sadness in coping with the loss of a caregiver, although the order, intensity, and length of each stage will vary according to the circumstances. It is important for parents to realize that grieving can take place even when a nanny or other caregiver that has been with the child for a long time leaves the family. Make suggestions for dealing with loss or separation if group members show interest in this topic. Make sure that the following points are made:

- Nurturing and calming should be provided by someone close to the child.

- The child needs to talk about and play out the loss. The child's feelings should not be avoided or left undiscussed, although this can be very difficult for a parent if they experienced the loss, too.

- The child needs assurance that he or she will be looked after by the family and provided with as much stability as possible.

Adults and Attachment

Point out that adults have attachment classifications just as children do. These attachments were formed originally out of their experiences with their parents. The questionnaire in Handout 3.6 describes the behavior and feelings of adults in the three adult attachment classifications. Adult attachment classifications parallel that of children and also influence the relationships that they have and their sense of security in the world. On the one hand, an adult who is preoccupied may find it difficult to trust in relationships, may be very emotional, and may struggle when it comes to being independent. On the other hand, an adult who is dismissive of emotions and relationships and who does not like to get too close to other people may push people away and focus on work instead. Also explain that people can and do change these styles according to various experiences that can happen throughout their lives. For example, someone who is dismissive of emotions can become more understanding of their child's need for emotional responsiveness if that individual is helped to remember how he or she felt when his or her own parent(s) were not available. The preoccupied parent may change if he or she is in a relationship in which his or her partner understands the parent's fear of abandonment and demonstrates availability and loyalty to the individual over time.

THE TREE

At the end of the group, before talking about homework, ask parents to write the principles of developing a secure attachment on pieces of cardboard and stick them on the Tree under one of the roles of parenting at the top of the tree.

HOMEWORK

Distribute Handout 3.11: Homework.

Describe the homework activities. Have parents choose one of the activities and have them do the self-care activity if the Step is given over only 1 week. If the Step is given over 2 weeks, they can do both activities under Parenting Activities and choose a second self-care activity for the next week that would be meaningful to them. Point out that the group will discuss them the following week.

1. Have parents notice and describe in writing the instances during the week when they provide comfort or nurture their child in some way.

or

2. Have parents remember good times they had with their parent(s), describe them in writing, and think about what it was about these good times that was so important.

Self-Care Activity

Have parents refer to the list of self-care activities provided in Handout 1.22. This week, it might be especially appropriate to choose an activity that has the parent connecting with his or her partner or a friend in an activity that is mutually enjoyable.

STEP 4

Encouraging Play and Imagination

MATERIALS

Required materials

Handouts 4.1–4.13 (on Pathways to Competence for Young Children CD-ROM accompanying this manual)

Self-Care Activities Handout 1.22

Suggested materials

Pathways to Competence: Encouraging Healthy Social and Emotional Development in Young Children (2002)

Three-ring binders with handouts

Overhead projector, blackboard, or flip chart

Tree picture cards to write principles on

Velcro or tape to stick the picture cards on the tree

Pretend play toys to role play what happens in play therapy and to illustrate some appropriate pretend play toys for young children. If possible, get some from a local dollar store.

Crayons, markers, pencils and/or pens for participants

Paper on which to draw

Markers and erasers for the group leader(s) for discussions

Self-care boxes for parents

Video clips of parent–child interactions if available

HOMEWORK REVIEW

Have parents review the homework activities from the previous week and, if they are comfortable, read what they listed as ways they comforted and nurtured their child during the week. For those parents who thought about good times they had with their parents, have them talk about the examples they came up with. Ask them also about the activities they enjoyed with someone else.

SETTING THE STAGE

Three-year-old Mary carefully tucks her doll into bed and reads her a story. Suddenly, John, Mary's brother, grabs the baby out of the bed and throws a tantrum, which infuriates Mary. She grabs the doll and puts it back into bed. The drama between Mary and John then begins all over again.

Parents of preschoolers like Mary and John often wonder if these noisy games are healthy and beneficial. They wonder if they should get involved in them or even if they should interrupt them and get the children involved in something else—perhaps something more useful or educational.

Ask parents to describe some of the types of play their children engage in.

Ask parents what kind of games their children play that may make the parents feel uncomfortable.

It is likely that the parents will mention aggressive games with guns or fighting. Explain to parents that these issues will be dealt with during this session and throughout the rest of the Steps.

121

Let parents know that despite parental concerns and certain attitudes of society, in general, play is an essential ingredient to children's development—and finding ways to relax and reduce stress helps the mental health of adults and children. In other words, play and relaxation are not a waste of time; they are an essential breath of life for children and adults of all ages!

UNDERSTANDING THE DEVELOPMENT OF PLAY AND IMAGINATION

Discussion of Key Terms Related to Play and Imagination

Those who have researched and written about the role of play in child development have had a great deal of difficulty in agreeing on the essential characteristics that can distinguish play from other behaviors that children engage in. Thus, many terms related to play and imagination seem to have some unavoidable overlap. After looking at the term *play*, related terms such as *fantasy, imagination,* and *symbolization* are explored.

Ask parents to discuss what they think are the essential characteristics of play.

Distribute Handout 4.1: The Essential Qualities and Types of Play.

Go through these qualities and point out that they can apply throughout life.

Play

Here is a simple definition: "Play is any voluntary activity engaged in for the purpose of enjoyment."

Point out that a number of different types of play come under this definition, such as

- *Social games* or play with others

- *Exploratory play,* in which objects are examined and explored

- *Play with objects,* such as putting things in and taking them out (for babies) and building with blocks (for older children)

- *Play to learn about the world,* such as when the child learns to plant seeds in the garden, or goes on a walk to see things in the world

- *Rough-and-tumble play,* such as when the child runs around, chases others, and wrestles with a parent

- *Pretend and sociodramatic play* during which children use pretend animals, things, and people to play out a story theme or play out an imaginary world assuming different characters (e.g., a pirate, a teacher)

Fantasy and Imagination

Much of what has been written and studied about play has concerned pretend play and fantasy. To many writers, this is the most important type of play and the most critical in terms of many aspects of development. Our fantasy world is important for all of us, and we dream occasionally about what we would like to do and what it would be like if something pleasant happened. During fantasy, we are freed for a while from the control of the immediate, concrete, and real aspects of the world.

Ask parents to fantasize for a moment about what it would be like to be rich or to win the lottery and to be able to do what they would like without the reality and restrictions of budget and obligations. Point out that imagining or fantasizing about something pleasant for a moment can be a way to calm down when they are feeling stressed.

Ask parents if they see any problems with engaging in fantasy.

Very young children, before the second year of life, do not have the capacity for fantasizing as yet, and for them, fantasy comes through pretend play. In its simplest form, make-believe play is expressed when children pretend an object is something that it isn't—a stick becomes a magic wand and a box, a stove to cook on. This type of play also allows children to assume different roles and become superman, a mother or father, or their latest television hero.

Have parents describe recent times that their child has engaged in pretend play. What are some of their child's favorite play themes that he or she engages in quite often?

Symbolization

Much of what we do as adults is based on the ability to use symbolization. When a young child uses a stick as a baseball bat, she is making that stick a symbol of a real bat. This substitution for or symbolizing is a step between acting everything out through banging, touching, and feeling objects as an infant does to abstract thinking that allows us to solve problems and to make predictions "in our heads" without having to go through the concrete steps. As such, the symbolization that appears in pretend play is crucial for intellectual development.

Ask parents to discuss whether they have seen their child use symbolization when they are playing. What has the child substituted for the real thing in play? How old was the child when the parent noticed him or her trying this kind of play?

Development of the Capacity for Play and Imagination

Distribute Handout 4.2: Development of Play.

For most children, play develops in a predictable way and seems to be fueled from the inside. A few children get stuck along the way, however, and have difficulty moving into pretend play or into cooperative and sharing behavior. The development of play in the typically developing child in different age groups is described in Handout 4.2. Children may be more interested and participate in one type of play more than another, so the designation of ages is somewhat arbitrary.

Birth to 12 months (See first three rows of Handout 4.2.)

In the first year, children do not pretend play but are busy with exploring objects, first by mouth and then by picking them up, feeling them, and looking at them. They are also beginning to understand about cause and effect; in other words, they are beginning to realize that they can make something happen. For example, if they pull a string, they can get an object that is out of reach or if they bang a drum, it makes a noise.

13 to 24 months

At this stage, a child likes to pretend that things are something else; for example, a pencil may be a bottle. By age 2, play has become a little more complex and the child may create a short routine of feeding dolls or driving a car to "work."

2 to 4 years

The child now enjoys playing out quite elaborate stories and may take the role of a superhero, teacher, or parent. Thoughts and feelings may be ascribed to the characters. Play themes about family life and "good" and "bad" characters are common.

4 to 6 years

Complex play themes continue, with the child at times "working through" issues in his or her life that are scary, frustrating, or sad. The child loves to engage in physical play and to test the limits of physical competence. By 6 years of age, pretend play usually drops off and games with rules become more common.

Have parents pick out some developmental characteristics of play noted in the age level of their child. Point out the difference in the three types of play: solitary, parallel, or cooperative play. Ask them which their child is primarily using.

Discuss the kinds of play parents may expect to see emerging in their child in the near future. Refer to the chapter in *Pathways to Competence* (2002), pages 221–224, for more details about development that could be useful for discussion. Highlight several key features of play that parents might see at different ages of development.

Handout 4.2 emphasizes the development of pretend or make-believe play and social play but also includes play in a variety of other ways—physical (gross and fine motor play), movement, and the other types of play listed above. All aspects of play have an important role in a child's development and can enhance development in areas iden-tified in the next section.

Importance of Play and Imagination

Although for some parents, play may seem like a waste of time or even dangerously unstructured, research has shown that it is critically important for a number of areas of the young child's development.

Have parents describe some play sequences they have seen their child act out and dis-cuss their significance.

Ask parents to think about what areas of development play can enhance in children. Ask them why they think play is important.

Distribute Handout 4.3: The Importance of Play.

Watching children of various ages shows us that children have a strong urge to play. Scores of research studies have found a strong relationship between how competent a child is and the frequency and elaborateness of his or her pretend play. So those games with monsters, doctors, castles, and trains really do make a difference, especially when they involve rich and elaborate stories and play themes. In addition to the advantages of play listed in Handout 4.3, play enhances development in a number of areas:

- Play encourages **learning.**

- Play enhances **self-esteem.**

- Play reduces physical **aggression.**

- Play encourages **language development.**

- Play improves **social ability.**

- Play helps develop a healthy and satisfying **inner world and fantasy life.**

See *Pathways to Competence* (2002), pages 217–220, for further elaboration of the im-portance of play.

Make-believe play can be the key that helps a child to unlock bottled-up feelings that may be getting in the way and causing problems. Fantasy provides children with a way to handle feelings of anxiety, frustration, and anger.

Distribute Handout 4.4: The Goals of Play Therapy.

If a child has a traumatic experience, passes through a difficult developmental stage, or lives in a stressful situation, he or she may use play to deal with the associated up-setting emotions—growing to understand the situation by repeatedly acting the emotions out in fantasy play and finding solutions in various scenarios. This need to act out the situation and the emotions related to it is why young children with a lot of emotional or behavioral problems may be recommended for play therapy. This kind of therapy is one during which an adult acting as therapist spends time playing with a child in a certain room with the same toys each session and at a preassigned hour. Using the same toys each session gives the child a sense of safety and encourages him or her to enlarge on the same themes. Toys are chosen with pretend play in mind rather than learning, although of course there is some overlap.

Although play therapists adopt different approaches, the purposes of play therapy listed on Handout 4.4 may explain how therapy can help children who are having problems to get back on track again. Also, read *Pathways to Competence* (2002), pages 245–249, for more information on these topics.

Parents may want to discuss the goals of play therapy if their child has attended play therapy sessions or to find out more about what play therapy is if they wonder whether their child should receive this kind of help. Ask group participants if they have any questions or concerns about using this kind of therapy with a child.

Group leaders may take the role of child and play therapist and illustrate how a child might be helped before a frightening event or when something has become frightening for a child (e.g., going to the hospital, going to school for the first time, or overcoming a fear of dogs). Parents may want to try out the role of the child.

Ask parents about questions they have about play and their child's play in particular. Do they worry that perhaps their child does not use pretend play enough or pretends too much?

Children vary in their interest and ability to play. Some of these differences appear to relate to the child's ability to concentrate and to his or her attention span. Some children have a great deal of difficulty staying with one toy or activity for more than a minute and pass rapidly from one activity to another without settling on anything for very long. Others are able to concentrate more and can sit or play for much longer.

Researchers have found that children tend to be one of two types of players: *patterners* or *dramatists.* On the one hand, patterners tend to concentrate on objects, typically spending a lot of time playing with play materials and toys by investigating their physical properties or building or constructing things with them rather than using them to pretend. Dramatists, on the other hand, typically use objects and toys to enhance their fantasy play. The dramatists usually adopt a particular style of pretending and build a repertoire of favorite play themes.

Distribute Handout 4.5: Types of Players.

See *Pathways to Competence* (2002), pages 245–247, for further information on types of players.

Without a rich inner world or imagination, a child may not develop a place to escape to and to use in order to calm down when upset.

Problems associated with a child who is primarily a patterner could include the following:

- The child may fail to develop ways to deal with conflicts and anxieties by playing out dramas.

- The child may not develop imagination and a fantasy life.

- The child does not have the opportunity to express emotions through play.

What can a parent do to encourage creative play when the child is more of a patterner and prefers to, for example, only use objects such as blocks to build with without making them into a building and making a play theme about what is happening with them? Mention to the participants that if their child is tending to play with objects without imaginative themes, they can encourage their child to introduce people in the "house" or "ship" or "castle," whatever the child happens to be playing with. By introducing the characters, it may spark more elaborate pretend play. Tell parents to make sure that they do not direct their child's play, however; it is better to let the child be the one to make up the play theme and lead the play. These activities will help parents to work with children who have difficulty pretending. Parents often ask, however, "Can a child pretend too much?" Occasionally, fantasy can become a problem when a child constantly escapes into a make-believe world instead of facing real situations. Parents should become concerned if a child becomes very withdrawn and does not want to play with other children or spend time with the family. Other danger signs include outbursts of emotion that do not fit the actual situations, strong and frequent anxiety, or an inability to try to solve problems, relate to others, or learn new skills.

According to psychologist Sebastien Santostefano, what a child needs is an ability to move between fantasy and reality and to bring information from one easily and regularly into the other. The child who is stuck in one or the other without being able to move easily between the two or to integrate information from one into another is likely to run into problems as he or she gets older.

Research Related to Play and Imagination

Refer to *Pathways to Competence* (2002), pages 225–230, including Important Research Findings and The Effects of Play on Various Areas of Development, and select some findings that would be of interest to the parents in the current group. Some suggestions to highlight include the following:

- Researchers have consistently found play and language development to be related, but it has been more difficult to find consistent relationships between play and other cognitive measures. Some studies have suggested that play can enhance *perspective-taking* and *problem solving*.

- There appears to be a *universal tendency* to play that is found in a number of cultures; however, when a parent encourages play, this has the strongest relationship with the child's ability to play. When mothers participate in play with their children and particularly when the play is reciprocal and includes turn taking, the children's level of play is generally higher.

- Children's play with their siblings is also linked to their level of solitary and peer play.

PARENTING PRINCIPLES AND TECHNIQUES

Ask parents to think about ways in which they might encourage pretend play.

If interactions were videotaped before starting the groups, select some good clips that show the parents in the group pretending with their children and ask them to list some of the things that they observe the parents doing when playing with their children.

Distribute Handout 4.6: Principles for Encouraging Play and Imagination.

PRINCIPLE 1: Spend time observing your baby or child and learning about his or her style of play, how the child interacts, what he or she enjoys doing, and about the child's inner world and feelings.

Distribute Handout 4.7: What to Look for in a Child's Play.

Explain that when observing their child's play or imaginative activities, listening and watching allows parents to begin to understand their child in new ways. A child's mood or feelings can be assessed by noting his or her tone of voice, facial expression, and use of words (or lack thereof). Watching themes of play as they unfold will also allow the observer to notice any play themes that come up frequently. Through these themes, parents can learn about their child's concerns and fantasies, needs and feelings, rivalries, and wishes and desires. Play may also reflect situations that their child may be finding difficult in life or issues that arise in achieving normal developmental milestones. These new insights can often help a caregiver to be more sensitive and understanding when reacting to a child. Observing children engaged in physical play can inform us about balance and fine and gross motor skills. As well, watching a child play with peers can be informational about his or her ability to play with other children.

Use a video clip of a child playing alone (not necessarily depicting a parent in the group and his or her child). You may want to use a clip of one of your own children or you may use one of another child as long as you have a parent or guardian's permission to show the video. Have parents look at Handout 4.7 and use it while they watch for aspects of the child's play.

Discuss what parents saw and suggest other aspects you may have noticed that they missed.

PRINCIPLE 2: Provide a special place or places where your child is free to play with objects, toys, and props that can encourage play and imagination.

Distribute Handout 4.8: Suitable Toys and Props and Handout 4.9: Toys for Pretend Play.

Research has shown that a child's play setting and toys can influence his or her ability to play. When a child first begins to crawl and can get around the house, it is critical to safety-proof the home. This not only keeps the child safe but also allows him or her to explore and to develop a sense of curiosity and excitement about the world. Remind parents to set up the space so that it does not overwhelm their child with too many toys. If parents have enough space to store toys somewhere else, changing toys to keep the novelty alive can be very helpful.

With the parents, create a list of appropriate toys for children. Choose toys to suit the age and interests of the child and that encourage pretend play. See Handouts 4.8 for suggestions. By having the right toys and materials available, this not only provides children access to tools for activities and experiences in which to engage but also it lets children know that play is something parents approve of and encourage. For the child who enjoys some of the other types of media, include plasticine or playdough, musical instruments, a sand tray, and finger paint. For the child who enjoys drawing, painting, or modeling, a child's table and chairs can be very helpul.

If possible, have these materials available for the parents to play with and examine during this Step. Also, if you offer child care to the parents who are attending the sessions, let them know that the toys the children are playing with have been chosen based on the principles of play taught during this Step. Encourage parents to enter into this play with the children when they drop their child off and during break time, if appropriate.

Discuss the list with parents. Would it be difficult for them to provide these things for play? Do they have other ideas of toys that encourage creative and imaginative play? Have parents give information about stores, libraries, and other places in which inexpensive pretend play toys can be found.

PRINCIPLE 3: Regularly assign time to join your child in play by giving the activity or game your undivided attention.

Sometimes the process of giving children attention in this kind of context (i.e., a regularly scheduled time) can change children's behavior dramatically. Negative symptoms often disappear when children know that they can look forward to playing with special caregivers. During play, children can experience a unique sense of closeness. They learn to feel accepted and secure as the caregiver becomes an active partner with them. For parents who find pretend time particularly difficult, setting a timer for 20 minutes or whatever amount of time they feel comfortable with can be reassuring because it lets them know that the play does not have to last beyond the time they are willing to spend. Moreover, sometimes taking the initiative and inviting the child to play will be particularly helpful.

Have parents discuss what it is like when they join their child in play. What should parents do when their child wants to do something that they have great difficulty enjoying? See pages 233–234 in *Pathways to Competence* (2002) for suggestions for making this time more exciting and interesting.

Ask parents to provide some examples of strategies for making play more exciting and interesting.

It is important to discuss why some parents may find playing with their children very difficult. Encourage parents to be open and honest about what it is that is difficult for them.

Play for fun may be difficult for some parents for the following reasons:

- They only use time with their child as a means of teaching about colors, words, letters, and so forth and not as a way to have fun or to follow the child's lead.

- The repetitiveness of the play may be experienced as tedious and boring.

- They view play as not having a time limit—that it is difficult to end.

- They perceive the child as controlling the situation, which may produce anxiety or anger.

- The child will often not join in activities that the parent wants to do.

- The parents may have so many things they have to do, it feels like time wasted.

- The sessions they have together always end in a fight or a power struggle.

- They may never have had the opportunity to play when they were young and do not know how to begin.

For parents who do not like pretend play, there are other activities that they can do to stimulate imagination and creativity (e.g., drawing, storytelling, walking). Think of ways these can stimulate imagination and fantasy.

Have parents think about how their parents played with them and what they enjoyed doing. If they never played with them, how would they have liked them to play with them?

PRINCIPLE 4: In pretend play, accept the feelings, join in the play, and—when necessary—extend play themes.

Even when parents spend just a few minutes a day following the child's lead in play—without teaching, structuring, or taking over—this can enhance a child's capacity for imagination. As the child's play themes are supported, he or she feels comfortable and acquires a sense of mastery. For parents or caregivers who are anxious that following the child's lead will result in losing control, it is important to explain that there will be certain restrictions that the child must adhere to even in free play such as not being allowed to intentionally break toys or to be aggressive.

Distribute Handout 4.10: Rules for Children During Pretend Play and 4:11: Rules for Parents During Pretend Play.

Go over Handouts 4.10 and 4.11 on what children and parents should not do during pretend play.

Rules for the Child

The child may not

- Hit, hurt, or endanger the parent in any way

- Keep leaving the play area except for one bathroom trip

- Willfully destroy the room or the toys

- Injure him- or herself

Rules for the Parent

Do not

- Criticize

- Keep questioning what is going on as if it should be something different

- Give advice or suggestions

- Interrupt the play

- Teach, preach, or moralize

- Initiate a new activity

Do

- Follow your child's lead and extend the play theme to make it richer

- Make comments about the child's play choices without being intrusive and turning the session into a teaching experience

- Talk for the toys and characters in the drama or assume a role yourself; this can keep the play going and stimulate imaginative and symbolic thinking

- Narrate what is going on, which will highlight for the child the value of his or her productions as well as help organize the child's play if he or she tends to be fragmented or disjointed in his or her play themes

- Describe the feelings of the toys in the drama. This can be extremely helpful for the child to begin to understand his or her own and other people's feelings

 Role play by taking the parts of a child and parent. As the parent, illustrate some of the strategies outlined above. It is particularly important to follow the "child's" lead, extend play themes, and describe the feelings or narrate the play theme.

PRINCIPLE 5: Encourage playfulness and joyous exchanges and experiences.

The transfer of affect or emotion between caregiver and child can influence the growing brain. Positive affective exchanges can promote the development of brain circuits, and positive facial expressions may trigger certain neurochemicals in the child's brain. Positive affective exchanges and playfulness with children can be essential for the child's emotional development.

 Ask parents about fun activities they and their child enjoy doing together. Point out that these activities must be something they both enjoy doing.

 Have parents recall a happy time they had with one of their own parents when they had fun together. Did they find that it was very meaningful? Do they think about it when they play with their children?

PRINCIPLE 6: Provide your child with the opportunity for a variety of different play experiences to encourage his or her imagination.

Children may enjoy using different media to express their feelings. These could include drawing or painting, modeling with plasticine, sand play, or telling stories.

 To illustrate a fun media activity, give one parent a large piece of paper and ask the individual to start a drawing. At a signal, have the person stop and pass it to the next person who will add something. The cycle is complete when everyone has had a chance to add something to the picture. Have the parents talk about their thoughts and feelings about the picture and what they found out about themselves they did not know before.

Some children may be reluctant to play, so it is important to find ways to encourage their imagination.

 ### Distribute Handout 4.12: List of Play Media that Can Be Used to Encourage Play and Imagination.

Ask parents if they enjoy using other types of play media. Go over the list of different play media and ask them if there are any that appeal to them or if they think there are some that would appeal to their child.

OTHER DISCUSSION TOPICS

Parents may want to discuss a number of other topics. These are discussed briefly next.

Imaginary Friends

Parents sometimes become concerned because their child suddenly introduces an imaginary friend. This "friend" may join the child on the bus, have breakfast with the child, and may even be blamed for spills and breaks around the house. In fact, it is estimated that about 65% of preschoolers have such a friend. Far from being a problem behavior, having an imaginary friend may be a sign of mental health. Children who have one tend to be less aggressive, to be happier, and to have more advanced language. Researchers theorize that imaginary friends may fill a gap between using external controls and developing a conscience of their own. After all they never criticize or answer back! Imaginary friends usually disappear by the time the child is 6 years of age to be replaced by real friendships. If this does not happen it can be a problem.

Parents may want to describe an imaginary friend their child has created or that they themselves created as a child. When was this friend used and when did the imaginary friend first appear and drop away (if not still present)?

Aggressive Play

Many parents are worried that if they allow their children to play with toy or pretend guns and to act out games such as cops and robbers, they will be encouraging their children to become violent. In fact, if such games do not escalate out of control or turn into real acts of hurting another person, when a child plays out these games it can reduce violent behavior, whereas observing real-life violence or violence on television will encourage it.

Have parents describe and discuss types of aggressive play that they may be concerned about.

Can Television and Computer Games Substitute for Pretend Play?

As just mentioned, ample evidence indicates that watching violence on television does increase aggressive play, at least in the short run, and some studies have shown a long-term effect over several years. Children are prone to imitate or model behaviors that they observe. Children who see a lot of violence on television may begin to see the world as a hostile, scary place, and violence as condoned by society. However, what may be as concerning is that television presents children with numerous rapid and disorganized stimuli that—while exciting—may lead to difficulty concentrating and problems with the development of imaginative skills. It's hard to conjure up fantasies and to create dreams if the images are always presented externally with few opportunities for fantasy play or creating images from stories. It is important to note that young children should not watch news programs that show dramatic events because they can be just as or even more terrifying for children. Certainly, most parents feel the need to let their children watch television at certain times of the day; they may feel that certain programs provide some educational value or they may just need a little break. It is important that the shows are monitored and when possible, parents spend time discussing a program, explaining material that may have been confusing, and clearing up any misunderstandings.

 Ask parents whether they find it difficult to monitor the child's television viewing. Here are some questions you can ask: "Are there shows that you have questions about whether it is appropriate for your child to watch? At what age would it be appropriate to watch these shows?"

Pathways to Competence (2002), pages 241–245, provides important information to help you to be prepared to talk more about these topics.

THE TREE

At the end of the group, before talking about homework, ask parents to write the principles on pieces of cardboard and to stick them at the top of the tree under one of the roles of parenting.

HOMEWORK

Distribute Handout 4.13: Homework.

Describe the homework activities. Have parents choose one of the activities and do the self-care activity if the Step is given over only 1 week. If the Step is given over 2 weeks, they can do both activities and choose a second self-care activity that would be meaningful to them. Point out that the group will discuss them next week.

1.   Have parents spend 15 minutes with their child 2–3 times during the week, joining the child in play and following their child's lead.

or

2.   Have parents observe their child at play a few times during the week. Ask them to use Handout 4.7 to help with the observation.

 Self-care activity: It is important for adults to "play" as well as children. For the self-care activity, ask parents to do something that stimulates their imagination or creativity, such as drawing a picture, writing in a journal, making something, or cooking a special recipe.

STEP 5

Encouraging Language and Communication

MATERIALS

Required materials

Handouts 5.1–5.15 (on Pathways to Competence for Young Children CD-ROM accompanying this manual)
Self-Care Activities Handout 1.22

Suggested materials

Pathways to Competence: Encouraging Healthy Social and Emotional Development in Young Children (2002)
Three-ring binders with handouts
Tree picture cards to write principles on
Velcro or tape to stick the picture cards on the tree
Overhead projector, blackboard, or flip chart
Crayons, markers, pencils and/or pens for participants
Paper on which to draw
Markers and erasers for the group leader(s) for discussions
Self-care boxes for parents
Cards with situations or feelings written on them such as those in Handout 5.2
Videoclips of parent-child interactions, if available
Cards with some of the examples on Handout 5.9 for role-playing

HOMEWORK REVIEW

Discuss with parents what they found out about their child's play themes. How elaborate did parents find these themes to be as they were observing their child playing or following their child's lead and playing with him or her? What did they think the child was expressing through any of his or her favorite or repetitive play themes? Did parents notice that their child was experiencing any emotions such as anxiety or anger? Did any of the play make the parents feel anxious or concerned? Also discuss the creative activity they engaged in and how it felt. Did it stimulate their imagination, and what did they find out about themselves?

SETTING THE STAGE

In almost every case in which a problem arises in an organization, a family, a marital relationship, or between a parent and child, communication is typically identified as an important component of the difficulty. One person is not letting another know enough about what is going on; feelings are not being discussed; there are no channels through which to resolve difficulties; and on it goes. The conclusion is often reached that if people could express themselves at work or at home more openly and listen to one another's point of view, relationships would be improved. Point out that although this Step will discuss language development, the emphasis will be on how best to communicate with the child and as a family so that messages are conveyed clearly and everyone feels heard and understood.

Ask parents what some of the other difficulties with communication are that are frequently identified.

Distribute Handout 5.1: Communication in My Family as I Was Growing Up.

Have parents complete Handout 5.1. Ask parents to discuss how communication took place in their family as they were growing up. Did family members yell? Did their parents listen to them? Did family members refuse to talk and sulk if they were upset? Did individuals talk their problems through? Ask them what they liked and did not like about these communication patterns and what they want to change in their own families. If they have difficulty coming up with answers, you might give them some of the following examples:

- How we were communicated with as children: *"Children were seen and not heard."*

- How problems were discussed and resolved: *"My parents handled them and we did not know about them."*

- How family members communicated: *"They yelled at each other a lot."* *"My parents sometimes refused to talk to each other for days."*

- What I liked about communication in my family: *"We often had meals together and talked about our day."*

Ask parents to discuss why communication is so difficult for families today.

Refer to page 265 in *Pathways to Competence* (2002) for some points of discussion about this question. A few reasons are listed here:

- Children and/or parents watch television excessively.

- Children are very involved with video or computer games.

- Parents are working and have extremely busy lifestyles, with little time for conversation.

Ask parents to try to remember the first words that their child said. If parents cannot remember any words, make some suggestions from your own experience with children you know or from Handout 5.3 on the development of language.

Did the parents find a difference in their child's behavior when he or she started to speak? Did they see improvements or did the constant talking and questions "get on their nerves"?

UNDERSTANDING LANGUAGE AND COMMUNICATION

Discussion of Key Words

People tend to use words such as *communication, speech,* and *language* interchangeably, but there are some important differences in the exact meanings of the words.

Communication

The word *communication* is used to describe the act of transmitting a message between people or places. For communication to take place, there has to be a message, a sender, and a receiver. Each person in this equation must also play a role, and if those roles are not followed correctly, things can go wrong and the message may not be received or responded to. For example, if a parent angrily screams an instruction across the room to a child, the child may not understand what was said or may be too upset to process the message. Communication between people can be transmitted by looks (scowls and smiles), silence (warm or cold), and words. Body language can also be a powerful tool for communicating. Correcting some of the things that get in the way of a message being received can enable us to communicate better.

Ask parents to think of ways in which they might express disapproval without words by just using body language.

Double-bind messages or communications occur when a person says one thing, but other signs indicate that the person really feels the opposite of the words he or she is saying; for example, the person may say, "I am so happy to see you," but the fact that he or she is looking the other way indicates otherwise. Also, a parent may have a pleasant expression on his or her face while calling the child something like "a little monster." When parents frequently use double-bind messages with their child, it can be very confusing and upsetting to the child.

Ask parents to think of any double-bind messages that their parents used with them. An example might be saying something that sounds nice on the surface such as, "Well that's just great," but using an angry or sarcastic voice or facial expression showing that they mean the opposite.

Speech

Speech pathologists distinguish speech from language. *Speech* refers to the movements of the vocal and articulatory system for making sounds. It is made up of the sounds that come out of our mouths that form the words.

Language

Language refers to the content of what is spoken, written, read, or understood. Language can be conveyed through gestures, body language, or sign language, as well as words, and it is divided into two types: receptive and expressive.

Receptive Language

A child usually understands more words, signs, and symbols than he or she can say or express. This is called the child's *receptive language*. The words that the child understands but cannot say are usually called *receptive vocabulary*. For many children who are late talkers, testing will show that they understand much more than they can express or say. Some of these children may have average receptive language development.

Expressive Language

Expressive language refers to the process of using a socially shared code or system to communicate. As mentioned, on the one hand, a child's spoken or expressive vocabulary may be more limited than his or her receptive vocabulary. On the other hand, some children use a lot of words in a parrot-like fashion but understand very little, which sometimes masks a significant problem. Many children have difficulty with both receptive and expressive language and may only be able to communicate using gestures, signing, and body language.

Distribute Handout 5.2: Situation or Feelings Cards (Samples)

Prepare cards with situations or feelings such as those written on Handout 5.2. Have participants pick one at random. Divide the group into pairs and have one from each pair communicate one of the situations or feelings without using words while the other one tries to guess what is being communicated. Switch roles and, using another card, have the parents repeat the activity. This exercise could also be done with parents trying to communicate the situations or feelings on their card to the whole group, depending on how the parents would feel about doing this. Even though the participants may think they are using their best nonverbal communication, they will quickly see that conveying the right meaning can be difficult to do.

Point out how difficult it can be to convey needs and feelings through body language, and that young children often lack words to fully describe what they want and how they are feeling. This can make a child easily frustrated and the child may give up and may withdraw or act out as a consequence.

The Development of Language and Communication

Distribute Handout 5.3: Development of Language and Communication.

Speech and language development go through significant changes in the first 6 years of life that can be divided into stages. These stages are usually referred to as the *preverbal* (or *prespeech*) stage (birth to 9 months); first words or beginnings of speech (9 to 12 months); first sentences (12 to 24 months); and grammatization and increased elaboration of language (24 months to 6 years). The explosion of vocabulary words that typically occurs at approximately 18 months of age and the beginning of the ability to use complex sentences that occurs in the third year are remarkable achievements in language development.

(See pages 270–272 in *Pathways to Competence* [2002] for more examples of significant speech and language developmental milestones.)

Birth to 1 Year: Preverbal or Prespeech Stage

The sounds that a baby makes before he or she reaches the age of 10 months to 1 year, when the child will likely speak his or her first words, are real language. However, in this prelinguistic or preverbal stage, several recognizable steps or stages appear to occur in the same order in all children. As with all development, the rates of progress through these steps vary from one baby to another, but the sequence seems to be consistent.

Have parents look at the language skills that babies develop in the first year of life (Handout 5.3). Ask them to discuss why these activities would be considered language skills and what children may be communicating.

12 to 24 Months: Beginning Speech Stage

A child has usually spoken his or her first word by the time he or she has turned 1 year old (i.e., 12 months). Sometimes, this first word is used to label an object or a person, such as "juice," "Mommy," "Daddy," "cookie," or "doll." The child's attempt at labeling may be clear and a good imitation of the intended word. Sometimes, however, a sound is only given meaning by gestures, intonation, and the context in which it occurs. Sometimes a single sound can stand for a number of things or a phrase or a sentence, such as when a child uses "dree" for any type of drink. When a child uses such a symbolic sound loudly with gestures such as pointing at the object he or she wants, parents are soon able to decode it. They receive the message and typically let the child know that they understand what is wanted.

Ask parents when their child said his or her first words. How did the child get the intended message across? How did he or she add words to his or her vocabulary? How did parents encourage their child's very early language?

2 to 6 Years: Sentences and Grammatization Stages

By 24 months of age, children typically have a vocabulary of between 200 and 300 words and can use two-word sentences, usually consisting of a noun and a verb. By the age of 4 to 5 years, most children have acquired the basic rules of grammar. They can change tense, pluralize, and construct prepositional phrases. Parents are sometimes confused about how much to correct their child's grammar. Discuss this question and suggest that it is all right to correct some of the time, but not so much so that the child feels bad about his or her mistakes and becomes too anxious and perfectionistic about how he or she speaks. One way to model better grammar without criticizing is to simply repeat the sentence as a question using the right grammar; for example, if the child says, "Her gave it to me," a parent could respond, "Oh, she gave it to you?" Children usually get the idea this way without feeling humiliated.

Have parents talk about how they deal with correcting their child's grammar when it is incorrect.

Have parents look again at Handout 5.3 at the age level for their child. What skills does the child currently exhibit and what skills do they think will be emerging next? If the child has achieved all of the skills in the handout, do parents remember the particular stages of the child's language development that were interesting to them?

Importance of Language and Communication

Children need good communication skills in order to achieve in a number of different areas of development. Language is one of the most important aspects of development and enables a child to communicate with others.

School Achievement

Although not all academic subjects are totally dependent on speech and language, many children who have delayed speech may lag behind in subjects such as language arts, social studies, foreign languages, general sciences, and so forth. In math, it is increasingly important in school and in life to be able to read and fully comprehend the meaning of problems and what is required, and some children can make mistakes because they misconstrue what is being required. Even in subjects that do not depend as much on language such as music and art, children still need to communicate, listen to, and read instructions—skills that depend on the use of language.

Peer Relationships

By the time children reach the age of 2, talking to peers and others becomes more and more central to the events of children's lives. In order to join in the play with their peers, children often rely on saying the right thing in the right way in order to gain acceptance. Popularity and acceptance have been shown to depend largely on a child's communication skills. Even for very young children, there are a number of unwritten rules that need to be adhered to in order to be accepted into a group, such as listening to what the children are saying as they play, understanding what is going on, asking if they can take a certain role, or joining in quickly by taking on a part or role in the play. A child who instead barges in or hovers on the edge asking distracting questions unrelated to the play is far less likely to be accepted.

Communication within the Family

Communication in the family relies on clear messages being given and understood by various members of the family. A child who has speech difficulties can be severely compromised by being unable to let other people in the family know how he or she is feeling and thinking and about why he or she behaved in certain ways.

Emotional Development

Children with better language development are less likely to have emotional and behavioral problems and often have higher self-esteem. With advanced speech, they are better able to get their message across and feel less frustrated and better understood. The ability to talk about feelings and emotions and to understand what others are saying can significantly enhance a child's capacity for self-control and reduce the incidence of acting-out behaviors such as aggression and noncompliance.

RESEARCH FINDINGS RELATED TO LANGUAGE AND COMMUNICATION

Research has concluded that the interactions children have with caregivers are critically important in terms of the development of language. Some of the most important factors have been found to be

- Following the child's interest in communicating

- Matching vocalizations to the child's age and level of language development

- Having positive emotionality during interactions with the child

- Being responsive and listening to the child

- Reading to the child

- Making sure that the child has opportunities to talk about things during family discussions such as at mealtimes

Research with young children has shown that children with speech difficulties often continue to have tantrums long after such behavior would normally be reduced. For some children, when speech blossoms, behavior rapidly improves almost miraculously. This is typically because, as a child is able to communicate and let his or her ideas and wishes be known, the child becomes less frustrated and more amenable to interacting and following directions.

Children are born with the innate capacity to learn language, but speech does not unfold without feedback from the human environment. Research has also shown clearly that the most critical variable for increasing speech capacity, regardless of the child's speech capability, is conversation with parents. For example, deaf infants start to babble at the same age as hearing infants. However, the development of speech falls off in a few months because their hearing deficit does not enable deaf infants to receive the usual stimulation of language.

Children raised in deprived environments or in abusive situations often show significant speech delays even though some other areas of their development may appear to be typical. It also seems that for language to develop past the two- or three-word level, the child must have extensive exposure to language **in the first 5 years of life.** Exposure after 5 years of age seems to be inadequate to make up completely for serious deficits or delays in language due to deprivation.

Distribute Handout 5.4: Am I Helping My Child Learn to Communicate?

Ask parents to look at the list of questions provided in Handout 5.4 and answer yes to the ones that they are already doing. Discuss the ones they are doing as well as the ones they are not doing but think might be useful. Do not ask parents to talk about their answers, but if they mention them, emphasize that the exercise is to give new ideas about communicating with their child. They may use some of these ideas as their child gets older.

Explain that the problems that children can experience with speech and language delays will be discussed later.

Leaders can review the research findings described in *Pathways to Competence* (2002), pages 275–281, and highlight additional information that they think the parents may find interesting.

PARENTING PRINCIPLES RELATED TO LANGUAGE AND COMMUNICATION

Although, for many children, language seems to unfold naturally and almost effortlessly, language development at all stages is enhanced by input from the child's environment (i.e., parents, other caregivers, and peers).

Distribute Handout 5.5: Principles for Encouraging Language and Communication.

Select video clips that illustrate positive communication between parent and child. Principles 2, 3, and 4 would be good to demonstrate with the video clips.

PRINCIPLE 1: Adopt strategies to encourage your child's speech and language development and communication skills.

Refer to pages 282–285 in *Pathways to Competence* (2002), which describe some of the activities appropriate for parents to try for each age level.

Distribute Handout 5.6a, b, or c (depending on the ages of the children): Strategies to Encourage Speech and Language Development and Communication Skills.

Ask parents to look at the strategies suggested in the handout for the age level of their child. Have they tried any of these suggestions? Select one or more to try in the coming weeks.

PRINCIPLE 2: Adopt strategies to ensure that your child receives and understands your communication.

Ask parents to talk about some of the strategies that they use to get children to listen.

The list should include the following suggestions. If parents do not bring these things up, suggest them and discuss them with the group.

• Get the child's attention before speaking to him or her.

• Call his or her name and insist that the child give his or her full attention. This will mean stopping what you are doing and turning off the television or other distractions.

• Communicate at eye level by stooping down or sitting at a table with your child.

• Do not stand over the child or sit at the opposite side of the room to talk to him or her.

• Touching in a supportive way can help foster positive attention.

• Make sure requests and statements are simple enough for the child to follow. One instruction at a time may be all some children can process, comprehend, remember, and follow through on.

• If you mean business, do not yell, but speak firmly and give a reason for the request.

• Use and maintain a warm tone in your voice while conveying the intensity and strength that is needed.

PRINCIPLE 3: Make conversation a two-way process of communication between you and your child.

Point out that even in adult conversations, it is very rare to have a conversation that goes beyond the superficial. People usually say nice but overused phrases such as "How are you?" "I'm fine. How are *you?*" Many conversations consist of one person telling another about what is going on in his or her life followed by the other person doing the same without responding to what the first person has said. Unfortunately, people don't often truly listen to one another. This can be even more the case for children who have limited conversational skills.

Distribute Handout 5.7: How to Listen to a Child.

Point out that one of the greatest gifts you can give a child is to really listen to him or her, to understand his or her ideas and point of view, and to show the child that you accept his or her feelings and opinions. Ask parents to talk about any of the strategies that they saw in the handout that they think could be useful.

Ask parents to discuss what gets in the way of them listening to their child. The list could include some of the following:

- Being very busy and not having time to sit down and pay attention

- Thinking about what I'm going to say next rather than fully listening to what the child is saying

- Expressing my own feelings rather than listening to the child's

- The content of what the child is saying makes me angry and then I stop listening to the child's point of view

- Having more than one child makes it difficult to give individual attention

Discuss how often the parents themselves really get listened to. Have parents describe situations when someone didn't listen to them. How did this make them feel? What would have made the situation better for them?

Distribute Handout 5.8: Opening Channels of Communication.

Go through the channels of communication, pointing out that they can be particularly important for a child who has some difficulty with processing language.

Ask parents if they felt listened to when they were children. If they did not, have them describe why and how this happened and what it felt like.

PRINCIPLE 4: Use special strategies to ensure that conversation is not cut off and is kept going so that issues can be discussed and resolved.

Distribute Handout 5.9: Keeping Communication Going.

Demonstrate the scenarios and point out the very different effects of positive and negative first responses to something a child says, and how what is said can make all the difference.

Group leaders could role play some of the examples. A sensitive remark can open communication lines and encourage the child to share information, whereas an accusatory remark can escalate negative feelings between the parent and child.

Have parents in the group comment on what went on. Following this discussion, invite parents to role play difficult exchanges they may have with their children.

A parent could take the positive role after the leaders have demonstrated the negative conversation. Ask parents to identify the type of situation in which the interaction with their child repeatedly results in a negative conversation. For example, a parent may say that whenever they tell their daughter she has to go to bed, she yells, "I hate you," and the parent finds it is difficult to respond appropriately. The parent and a volunteer could role play the situation, with the group supporting the parent in strategizing alternative and more positive responses.

Distribute Handout 5.10: Preparing a Positive Response.

Have parents suggest ways that they could respond to the child's comments on the handout that would end up with a more positive discussion.

PRINCIPLE 5: Communicate acceptance and respect for your child, even when the content of the message may be difficult.

It is interesting how positive messages given by someone who is sincere can make a difference to anyone's day. For example, if someone positively comments on our appearance on a certain day or notices how hard we've worked to do something, it can lift our spirits. Conversely, we can be sensitive and feel hurt when someone fails to greet us, makes an angry comment, or even frowns at us. A child who is influenced deeply by parental disapproval may find a harsh response from parents upsetting and it may inhibit interaction and communication between parent and child.

Distribute Handout 5.11: Changing the Don'ts into Dos.

Explain the principle of giving difficult information with as positive a message as possible. Ask parents if, on some days, they feel as if they keep saying "no," "don't," or criticizing. Indicate that the next few handouts will suggest ways to change such interactions with children. Refer to page 290 in *Pathways to Competence* (2002) under Principle 5.

Explain to participants how to complete the activity handout of Changing the Don'ts into Dos. Use an example such as changing "Don't run in the house" to "You can run outside if you want to." Have parents complete the other examples and discuss these ideas in the group.

Distribute Handout 5.12: Changing "You" Messages into "I" Messages.

Discuss why using "I" rather than "You" messages is helpful for children. Give an example of changing "You" to "I." For example, change "You're just a lazy 'good for nothing' when you don't clean up the toys" to "It upsets me when you won't pick up your toys." Explain how "I" messages are much less likely to bring on resistance and anger and can soften the message as much as possible. They can also change how the child feels about him- or herself and do not shame the child into feeling badly about him- or herself. Parents should also be aware of their body language and gestures.

Have parents complete the other messages on the handout.

PRINCIPLE 6: Create a language-rich environment and make conversation and discussion a valued part of the caregiving environment.

Ask parents to think again about how communication took place in their family as they were growing up. Point out that having a language-rich environment or one in which conversation is valued can take time and effort; however, it can significantly enhance language, emotional, and social development and provide opportunities for parents and children to share ideas. Encourage the family to have at least one or two family meals together each week. This should be a time when all family members have the opportunity to share ideas and contribute to the discussion. Be sure that everyone's opinion is heard. This not only supports the development of language and communication but also enhances self-esteem and problem-solving abilities. Some families give all of the members a chance to talk about a positive and a negative thing that happened in their day and how it made them feel, as a way to get discussion started.

Distribute Handout 5.13: Suggestions for Creating a Conversational and Language-Rich Environment.

Have parents go through the list and check off what they do and would like to do.

PRINCIPLE 7: Help your child learn to communicate with his or her peers.

Talking to peers can be very difficult for some children who have delayed language skills or some other problem communicating.

Ask parents if their child has difficulty communicating with peers. What is difficult for them? What has helped them in interacting with others?

If parents have difficulty thinking of things that would help their child interact with peers, group leaders might suggest the following:

- Coach the child to use phrases that might help him or her join in the play with others; for example, "Johnny, can I be an astronaut?" or "Can I play too?"

- Teach the child about taking turns and sharing his or her toys and other possessions.

- Make it clear to the child that aggression is unacceptable and help the slow-to-warm-up child to gradually become more comfortable being in the group.

Other examples and more details on this topic will be given in Step 10.

OTHER DISCUSSION TOPICS

Refer to *Pathways to Competence* (2002), pages 293–299, on commonly raised issues around language and communication, and discuss any topics in which parents have a particular interest (e.g., stuttering, ear infections or otitis media, bilingualism). These could be discussed if parents have concerns in these particular areas. For example, if children of some of the parents in the group have speech delays, talking about the effects of ear infections on language development might be relevant. If parents are recent immigrants they may want to discuss whether it is a problem if they use two different languages with their young child. These topics frequently become important when the child starts formal schooling. It is important to draw parents' attention to the need for assessment and possibly early intervention if children are having difficulties with language.

Speech and Language Delays

Not all children develop speech and language effortlessly. Approximately 7% of children have difficulty learning communication skills. With some children the cause of speech and language impairment is easy to determine, whereas for many children the reasons for their language delay are unclear and no identifiable physical or psychological basis is found. When a child is showing delays in speech or other language difficulties, it is critical that a speech and language pathologist (SLP) and/or an audiologist assess the child as soon as possible so that if difficulties are identified early, intervention can begin.

Distribute Handout 5.14: Warning Signs of Speech Problems.

Handout 5.14 provides a list of warning signs that indicate that a child needs a referral for an assessment. Highlight some of the most important ones.

THE TREE

Before talking about homework and ending the session, ask parents to write the principles on cards and to stick them at the top of the tree under one of the roles of parenting.

HOMEWORK

Distribute Handout 5.15: Homework.

Describe the homework activities. Have parents choose one of the activities and do the self-care activity if the Step is given over only 1 week. If the Step is given over 2 weeks, parents can do both activities and choose a second self-care activity that would

be meaningful to them. Point out that the group will discuss them next week.

1. Ask parents to observe themselves or others in the family. Did they tend to cut off discussions? What about someone else in the family? Did they cut off discussions or keep them going? What could they have said that might have helped resolve issues and keep communication flowing?

or

2. Encourage parents to have a meal with everyone in the family present. Give each person a chance to talk about how his or her day went and what he or she felt about it. Jot down what each person noticed about the effect of doing this.

Self-Care Activity

Ask parents to make time this week to talk with a friend about something important to them. Choose a friend who they think will listen to them.

STEP 6

Laying a Foundation for Positive Self-Esteem

MATERIALS

Required materials

Handouts 6.1–6.16 (on Pathways to Competence for Young Children CD-ROM accompanying this manual)

Self-Care Activities Handout 1.22

Suggested materials

Pathways to Competence: Encouraging Healthy Social and Emotional Development in Young Children (2002)

Three-ring binders with handouts

Tree picture cards to write principles on

Overhead projector, blackboard, or flip chart

Crayons, markers, pencils and/or pens for participants

Paper on which to draw

Markers and erasers for the group leader(s) for discussions

Self-care boxes for parents

Videoclips of parent–child interactions, if available

Cards for parents to write down their positive attributes and to write any parenting behaviors they would like to improve

HOMEWORK REVIEW

Encourage participants to report on their observations of the homework activities from Step 5: Encouraging Language and Communication. What did they notice about their child's language and communication, and how does communication take place in their family? Inquire about any changes they were able to make in talking and listening to their child and if they noticed any changes in their child's behavior as a result.

Also ask parents about how it was for them when they talked with a friend about something that was important to them. Did their friend listen and pay attention to them? Did they notice how important it is to really be listened to and did it make the conversation and the relationship feel more meaningful?

SETTING THE STAGE

The importance of self-esteem in people's lives has been a hot topic of discussion in the popular press. Some have described high self-esteem as an inoculation against social ills such as drug use and dependence on welfare, whereas a diminished sense of self-worth has been perceived as predictive of behavioral difficulties and/or mental health problems. Less dramatically, high self-esteem has been linked to feelings of competence, a sense of well-being, and even to parenting competence. Other views of self-esteem are often quite simplistic and do not distinguish between having a realistic understanding of self and the negative effects on behavior of grandiose self-esteem.

Ask parents if they have ever thought about their own self-esteem. Has anyone ever told them that they seem to have high or low self-esteem? Have they ever thought of themselves as having high or low self-esteem?

149

Write one or both of the following comments on a flip chart and read them to the group. The comments have been written by people in the fields of psychology and social work, addressing the importance of self-esteem in people's lives.

A great self-image is the single-most important tool for successfully facing the problems, issues and crises that arise in everyday life. Self-image is central to how your child learns, achieves, works, socializes, and lives. Self-image is the key to the way your child treats himself and is treated by others. (Phillips & Bernstein, 1989, p. 7)

Self-esteem is essential for psychological survival. It is an emotional sine qua non—without some measure of self-worth, life can be enormously painful, with many basic needs going unmet. (McKay & Fanning, 1992, p. 1)

Add other quotes or comments about self-esteem that you find helpful or interesting.

UNDERSTANDING SELF-ESTEEM

Discussion of Key Words

Self-Esteem

Before explaining the meaning of the term *self-esteem,* it is important to define the meaning of *self* or *selfhood,* which refers to an individual's distinct personality or identity. **Self-esteem** is primarily about an individual's reflective self or evaluation of him- or herself.

Self-esteem is a subjective evaluation (both cognitive and affective) that an individual holds about him- or herself. Some of the important facts about self-esteem are that it is

- Multidimensional: Self-esteem may vary in different dimensions of our lives. For example, an individual may feel confident about his or her physical skills but less so in academic or cognitive abilities or in interactions with others.

- Dependent on a feeling of worthiness coming from others (i.e., on how much a person feels himself worthy of others' love)

- Capable of giving one a sense of control over life

Global Self-Esteem

While we feel differently about ourselves in different aspects of who we are, global self-esteem refers to an overall sense of self-esteem or self-worth and may provide us with a feeling of acceptance of ourselves or in some cases a sense of deep shame about who we are. In order to understand global self-esteem and how one arrives at it, it is important to understand the terms *ideal self* and *perceived self.*

Distribute Handout 6.1: A Formula for Global Self-Esteem.

Handout 6.1 illustrates how ideal self and perceived self work together to determine one's global self-esteem. Positive self-esteem happens when there is a balance between the ideal self and the perceived self. Low self-esteem occurs when a person's perceived self is out of balance with the ideal self or when the person sees him- or herself as not as good as he or she should be. For example, even though an individual gets good grades in school, his or her ideal self may feel that unless he or she gets a perfect score on all the tests, he or she is a failure (perceived self).

Ask parents to discuss how a person's perceived self and ideal self can be out of balance. Write down the ideas for the group to see. For example, someone may dream of being a singer but have more success with academic activities such as writing essays or mathematics. This could lead to a sense of low self-esteem.

Optimal Self-Esteem

Optimal self-esteem is not just about feeling successful in certain areas of functioning but has a number of other characteristics.

Distribute Handout 6.2: Optimal Self-Esteem: What Do We Look For?

Go over the handout with the participants and explain the items. A person with optimal self-esteem has

- A global self-esteem or a basic core feeling of being worthy of love and respect and being accepted by others

- A basic core belief that one has the competence to survive and live a productive life and has a sense of control over life and a sense of self-efficacy

- A realistic view of strengths and weaknesses in areas such as physical ability, intellectual capacity, moral worth, and kindness to others

- A sense of self or who one is that can adapt to and accommodate new information about one's self as it becomes available

- A sense that perfection is impossible. In other words, the person is not trying to live up to an ideal standard that cannot be met.

Have parents comment on how any of these concepts may apply to their child, themselves, or someone close to them. Jot down the comments that they make.

A number of other words relate to self-esteem including *working models of self, self-concept, self-image, self-confidence,* and *self-efficacy. Self-esteem* is a unique term, however, because it is about an individual's evaluation or judgment about his or her self-worth. If possible, refer to *Pathways to Competence* (2002), page 321, for more on these terms.

Another aspect of self-esteem focuses on how parents view themselves as parents. Parent self-confidence or self-esteem can be defined as the belief that parents develop about their ability to care for and enhance their child's development. This can be described as their expectations of the kind of parent they *should* be.

The Development of Self-Esteem

Distribute Handout 6.3: Development of Self-Esteem.

Using the chart in Handout 6.3, explain how the view of self develops.

Pick out some developmental characteristics of self-esteem that are relevant for the ages of the children being discussed in the group. For example:

19 to 24 months

The child typically becomes more and more aware of the self and its continuity. He or she uses self pronouns such as "I" and "me" and pushes for things with "I want" and "mine." At this age, a sense of omnipotence and a grandiose sense of self is predominant. The child begins to show pride in doing a task and is self-admiring when looking at his or her mirror image.

2 to 3 years

The child can now experience the self-conscious emotions of pride, shame, and guilt. The child may show these emotions if he or she can or cannot complete a task and even if he or she breaks a toy or other object by accident.

3 to 5 years

The child can now compare his or her actions with those of another child. He or she can feel pride in winning and doing well or shame because of not meeting the standard that other children reach.

5 to 8 years

By 8 years of age, a child is capable of evaluating him- or herself in a number of areas. He or she continues to compare his or her performance with that of others and is also more aware of the need to achieve certain abilities such as learning to read and write. In fact, some children with learning challenges who had positive self-esteem until they started school may suddenly feel less competent when they try to learn to read and write and compare themselves with the other children in the class.

Development of self-esteem or one's view of one's self can continue into adolescence and adulthood as new experiences are encountered. However, the sense of self or of who one is, developed in the first 3–5 years of life, can continue to influence how one feels about one's competence, how things are experienced, how one reacts, and even how memories are formed for a lifetime.

Have parents come up with ways in which they, as parents, can contribute to their child's development of positive self-esteem. Jot them down on a flip chart or overhead projector and share them with the group.

Distribute Handout 6.4: Self-Esteem in My Family as I Was Growing Up.

Have parents think about how their own parents helped them develop positive self-esteem or any of the things they remember that their parents did to make them feel negatively about themselves. How do they think it has affected how they feel about themselves now?

Here are some examples:

- *My parents always believed in me and encouraged me to try new activities like learning to swim or to cook a recipe.*

- *My mother was so protective that I was never allowed to try new activities for myself like painting a picture or playing with my friend.*

Importance of Self-Esteem

Point out that children who have optimal self-esteem are

- More likely to have friends and to have **good social skills** leading to popularity with peers

- More able to **persist at tasks** even when they are challenging and to **problem solve** in order to come up with solutions and different ways to do things, even though self-esteem is not directly related to intellectual functioning

Low self-esteem can lead to anxiety and depression, whereas high self-esteem has been shown to be related to a sense of **well-being, adaptation,** and **resilience.**

Ask parents in what areas they feel their child has positive self-esteem and if there are some areas in which their child does not feel good about him- or herself.

Ask parents why they think that their child's sense of self-esteem has developed in this way. Note their ideas on a flip chart or overhead projector and ask the group for ideas as to how the parent could support the child to feel better about him- or herself.

Research Findings Related to Self-Esteem

Read pages 330–335 in *Pathways to Competence* (2002) and then highlight some interesting research findings that would have relevance for parents in the group. Highlights that your group may find interesting include:

- Researchers have identified a number of parenting qualities used in interactions or relationships with children that are related to a child's sense of self-esteem. These will be discussed in the next section. Some of the parental qualities that have been found to relate to the child's self-esteem include acceptance, warmth, granting of autonomy, nurturance, or authoritative parenting (see Step 7).

- Depression has consistently been linked to low self-esteem. Conversely, high self-esteem can be a protective factor for children living in high-risk situations such as in poverty. Self-esteem has been found to be fairly stable over time, although some children who may have more fragile self-esteem may show short-term fluctuations in response to adverse events.

- Unrealistic views of one's self can lead to frequent lack of confirmation when a child relates to others. Some children can respond with aggression or destructive behavior when they feel that their self-esteem is threatened by any negative feedback.

- Parental confidence or feelings about being a "good parent" can contribute to parenting skills and child outcomes. However, parents who are very confident about parenting but have little parenting information can have problems with parenting, particularly if they are not willing to listen to new information or ideas or to examine how they are parenting.

- Some parents may have recalled that in their own families of origin, their mother or father had strong ideas about parenting that might be considered poor parenting practices today. Group participants may be able to relate how their parents' strong ideas or opinions affected the kinds of parenting they now practice with their own children. Parents need to understand that knowledge as well as confidence is important and that it is sometimes important to step back in order to consider why they do things and how they are affecting their children.

Distribute Handout 6.5: How I Can Help My Child to Develop Positive Self-Esteem.

Ask parents to list ways that they can help enhance their child's self-esteem on Handout 6.5.

Have parents talk about some of the ways they listed in which they are enhancing their children's self-esteem and how their parenting style differs from their own parents' as a result of information they have about child development.

PARENTING PRINCIPLES AND TECHNIQUES

Distribute Handout 6.6: Principles for Encouraging Self-Esteem.

Show video clips of the parent–child interactions if available. Principles 2, 3, 5, and 6 would be particularly suitable to illustrate through video clips, if available.

PRINCIPLE 1: Show unconditional love and let your child know that he or she is valued and accepted.

The concept of unconditional love is demonstrated when a parent conveys to his or her child that the child is loved as he or she is and not because of what he or she can or cannot do. The basic message is that the child is accepted "no matter what happens" and that the adult intends to always be there for the child.

Distribute Handout 6.7: Showing Unconditional Love.

Ask parents to complete this form. Have the group discuss the ways in which they provide unconditional love to their child and in which circumstances they may find it more difficult. Discuss with the parents the time they spend with their children and positive words they use with them. Also point out, "As children get a little older, let them know that you trust in their ability to be independent and do not overprotect them, which can help build their self-esteem."

The basic message must be that we accept our children as they are, and comments such as "I wish you were never born," "I'm going to send you away (to a foster home)," "Why can't you be more like your sister," "You're just like your stupid father," or " I should never have had you—you've ruined my life" are unacceptable. These types of statements can stay with a child and become the core of the child's sense of self—constantly dragging him or her down just like physical abuse and neglect. Children need our attention and concern; they need to know someone cares, and this concern can be given in a variety of ways by each parent in his or her unique style and at different times in the children's lives.

See *Pathways to Competence* (2002), page 349, for more suggestions.

PRINCIPLE 2: Acknowledge your child's successes and abilities.

Children need to be noticed for their good qualities and to have their behavior acknowledged—particularly any efforts that they make to accomplish some desired task. Whereas praise is usually given for something the child completes or accomplishes, encouragement is given when the child is acknowledged for trying and efforts are supported to help the child keep trying to learn or do something that may be difficult for the child. Parents may use words to encourage the child, or sit with him or her and "scaffold" the task with a touch or a positive tone of voice or facial expression. In this way, even if the task is not completed, the child knows that the parent appreciated his or her efforts and will support the child if what he or she is attempting becomes too overwhelming for them. Children do not need to be praised all of the time for completing every activity and task that they are expected to do. Praise and encouragement is best given on an ongoing basis rather than only for task completion. In fact, hearing praise all of the time can lead to some negative consequences. Have parents suggest ways to encourage their child, instead of using constant praise for task completion. Write down these ideas on a flip chart or overhead projector.

Point out, if the issue has not been raised already, what some unintended consequences of constant and unnecessary praise may be:

- The child may learn to **rely on external praise** instead of doing something because of the desire to do it or motivation from within.

- Praise can seem **empty and insincere** if it is used all of the time for things that should be done anyway. Praising the child too frequently can lead to a child being **passive or unenthusiastic** about trying.

- Praise can **lead to perfectionism** because the child may believe that what he or she does is not acceptable unless it can be completed and perfect.

- The child may only do things **because caregivers notice** and praise the behavior and may stop doing things for pleasure and fun.

Some encouraging phrases that could be used include the following:

- "That's really coming along well."

- "I liked the way you put your toys in the right bins."

- "You really worked hard on that painting. I like the way the sky comes all the way to the ground and the bright colors you used."

Ask parents to suggest comments that they find helpful with their child.

Add some suggestions listed on page 338 in *Pathways to Competence* (2002) if parents cannot come up with many ideas.

PRINCIPLE 3: Structure situations to help your child to experience feelings of success.

Point out that, although parents should not try to protect children from all difficulties, having experiences of success can give children a positive sense of self that will allow them to face the larger difficulties they will inevitably be confronted with throughout their lives. For example, put a rattle close to a baby's hand so that he or she can reach out and grasp it or hold a toddler's hand when he or she takes those first steps.

It can be very helpful for some children who may be struggling to do something that may seem to be a relatively simple task (e.g., cleaning their teeth) to break the task into simple steps and to notice efforts along the way to completing it.

Distribute Handout 6.8: Breaking Down a Task for Success.

Have parents fill in the steps to support a child when completing the tasks listed. Discuss what they noticed when doing this activity.

Ask parents to suggest strategies that have worked for them when encouraging children to do tasks that may be causing them difficulty.

Distribute Handout 6.9: Helping to Encourage a Child.

Review some ways to express encouragement to a child who is having difficulty completing a task. For example, if the child cannot do something, tell parents to let the child know that it can take a long time to learn, and offer to help them with their efforts. Explain to the parents that it is also very important to remember that when a child is struggling to do something, although it is tempting to take over, the child needs to be able to experience the success of completing the task him- or herself. So it may be important to show interest and to help along the way but to make sure that the child has the experience of putting the last piece in the jigsaw, of painting the last stroke to finish a picture, or of reading the last page of a book.

Take the role of a parent while a group participant takes the role of a child. Demonstrate how to encourage the "child" to do a task that has become frustrating and difficult, such as building with blocks that keep falling down. Show how to encourage the child and acknowledge the child's attempts and efforts.

PRINCIPLE 4: Give your child a feeling of reasonable control over his or her life.

Children need rules and structure in their lives, and they need to know that certain rules are not to be negotiated. Small children can make some choices, as long as these choices would not threaten their safety, be contrary to their parents' morals, or endanger anyone's health. For example, the child may choose to eat peas instead of broccoli or wear the blue dress instead of the green dress. Have parents discuss the difference between absolute rules and parental decisions a child must follow and structures and limits in which some flexibility can be allowed.

PRINCIPLE 5: Value each child's uniqueness and tell each child about his or her special qualities.

On a daily basis, children can be made aware of their special qualities. These may include personality traits, physical attributes, things the child does well, and positive behaviors. Children need to be genuinely accepted as they are and to be told how much they are valued for who they are. Avoid comparing children. Have children realistically evaluate their own efforts over time. Avoid labeling children, particularly with negative labels. Even very positive labels can become very difficult to live up to, however. Imagine feeling like you have to be "The best, the prettiest, or the smartest girl in the whole wide world" your whole life.

Distribute Handout 6.10: My Labels.

Have participants list the labels that their parents or others used with them. Discuss the labels that were used with them when they were growing up. How did the labels make them feel?

Here are some examples you could give to the parents:

- The "difficult one": *"Made me feel like I should live up to the label."*

- The "smart one": *"Made me feel like I always had to get top grades and I wasn't allowed to fail. I felt very pressured."*

Did the labels their parents gave them affect the way they see themselves today?

Have parents identify negative labels that they use with their children and ask the group to help them come up with more positive alternatives.

PRINCIPLE 6: Intervene when your child puts him- or herself down and expresses a sense of failure or hopelessness.

Use role playing between the group leaders to show how children can put themselves down and express a sense of failure and hopelessness. Demonstrate with the example of the role plays set out in Table 6 on the next page, showing the difference between the positive and negative result. Have parents take turns to role play the negative feelings and experiences their children may seem to be having and have them try ways to respond to help children feel better. This will also reinforce with parents that there are ways they can support their children when they are feeling down or when something difficult has happened.

Distribute Handout 6.11: Important Tasks to Help a Child Deal with Feelings of Failure.

Point out that the important steps for the parents to remember are the following:

- Hear and acknowledge the child's discouragement and frustration, and tell the child that you understand that he or she feels upset.

- Remind the child of a similar time when the situation had worked out or was positive (e.g., "Remember when you and your sister had such a good time playing together last week").

- Suggest some ways to overcome the difficulty. Make sure that the child follows through with the suggestions and assist him or her to do so if necessary to ensure successful completion or a more positive experience for the child.

Ask parents to describe what happened when they expressed feelings of failure or inadequacy to their parents.

PRINCIPLE 7: Establish a realistic view of self-esteem in your child and help him or her to cope with experiences of failure.

Remind parents that it is important that children establish a realistic and accurate—and not a grandiose—sense of self-esteem. If they feel grandiose and omnipotent they will frequently be disappointed and upset when they have difficulty doing something. For this reason, children need clear limits and structures, and they need to hear

Table 6. Examples of role plays

Role-play demonstration: Negative result		Role-play demonstration: Positive result	
Child:	"Johnny hit me; everyone hurts me."	**Child:**	"Johnny hit me; everyone hurts me."
Parent:	"Don't be silly. Everyone is nice to you."	**Parent:**	"What Johnny did makes you feel sad? You wish he would stop doing that."
Child:	"No they're not. And you hurt me too."	**Child:**	"Yes! He did it yesterday, too!"
Parent:	"I'm always doing things for you."	**Parent:**	"Didn't you two have fun together the other day in the water?"
Child:	"You never listen. You don't understand!" (slams out of the room).	**Child:**	"Yes. Johnny can be nice, too."
Parent:	"You rude little thing—come here!"	**Parent:**	"Perhaps you could ask him over to play in the water again one day."

the message, "You can do it—not by magic, but by trying hard and finding solutions to the problem." A balance needs to be provided in terms of these types of encouragement by parents:

- Acknowledgment of efforts made

- Support when things do not work out

- Encouragement to find new ways and a solution to a problem when they have become stuck

- Helping them to keep trying by reminding them that many worthwhile achievements require a lot of trying and effort before they are achieved

Ask parents to think about someone they know or someone in public life who seems to be extremely grandiose and self-absorbed. Have them describe the individual's characteristics and discuss why the person may act in the way he or she does. Write down the parents' thoughts. If someone does not come up with some of the following ideas, remind him or her that these are some important reasons:

- When people are dependent on someone outside themselves for confirmation of being worthwhile, they will be very vulnerable to criticism.

- These very narcissistic types of people have often not received the appropriate nurturance during infancy and the preschool years.

- Some people may be "stuck" at a level of egocentricity and omnipotence because they did not receive adequate limits and rules that gradually enabled them to accept the reality of the outside world.

If the suggestions in Principle 7 and other Principles in this Step are used, children can establish a sense of positive and realistic self-esteem and gradually give up on their sense of grandiosity and omnipotence.

Point out that parents may be idealistic and perfectionistic and have unreal expectations about being a parent. This can make them feel inadequate, because no parent can be perfect. Have parents discuss what realistic expectations mean for them as parents. Point out that all parents feel at times that they have failed their children.

Distribute Handout 6.12: My Expectations as a Parent: Changing the "Shoulds" to "I Will Try Tos."

Indicate that parents need to change the "shoulds," or their unrealistic expectations for themselves or their child, to the "I will try tos" or something that is more realistic.

For example, the "shoulds," or what parents expect themselves or their children to be like, might include

- *My child should always be polite.*

- *My child will always behave well when we go shopping.*

The corresponding "I will try tos" for this list could be the following:

- *I will encourage my child to be polite by noticing his or her good manners but I will try to accept that my child is still learning.*

Have parents complete Handout 6.12 and discuss their responses.

PRINCIPLE 8: Model a sense of optimism and a positive view of yourself to your child.

Between 3 and 5 years of age, children increasingly identify with their parents and begin to imitate what their parents do and say, including the ways in which parents express a sense of competence and strength. Parents should, as far as possible, try to present an image of being positive and optimistic about their own ability and sense of control. It is also important to give children a feeling that things will generally turn out all right and to model ways of helping this happen. Pointing out positive models of people outside the home can also be helpful. Have children read books or watch movies or television shows that include people who have succeeded even in difficult circumstances.

Distribute Handout 6.13: The Self-Acceptance Game.

Explain the self-acceptance game and read the phrases that are listed in Handout 6.13. After each phrase, ask participants to write down "yes," "no," or "uncertain," or pass on to the next item if they don't want to comment on the phrase. Read these phrases out loud:

Good writer	Good parent	Good speaker
Good sibling	Good friend	Good athlete
Good thinker	Good lover	Good singer
Good neighbor	Good dreamer	Good organizer
Good leader	Good student	Good artist
Good dresser	Good swimmer	Good citizen
Good handicrafter	Good spouse/partner	Good dancer

Ask parents to add other descriptive phrases that might have been left off this list. Add the suggestions to the list.

Then, ask parents the number of "yes" responses they had and to comment on anything they rediscovered about themselves that they had forgotten. Have participants comment on three to five things that are unique about themselves that they have done or do well. This could be especially interesting for multicultural groups who have had very different experiences. Have parents write down these or other positive attributes about themselves and write down about 15 on a card. Remind parents that these can be read over when they are feeling discouraged or negative about themselves.

Ask parents what may have raised and what may have lowered their self-esteem in childhood and how they want to make their children's experiences growing up to be different. Was a positive view of the world presented in their family of origin?

If the discussion is relevant, explain that there is danger in overcompensating for negative patterns of parenting. Examples include an abused parent who fails to provide adequate discipline for a child because the individual doesn't want the child to experience the harsh discipline he or she suffered, an emotionally neglected mother who makes the child the center of her life and overindulges the child—ignoring her own and other people's needs and other activities completely, or a father who insists his child go to college regardless of the child's interests or talents because he himself never had the opportunity to do so.

Distribute Handout 6.14: What Makes Me Feel Down?

Have parents identify any triggers that make them feel low, depressed, or unworthy and what cheers them up. After the charts have been completed, have parents identify any ways in which they think the triggers that make them feel down could be avoided.

Give group participants a 3″ x 5″ card or piece of paper and ask them to list any faults or parenting behaviors they would like to improve. Collect the cards, shuffle them, and redistribute them to everyone so that no one knows which belongs to whom. If someone gets his or her own card, tell the person to ignore this and proceed in the same way so no one is aware whose parenting behavior it is. Have each parent read the fault or parenting response and have the group brainstorm possible solutions. Write all of the identified faults on the board. Participants will notice similarities to their own problems and see the range of concerns that have been shared. Comment on solutions and suggest some parenting techniques that may be helpful.

Explain that burnout is a stage that anyone can reach in a work situation or as a parent. Signs of burnout include feeling depressed, helpless, and irritable. When burnout is extreme, a parent may feel tired, drained, and exhausted all of the time and have physical symptoms as well, such as aches and pains, headaches, and an increase in minor illnesses and infections.

Distribute Handout 6.15: The Experience of Burnout.

Have parents complete Handout 6.15 to get an estimate of their level or degree of burnout. Point out that parents who check four or more of the statements as applying to them should look for ways to overcome burnout. Explain that when choosing ways to overcome burnout, parents should look for things they find enjoyable, relaxing, and fulfilling. Refer back to the expectations parents wrote down about themselves and emphasize some of the positive things they are doing as parents.

OTHER DISCUSSION TOPICS

If possible, refer to *Pathways to Competence* (2002), which describes other issues related to self-esteem such as helping children who have low self-esteem and developing a healthy self-concept in children with physical and intellectual challenges. Consult this book if either of these issues are raised by parents in the group.

THE TREE

At the end of Step 6, before talking about homework, ask parents to write principles 1–8 on pieces of cardboard and to stick them on the tree under one of the roles of parenting.

HOMEWORK

Distribute Handout 6.16: Homework.

Describe the homework activities. Have parents choose one of the activities and do the self-care activity if the Step is given over only 1 week. If the step is given over 2 weeks, they can do both activities and choose a second self-care activity from Handout 1.22 that would be meaningful to them. Point out that the group will discuss them next week.

1. Have parents avoid saying negative things to their child during the week following the group session. Have them comment on the experience and how they thought it felt for their child.

or

2. Have parents make a note of any positive behaviors that their child displays during the week.

or

3. Have parents note the words or actions they used during the week to encourage their child when they were attempting to do something.

Self-Care Activity

Have parents make a list of 15 or so positive qualities or attributes about themselves on Handout 6.16. These can be added to during the week as they think of other things. These need not be significant achievements, but instead, they can be little things they do well, such as being cheerful in the morning, baking great pies, and so forth. Then ask parents to read their list in the morning and evening throughout the week.

STEP 7

Encouraging Self-Regulation, Morality, and a Sense of Conscience

MATERIALS

Required materials

Handouts 7.1–7.14 (on Pathways to Competence for Young Children CD-ROM accompanying this manual)

Self-Care Activities Handout 1.22

Suggested materials

Pathways to Competence: Encouraging Social and Emotional Development in Young Children (Landy, 2002)

Three-ring binders with handouts for group leaders and for parents

Overhead projector, blackboard, or flip chart

Tree picture cards to write principles on

Velcro or tape to stick the picture cards on the tree

Self-care boxes for parents

Video clips of parent–child interactions if available

HOMEWORK REVIEW

Ask the parents about the list of positive personal qualities they compiled after the last session and have them talk about some of the qualities that they listed. How did they feel about reading the list every day? Did it change the way they approached their interactions with others and with their children?

Suggest that when they are feeling stressed or deflated, they read the list and focus on their strengths (i.e., concentrate on what they do well rather than on what they have more difficulty with).

Ask parents if noticing their child's positive behaviors or not commenting on the negative behaviors helped them to interact in more positive and less conflicted ways with their child. Did parents notice an increase in the amount of positive behaviors their child exhibited as a result of these changes?

SETTING THE STAGE

Most people with children get parenting advice from everyone— friends, relatives, and even strangers! Sometimes the information is welcomed, but at other times it can be frustrating, annoying, and/or confusing. Ask parents to comment on the best piece of advice and worst piece of parenting advice they received. Did any of the advice they were given make parenting more confusing? Write their comments down on a flip chart and/or overhead projector.

All Young Children Misbehave

Parenting courses often center around developing obedience in children and controlling their negative behaviors. When parents attend such courses, questions about managing behavior tend to be uppermost in their minds. It is not surprising that parents' concerns for their toddler or preschooler center around misbehavior. Toddlers' acting out episodes in which they disobey the rules may occur at home every 10 minutes or so.

Parents often have the idea that "If I could just find the magic solution to my child's bad behavior or the ideal discipline techniques, our problems would be over." The fact of the matter is that there is no magic solution. To some extent, all young children misbehave sometimes. Realistic expectations for obedience need to be set and will be markedly different depending on the age of the child, the type of discipline that a child responds to, and the child's temperament. And even when a successful strategy is found, it sometimes seems to only last for a while! A variety of factors contribute to the problems that children experience in following the rules or doing as they are told.

Children Want to Be in Control!

The widespread need for information on discipline and how to encourage compliance arises out of the universality of misbehavior in children. All children misbehave at times because they want to be in control of situations and their parents. Everyone can dream about having everything they want, especially children; however, if adults give in to young children all of the time, the children's sense of power can be overwhelming and extremely frightening. An all-powerful child has no sense of anyone being able to control him or her and never has to learn how to deal with the normal frustrations of life or how to adapt to the routines and needs of others. In other words, whereas the child who loses all of the battles quickly becomes defeated and dispirited, the child who wins all of the battles never learns to be socialized or to adapt to the world and the needs of others.

Ask parents if they know any adults who seem to have been over-disciplined or under-disciplined as children.

Establishing a Discipline Plan

Most parents would agree that children need some discipline, but amazingly, in many homes, it just doesn't happen. There are all sorts of reasons for this, and some of them have been talked about in other Steps of this program. Sometimes busy parents may find it easier to give in to a child, at least at the time! Some parents may not know how to set limits that are realistic or appropriate for the age of their child, but perhaps more often, a parent avoids imposing limits because he or she thinks that doing so will destroy a child's creativity, injure the child's self-esteem, or make the parent a monster in the child's eyes. Sometimes parents discipline inconsistently, letting negative behavior go sometimes and at other times, exploding because they cannot stand the behavior anymore.

A plan for discipline is absolutely essential for every child and in every home, but it needs to be built on the foundation of strategies that can foster the other capacities that have been outlined in this parenting course. For example, the discipline plan needs to be based on a secure relationship or attachment with the child and on parenting principles that help the child to build positive self-esteem.

Distribute Handout 7.1: What Kind of Discipline Do I Provide?

Have parents complete this form in Handout 7.1, but ask them to keep their answers to themselves at this time. This handout will be referred back to later in the session.

UNDERSTANDING SELF-REGULATION, MORALITY, AND A SENSE OF CONSCIENCE

Discussion of Key Words

Point out that some words that are commonly used when talking about disciplining children have different meanings for people.

Discipline

Ask parents what they think the word *discipline* means. Write their answers down on a flip chart and/or overhead projector.

Discipline is often seen as synonymous with punishment and as a negative word conjuring up visions of harshness and control. Thus, some parents will probably emphasize the control aspect of discipline and may begin to talk about some of the things they do to control their children. If this happens, make the point that discipline is not simply control or punishment. In fact, the word *discipline* comes from the root word *disciple,* which means to lead and to teach. So discipline is really less about control and much more about helping children learn new strategies so that they can grow and develop in the right directions. It's about helping children to gradually gain self-control so they no longer have to rely on people outside of themselves to control them and will want to obey the rules of the home and society. In other words, a desire to be helpful rather than to do things that will get them into trouble or will hurt other people.

Compliance

Ask parents what they think of when they hear the term *compliance.*

The word *compliance* may conjure up an image of a child who will grow up to have no backbone, who will not have a mind of his or her own, or who will not be able to stand up for him- or herself and who does everything peers do without questioning it. In the context of developing self-regulation and a conscience, compliance is a more positive attribute. It is when the child is able to follow through with directions and do what he or she is asked to do. This has to do with cooperation and wanting to please, and the *reason* the child is compliant makes all of the difference. If the child is compliant because he or she is too scared to do anything else, this is different from being compliant because the child has a real wish to please and feels good about what he or she has been asked to do. In fact, compliant children like this often do extra things they have not been asked to do in order to help out and to give their parents pleasure. Also point out that a child who is noncompliant and defiant and oppositional all of the time creates serious problems for him- or herself both at home and at child care or school.

Conscience

Ask parents what the term *conscience* means to them in the context of having children behave appropriately.

A conscience is a person's internal system of moral values that not only allows him or her to judge whether certain acts are right or wrong but also makes the individual feel guilty or uncomfortable if he or she does not live up to the moral code or does something that does not fit with it.

Selma Fraiberg, in her book *The Magic Years* (Scribner, 1996), notes that children do not develop an internal standard of behavior (i.e., a sense of what is morally right or wrong) or conscience without teaching. A child has no inherited tendencies "to be good," to be unselfish, or to control his or her temper. Parents provide the incentives, and much later in the child's development, the child will make these incentives his or her own. She contends that conscience is built, not inherited, and is developed out of the relationships the child has with those around him or her.

Moral Development

Moral development refers to a process whereby the norms, rules, and values of the family and society become part of an internal motivational system that guides behavior even without anyone enforcing the rules.

Most parents would agree that one of their goals for their children is for them to be moral. But what is morality? The definition may be different depending on the individual.

Ask parents what qualities they want their children to develop that would demonstrate morality. How are they teaching morality in their family? Parents may list some of the following qualities when describing morality:

• Basic ideas of right and wrong

• Standards concerning sexual behavior

- Tolerance for people of different races, ages, and values

- A belief in the importance of a lifelong commitment to a partner and family

- A respect for the value of friendship and empathy and caring for others

- Good manners and appropriate social behaviors

- Religious beliefs

- A realization of the importance of hard work and the delay of gratification in order to get through school and to finish a task

Discipline is not just about punishment—it is about teaching and socialization, and although very little has been written about it by developmental theorists, choosing the right method is often challenging and can be quite a complex task.

Ask parents what gets in the way of them disciplining their child. Show understanding of the issues raised, but reiterate the importance of discipline.

Parents may list as examples feelings of guilt that a child is not happy; sadness for the child; fear that the child's feelings will get out of control in a discipline situation so they give in to avoid the tantrum and screaming; and worry about what other people will think if their child has a tantrum in public. They may also mention that it is hard to be consistent in providing discipline, especially if one is tired or busy.

THE DEVELOPMENT OF COMPLIANCE AND A SENSE OF CONSCIENCE IN YOUNG CHILDREN

Read *Pathways to Competence* (2002), pages 372–376, for a full explanation of the development of compliance.

The capacity for compliance and a sense of conscience develop much more slowly in young children than do many of the other capacities that have been discussed in this parenting program. This relative slowness to develop can be frustrating for parents. In addition, sometimes there can be regressions in behavior during development, for example, during disruptions in the family (e.g., a new sibling, a death, hospitalization). However, if parents adhere to appropriate parenting and discipline strategies, they will usually find that by the time a child is 6 years of age, he or she is quite strict about following rules and directions at home and at school and identifies with his or her parents and wants to be helpful.

Distribute Handout 7.2: Development of Self-Regulation, Morality, and a Sense of Conscience.

Review Handout 7.2 on the development of self-regulation, morality, and a sense of conscience, and discuss with the group some of the highlights of the different ages and stages of development.

Birth to 12 months

From birth to 1 year of age, babies are unable to respond to the needs or desires of others. However, they can gradually learn to wait a little while to be fed. In this way, babies first learn to regulate their behavior and that they cannot have everything that they want immediately. The parent's task is to begin to set some routines and structures, not rigidly, but enough to help the child get some internal management strategies around eating and sleeping.

12 to 24 months

Between 12 and 24 months, the rapid acquisition of developmental milestones takes place. These include the ability to walk and the development of speech and language, both of which encourage children to explore their independence. This desire for independence and the struggle to master these skills can lead to frustration, both on the part of the child and parents, and thus temper tantrums are usually at their height.

 Ask parents if their children have gone through a period of increased temper tantrums. Did these tantrums decrease as the children got older? What seemed to help decrease their occurrence?

2 to 3 years

Children between 2 and 3 years of age often imitate what their parents say and can be seen disciplining dolls, pets, or friends in play. This is a sign that children are beginning to internalize the rules that parents set, but they still need the physical presence of the parent to contain their impulses. Children of this age only obey the rules about 45% of the time and the rest of the time, they find impulses to respond in other ways too strong to resist.

 Ask parents if they have heard their child repeat something that they themselves have often said when the child was playing. If so, what was it?

3 to 4 years

By the time children are 3 or 4 years old, they are generally complying with 60%–70% of what parents tell them not to do. However, they may do what they are asked to do (e.g., pick up their toys, set the table) somewhat less frequently. Children at this age may know what is right and wrong, but they do not always do it.

4 to 6 years

Children between the ages of 4 and 6 years old are beginning to identify with people who are close to them. A child now wants to be "like Mommy" or do things "like Daddy does." This important desire to be like parents and significant others can help the child to internalize the wishes and moral values of parents, caregivers, and other significant people in the child's life. If a parent demonstrates caring, responsible behavior, then the child will want to emulate that behavior.

Have parents review Handout 7.2 on the Development of Self-Regulation, Morality, and a Sense of Conscience, and discuss how their child seems to be acting in terms of these stages, regardless of age.

The Importance of Self-Regulation, Morality, and a Sense of Conscience

Achieving self-control and morality is crucial to a child's development, and helping a child to develop these skills is probably one of the main reasons parents decide to attend the Pathways to Competence group. Without self-control, a young child will constantly challenge parents and other caregivers, may upset or even harm peers, and will eventually become overwhelmed with feelings of lack of control. A child without a sense of morality can be destructive in relationships with others. Self-control can influence development in areas such as

- **Concentration and attention that can be affected if the child cannot self-regulate his or her behavior:** The child would not be able to delay gratification or follow the instructions or the requests of caregivers.

- **Peer relationships:** Typically, a child with little self-control may be unable to understand the perspective of others and can be quite hurtful to them. As a consequence, the child will not be well liked by others and may have few friends.

- **Behavior:** One of the areas in a child's life most likely to be affected by failing to develop self-regulation is behavior. The child may be aggressive and oppositional and have other behavior problems.

See *Pathways to Competence* (2002), pages 370–372, for more information on these areas of development.

Research Findings Related to Self-Regulation, Morality, and a Sense of Conscience

Although most parenting books give some advice on discipline, it is not all based on research about the early years and often only focuses on behavior modification principles without considering an attachment or relationship perspective. However, a number of research studies are beginning to clarify what is critically important in parenting for helping children to develop self-regulation. Read *Pathways to Competence* (2002), pages 376–382, for an overview of this research. Information on a few relevant studies is summarized briefly.

In the 1970s, Diana Baumrind and associates followed preschoolers into middle childhood and then into adolescence and linked components of family interactions and discipline style to a number of developmental outcomes. The styles known as permissive, authoritarian, and authoritative are described in Handout 7.4, and are to be discussed with the group later.

The researchers found that by 8 or 9 years of age, children who had received the different styles of discipline showed different outcomes. Children with parents whose style would place them in the authoritative group were more competent, capable, and responsible (achievement-oriented and independent) and socially responsive (interpersonally cooperative and friendly) than those children who received the other styles of discipline. The children of these authoritative parents were also more self-confident, self-controlled, and assertive, and they tended to achieve higher grades in high school than did those with parents who exhibited other styles. Children with parents falling into the other two types or styles of discipline had lower social and cognitive competence. Specifically, adolescents of authoritarian parents were discontent, submissive, whiny, withdrawn, and often aggressive. Permissive parents produced adolescents who were immature and lacking in self-reliance and self-control. Those whose parents were not only permissive but also neglectful tended to become adolescents who were more likely to get into trouble with the law and to abuse substances.

Ask parents what kind of parenting their parents provided. Do they want to use the same or different ways to discipline from the style of discipline they received?

Research has demonstrated that 90% of parents in the United States use corporal punishment including spanking, slapping, grabbing, and shoving at one time or another. Yet research has shown that this kind of discipline can actually increase aggression and defiance in children. As well, physical punishment has been associated with a variety of other negative outcomes including poor impulse control, impaired psychological adjustment, and abusive parenting when the child reaches adulthood. On a societal level, in countries such as Sweden in which the use of corporal punishment has been banned, there is less violence and lower crime rates.

Approaches such as time-out used appropriately and positive discipline strategies based on building a secure attachment with the child are much more successful, and they tend to encourage children to be cooperative and compliant with parents' requests.

Scientists have also determined that explaining to children the effect their behavior has on others can increase children's compliance (e.g., When you hit your brother, it hurts him and he cries and needs a Band-Aid). This is called *induction,* and it develops the child's sense of conscience because it helps him or her to see the perspective of others and can enable the child to develop empathy for the other person and feelings of guilt when he or she hurts someone else. It would seem that the words and explanations can get internalized and are remembered and form a part of a conscience for the child later and the child will feel guilty if he or she disobeys them.

PRINCIPLES FOR ENCOURAGING SELF-REGULATION, MORALITY, AND A SENSE OF CONSCIENCE

Distribute Handout 7.3: Principles for Encouraging Self-Regulation, Morality, and a Sense of Conscience.

Show video clips of parent–child interactions if any illustrate a parent using appropriate discipline techniques (e.g., using distraction appropriately, explaining reasons for not doing certain behaviors, following through with setting appropriate limits).

PRINCIPLE 1: Set up a warm, reciprocal, and responsive caregiving environment within which limits and standards are firmly enforced, so that your child wants to be cooperative with most of the requests made.

Research has shown that it is the emotional climate within a home and family that sets the stage for children's gradual internalization of values and ability to follow standards and rules smoothly and cooperatively. In a healthy emotional climate, the parents are loving and warm and love the children unconditionally but also set clear boundaries so that children feel secure about them and know what is acceptable and what is not. At the same time, children are encouraged to be independent and to have a say in what happens in the family.

Distribute Handout 7.4: The Styles of Parenting.

Remind the group about Diana Baumrind's styles of parenting (i.e., authoritative, authoritarian, permissive) and the outcomes that resulted from them. Go over the styles as they are described in Handout 7.4. Discuss with parents the different styles of parenting and ask how their styles fit with one or another of these styles.

Distribute Handout 7.5: My Parents and Me.

Have parents complete Handout 7.5 and discuss what they found out about how they and their parents discipline. Have them discuss similarities and differences in the way they parent compared with how they were parented as they were growing up. Point out that some parents repeat patterns of how they were parented, whereas some parents may try to parent very differently.

PRINCIPLE 2: Be clear about who is in charge. Do not try to be an equal and a friend to your child.

Although parents hope to be good friends with their children eventually, while children are young and even in the teenage years, they need a parent, not another friend. They will have many friends over the course of their lives, but they will probably only have one or two parents, and friends and parents play different roles in children's lives.

The role of parents should not include sharing all of their worries or information about their love lives, and children should not be allowed to take on the roles of friends, supporters, or caregivers of their parents. A child has to know that parents manage things and that they can look after his or her interests. When a parent tries to become an equal and encourages inappropriate closeness with a child, this can lead to role reversal, and the child may feel that he or she is expected to take care of the parent or to be in charge and responsible both for his or her own life and that of the parent at a time when this is too overwhelming.

Ask parents to discuss the differences between being a parent and a friend to their child.

PRINCIPLE 3: Present a united front with other caregivers. Keep channels of communication open so that any differences can be identified and discussed.

It is extremely important, whenever possible, for couples to support one another when imposing rules and not to allow their child to play one against the other. If partners disagree in terms of a consequence or how to discipline, it should be discussed without the child present, and parents need to be careful not to be coerced into disagreeing in front of their child. Sometimes children visit grandparents or noncustodial parents who do not follow the same discipline rules with the child, which can present a difficult situation. It may be necessary, especially with caregivers such as grandparents who see a child frequently, to insist on certain parenting behaviors from them such as that they pick up the baby when he or she cries or that they do not use corporal punishment with the child. Sometimes children may have to learn to adapt to differences in styles of discipline and rules, and parents should continue to enforce their own rules. Daily communication through notes in a book can help keep channels of communication open between child care or classroom and home.

Ask parents to describe examples from their own situations in which different caregivers have different rules. What have they done to help the caregivers follow the same rules as their own?

PRINCIPLE 4: Draw up a list of absolute, nonnegotiable rules and standards that your child must adhere to. Communicate them clearly to your child and be consistent in enforcing them.

Children need a set of rules that they must adhere to. Some of these will relate to issues of safety. Others will be about moral issues such as a rule that no one is to hurt anyone else in the family. Some rules will relate more directly to following routines and showing politeness to others. It is important to remember that these are intended to be rules for which there is no latitude and therefore no discussion allowed. Of course, as children get older, some of the rules may change, and family routines need to be adjusted to fit the changes. Because these rules are not negotiable, they need to be kept to a minimum or parents will find it very difficult to enforce them consistently. There is no point in having rules if they are not understood by everyone. Some families write such rules down or use pictures (e.g., photos or illustrations) to make them understandable and clear for younger children who cannot read yet.

Ask parents to discuss how the rules of their family are decided and communicated to everyone.

Distribute Handout 7.6: List of Nonnegotiable Rules.

Ask parents to divide into groups of three or four and discuss the critical rules that must be enforced in their family. Then, have the groups decide on the rules that children must follow. Remind them to keep the list short.

Have parents share their rules with the rest of the group and write them on a flip chart and/or overhead projector so they can see how similar and dissimilar they are.

PRINCIPLE 5: Explain the reasons for certain behaviors that are expected and requested.

In a variety of research studies it has been found that children do not learn morality by parental power assertion methods (i.e., giving strict controls) alone. Learning morality depends on caregivers using inductive methods (i.e., pointing out the other person's point of view), explanations, and reasoning. Children need to learn why it is important to share with or not hurt others in order to be able to internalize the rules and values of their family. A child does not learn values just from being sent to his or her room, but instead, develops them out of **discussions, explanations, and the sharing of emotional responses.**

The other important characteristic for encouraging moral behavior is showing affection in nondisciplinary situations. It is important to **model caring behavior,** discuss the reasons for the rules, read stories about brave people who have done courageous things, and explain how others feel in different situations. A child needs to not only experience the consequences of his or her actions but also to understand the reasoning and explanations for the rules. Once children understand the rules and expectations, consistent implementation of the rules is crucial to changing behavior. Parents need to learn to apply these absolute rules, of which the child must be aware, without explanation or discussion and to use reasoning and explanations only when a situation is new or when it is important for the child to learn about the perspective of another person.

Ask parents if they use reasoning and explanations when their child is learning what behaviors are expected in new situations. What do they find difficult about providing explanations? Discuss the importance of balancing reasoning and explanation with consistently enforcing the "bottom line rules." Give examples if necessary (e.g., If a child has been told repeatedly that he or she can only have a healthy snack before dinner, then there is no need to repeat the reasons why the child cannot have an unhealthy snack every time the issue comes up).

PRINCIPLE 6: Decide on areas in which there can be some flexibility, and let your child express his or her point of view around these issues.

Children can grow in responsibility if they are allowed to contribute their ideas to the development of certain family rules. This allows them to learn the skills needed in making and living with certain choices. For example, a child cannot decide whether or not to go to school because it is the law! However, he or she can decide whether to choose the brown pants or the blue pants to wear to school, or what sandwich to take for lunch.

Ask parents if they have involved their child in discussing discipline rules. What did they observe about their child's ideas for rules and his or her ability to make choices?

Have parents select a partner and have one assume the parent role and the other, that of the child. Plan a family activity (e.g., a trip to the park). Make sure that the "child" is encouraged to make some suggestions about the trip. Ask for volunteers to role-play their planning for the whole group, and have the group note how much the child's ideas were included in the plan for the outing.

PRINCIPLE 7: Make sure that good behavior is noticed and acknowledged and that negative behavior is stopped.

It is critical to notice and acknowledge positive behaviors and to let a child know that efforts to behave, cooperate, and show caring behavior are appreciated. Noticing positive behaviors that follow the correction of negative ones can be very valuable for bolstering self-esteem and increasing positive behavior.

When a child is having difficulty modulating his or her behavior to meet parental expectations, parents must not only ask the question, "How do I get rid of this negative behavior?" but also they should always ask the question, "What positive behavior do I want my child to do instead of the negative behavior?" The job of parents is then to find a way to teach the behavior that they want the child to do. Positive reinforcement is something that increases the frequency of a response when it is immediately followed by certain favorable consequences. Often, people think of positive reinforcement as giving the child something tangible (e.g., a toy, a treat). However, the most powerful reinforcer that will encourage a child to continue a positive behavior can be noticing and showing positive attention to the child. Smiling at, clapping for, or cuddling with the child after he or she completes the positive behavior are all very powerful approaches to increasing the child's compliance and self-regulation. Often, reinforcing the appropriate behavior increases the positive and thus, the negative behavior automatically decreases. If the negative behavior is something a parent needs to eliminate immediately or that needs to be addressed specifically, then providing consequences for the negative behavior may also be warranted. Always encourage the behavior you want to occur.

A child should be encouraged to recognize that not only is Mom and/or Dad pleased with his or her performance but also that he or she should be pleased with his or her own performance. This could be done by pointing out how much improvement the child has shown and how hard he or she tried to get the task finished. In this way, the child feels that he or she is growing up and is developing a sense of personal pride in his or her ability to use self-control. As this happens, the child internalizes the rules and moral values of his or her family.

Ask parents what works as a positive reinforcer for their child.

Ask parents about some of the positive approaches they are using with their child. Make sure to acknowledge these efforts and to put together a list that can be kept in their self-care box.

Making Star Charts and Other Techniques

One way to provide reinforcement is through the use of a system of immediate rewards such as a star or responsibilities chart, a marble jar, or a bank with tokens. With each method the child receives an immediate reward and can accumulate these rewards over time to "cash in" for an outing, time with the caregiver, or an appropriate small gift or token. Charting is used for increasing a type of behavior or behaviors that a parent believes is important. Often, these charts are helpful for parents as well, because they remind them to reinforce the behavior consistently, and children enjoy participating in creating and maintaining the chart.

Once a child has learned the new skill, it is not necessary to continue the charting program at the same level. Instead, as the skill is learned, the child can receive a reinforcement less frequently and the formal program can be gradually eliminated. Children are generally so pleased with their ability to self-regulate and to be responsible that they want to continue the good behavior. In addition, it is useful to always pair the tangible reinforcer (e.g., the toy or treat) with a social reinforcer (e.g., praise and self-affirmation statements for a job well done). Later, the social reinforcement and internalization of values will be sufficient for the child to maintain the behavior on his or her own.

Distribute Handout 7.7: Using a Star Chart or Token System to Encourage Positive Behaviors.

Review Handout 7.7 with the group. Have the group divide into groups of two or three and have each group pick a child behavior that they want to increase for a child. Have the groups design a chart and suggest a method of feedback and reinforcement.

PRINCIPLE 8: Select consequences for not complying with rules, and let your child know ahead of time what these consequences will be.

Although methods of discipline vary somewhat at different ages, certain fundamentals of discipline are helpful for making it work at all ages.

Distribute Handout 7.8: Fundamentals of Discipline.

Have parents read the list of tips. Each of these ideas can generate discussion, and leaders should follow the interests and questions gleaned from parents.

How I Would Like to Be Disciplined

Ask parents to write down five positive characteristics and five negative characteristics that they have experienced with supervisors.

Parents commonly list positive characteristics such as being fair, being respectful, listening, setting clear rules, being firm, and modeling good behavior, whereas they typically list being too strict, playing favorites, not appreciating work, knowing little about what they are supervising, and unpredictability as some negative characteristics.

Have parents think about how the positive qualities they identify may relate to good parenting strategies.

Ways to Avoid Problem Behaviors

Humor

Humor can be used occasionally as a way to turn a negative situation back to positive. Kind imitation of a child, done sensitively, may help a child to see the funny side of what he or she is doing and turn a negative situation around. Teasing, laughing at a child, and cruel joking is destructive and demeaning, however. If parents use humor frequently, they should have an outside observer give them feedback on how they believe the child is receiving the humor they are using. This will help ensure that the child understands and feels that what is said is funny and actually diffuses the situation.

Dealing with Transitions Using Preparation

Distribute Handout 7.9: Helping with Transitions.

Transitions are very difficult, especially at certain times or in certain situations. The times that parents often report as being the most difficult for children include leaving home in the morning, returning home at the end of the day, and going to bed. Certain situations are stressful because of the difficulty in transitioning; for example, keeping appointments and doing errands. When a child is taken to the grocery store or doctor, or is changing from one place or situation to another (leaving the park to go home), establishing a routine for preparing for this can be very helpful to avoid the behavior problems that can frequently occur. New places or situations can be over-stimulating and difficult, especially for some children, and especially when a child is tired or not feeling well. Some ideas for dealing with situations that are more difficult are set out next:

• Prepare the child for change or outings well ahead of time.

• Give up to three warnings that it is time to get ready.

• Explain what will happen and for how long.

• If possible, let the child have a role when you go on outings (e.g., finding some things at the grocery store).

• Remember to keep the outing manageable and vary it according to the child's level of coping.

• If appropriate, compensate in some small way for good behavior.

• Choose the time of day for the outing when the child is likely to be at his or her best.

 Have a parent act out how his or her child behaves in the morning while leaving for school or child care. Play the role of the parent, showing ways that the child's behavior might be modified.

Distraction

Distraction, turning an individual's attention away from the source of the bad behavior, is a great method for younger children and can even work for older children. It can be used to keep difficulties from developing, to turn a child's sad and angry feelings into positive ones, or to divert attention away from a problem once it has been initiated. Examples of using distraction are described next.

Louise could tell that her children, 2 and 4 years old, were getting tired and irritable. She quickly changed the pace, suggesting a snack, a rest, and a trip to the park. After a few protests the children happily complied and the day progressed without major problems.

Phyllis heard screams from the family room and found her children, who were 1 and 3 years old, pulling at the same toy, both red in the face. She took the toy away calmly and began to sing an action song that the children both loved. Before long, they were all laughing together and the struggle over the toy was forgotten.

Alternatives to a Straight "No"

Tell parents that they and their children will both feel better if they can avoid saying "no" or "don't" all day. In fact, using "do" instead of "don't" can often increase compliance in the long run. When we cut off requests and activities with continual "nos," we can add to a child's sense of helplessness and increase his or her desire to be in control and set up negative patterns of interaction. (Suggestions for alternatives to using "don'ts" and "Nos" all day are provided in Step 5 on communication.) There are a number of ways that can make a child feel more in control while at the same time enforcing necessary limits and structures.

Dealing with Problem Behaviors and Breaking Rules

Unfortunately, a number of parents of young children still use spanking as a way to discipline their children. In order for parents to stop this behavior, it is crucial to provide them with successful alternatives and to inform them about the adverse effects spanking can have on children's development in the long term.

What About Physical Punishment?

Ask parents what their views are on spanking and to think about alternatives to using spanking.

Distribute Handout 7.10: Spanking: Why It's Bad.

Recall the negative outcomes of spanking in the Research Findings section. You may want to refer to pages 377–378 in *Pathways to Competence* (2002) for a further discussion of this topic. Go over the reasons for not spanking with the group.

Ask the participants if spanking was used as they were growing up and, if they were spanked, how they felt about it. What disciplinary methods do they use?

Make sure that the point is made that spanking probably made them feel powerless and sad and increased their feelings of resentment. If a parent says that they deserved it and it made them better, suggest that there are other ways to help children learn self-control and to internalize rules so that they will continue to behave in acceptable ways as they get older.

Time-Out

Time-out is probably the most commonly used method of disciplining young children. Used appropriately, it can be an excellent strategy as long as it is not used to shame the child, such as when a child is told to "sit in the corner." As one expert put it, "time-out" works if "time in" is positive. Things to remember about how and when to use time-out are outlined in Handout 7.11.

Distribute Handout 7.11: Guidelines for Using Time-Out.

Go through the guidelines given in Handout 7.11. Time-out can be used as a way to encourage the child to calm down and to get control of his or her behavior, not only as a punishment. Time-out is most effective if it has been explained to the child before an event occurs, including how it is going to be used and what specific behavior will result in time in the time-out location. A simple explanation of its use and for what specific behaviors it will be used needs to occur in a dialogue with the child. After explaining in simple words and a calm voice, have the child explain when and how he or she will go to time-out to ensure that he or she really understands. When a problem behavior arises, parents do not need to engage the child in long discussions, just send or take the child to time-out. Remember, once a decision has been made to use time-out for a specific behavior, parents must use it consistently every time the behavior occurs. Generally, time-out is most successful if it is used only for the behaviors that have been discussed with the child and are specifically being worked on. Remember to be consistent in reinforcing/encouraging the child for completing the desired alternative behavior.

Review with the parents the use of time-out. Ask them if they have used these techniques before and how it has worked for them. Many may have used variations of time-out but have found it difficult to implement without professional support. Take this time to discuss the problems they may have experienced and to troubleshoot the issues.

Natural and Logical Consequences

Natural and logical consequences allow children to experience the consequences of their actions and to understand the reasons for limits that are imposed. The effectiveness of these natural and logical consequences is based on the fact that motivation for good behavior comes from a child's personal experience. Natural consequences are those that follow naturally from certain behavior. For example, the consequence of not eating lunch may be feeling hungry until the next meal, or the consequence of dawdling when getting ready to go to the park may be that there is not enough time to go. Obviously, in many instances, a child must be protected from the natural consequences of an action; for example, the dangers inherent in running across the street or climbing on the stove.

When natural consequences cannot be applied, logical consequences may be used instead. Logical consequences are a direct and logical result of the child's behavior and are typically established by the caregiver. A child who runs outside without permission has to stay inside for the rest of the day, for example, or a child who refuses to pick up toys has the toys removed out of reach for a period of time. What is important is that the child can see some link between the consequence and the behavior, making the consequence seem more acceptable and understandable.

Distribute Handout 7.12: Natural and Logical Consequences.

Ask parents to think of negative behaviors that their child might do that would have a natural or logical consequence. Have them complete the handout and share it with the group. Other parents' ideas might help them to think of opportunities to use with their own child.

There are other ways to discipline children, of course, including earning and withdrawal of privileges. Parents may have suggestions of other ways they have helped children to learn self-regulation, morality, and a sense of conscience. Have parents share their ideas of what has worked in their family.

Have a parent volunteer to act out how his or her child typically responds when told to do something or to stop doing something. Ask parents how best to respond, model a good response, or respond to the "child" in a way that will be likely to reduce misbehavior.

PRINCIPLE 9: Use problem-solving strategies to find solutions to discipline difficulties.

When a caregiver is continually confronted by the same behavior problem with a child, they may want to step back and observe the specific behaviors that are causing the difficulty and think of possible reasons for them and then implement a behavioral strategy.

Distribute Handout 7.13: Steps in Solving Behavior Problems that Are Resistant to other Discipline Strategies.

Go over Handout 7.13, explaining in detail as set out next.

Sometimes, parents encounter discipline problems in their children that have not responded to the usual discipline techniques, such as those described previously. The following describes the steps that can be used to problem-solve to come up with a new approach for solving these difficult-to-resolve behavioral issues. Explain to parents that it is best to use them with one problem at a time and continue to use the general principles of discipline with all other behavior problems.

The steps involved in solving such behavior problems include the following:

1. Pick a behavior to change. It is necessary to specify the behavior you want to eliminate and the behavior you want to encourage in exact terms. Make sure the behavior is defined in such a way that you can count or measure it. For example, you can't count "being good" but you can count the number of times a child picks up his or her toys after playing. You can't count "hyperactivity" but you can count the number of times a child jumps up from the table.

2. Measure or count the behavior for a short period of time before you start to implement the discipline strategy. Count the number of times the child takes the toy from his or her sister or measure the length of time the child can play cooperatively with a sibling, for example. This process is called *taking a baseline.* This is a "before"

measure that can be used, when compared with an "after" measure, to determine whether a change that has been implemented is working in the desired direction.

3. Identify the ABC pattern.

    A: Observe the situation and identify the *antecedents* (A), or the factors that set up the behavior to occur. For example, every time you take the child with you to the grocery store late in the afternoon, he has a temper tantrum. The antecedents for this child's temper tantrums might be the act of going to the grocery store or the time—late afternoon—or both factors combined.

    B: Identify the *behavior* (B) you have pinpointed or identified to change in step A. In this case, you would like the child to get through the trip to the store without throwing a tantrum.

    C: Identify the *consequences* (C)—what follows the behavior that either discourages it or may be encouraging the behavior to continue. In this situation, if the child usually gets what he wants after throwing a temper tantrum, such as treat to keep him quiet, this payoff may be encouraging the child to continue to tantrum when he goes to the grocery store.

4. Change the *antecedent.* Arrange to leave the child at home with another caregiver for those pre-supper trips to the grocery store. If you do take the child, make the trip at a less volatile time of the day. Shorten the trip to 15 minutes instead of the usual 45. Distract the child with another activity during the check-out time.

5. Change the *consequences.* Prior to the visit, explain that if the child is able to get through the short visit without yelling or crying, Mother will have a game with him or her as a special treat at home. Remove the child from the store as soon as he or she starts to tantrum. In order to change the behavior, change the antecedents or the consequences or both if necessary.

6. Keep measuring the behavior while you make the changes and note if the appropriate behavior increases and the inappropriate behavior decreases.

Choose a behavior that you or a parent suggest and work through the steps with the group. Use several examples if there is time. Parents usually need support as they learn to implement these steps, and review is important.

Ask parents to come up with a way that they use to get some relief if they are finding their child's behavior very difficult to manage (e.g., their baby is very colicky, their child is quite oppositional). Get other parents to suggest things that have worked for them. Make a list to put in their self-care boxes.

OTHER DISCUSSION TOPICS

The book *Pathways to Competence* (2002), pages 396–398, discusses ways to cope with some specific behaviors children exhibit from time to time that are of concern to many parents. These include lying, swearing, using "bad" language, answering back, stealing, and misbehaving in public (see a list of rules for public behavior on page 398 of *Pathways* [2002]). It is important to make the point that the same rules need to be applied in public as are used at home. These areas of misbehavior can be discussed if parents show interest.

 At the end of the session (the second session, if two sessions are used for this step), have parents look at Handout 7.1 (What Kind of Discipline Do I Provide?), the form they completed at the beginning of Step 7, to see if they would answer the questions differently now. Discuss what they found with the group.

THE TREE

 At the end of the group, before talking about the homework, ask parents to write Principles 1–9 on pieces of cardboard and to stick them on the tree under the various parenting roles.

HOMEWORK

 Distribute Handout 7.14: Homework.

Go through the homework suggestions. Have parents choose one of the activities and do the self-care activity if the Step is given over only 1 week. If the Step is given over 2 weeks, they can do one of the activities following each week of the Step and choose a second self-care activity from Handout 1.22 that would be meaningful to them. Point out that the group will discuss these assignments next week.

1. Have parents pick a behavior that they would like to work on this week and begin to complete the steps of solving that problem behavior. The first week they could pinpoint a behavior and take a baseline and then the second week they could implement a behavior change strategy.

or

2. Have the parents implement the time-out strategy with their child for a specific problem behavior.

or

3. Make a star chart to eliminate one difficult behavior and encourage an alternative behavior.

Self-Care Activity

 Discuss with your partner some ways to share the load in terms of discipline and agree on methods of discipline. If you are a single parent, meet with a friend and discuss the issues that you find particularly difficult in teaching your child self-regulation, morality, and a sense of conscience.

STEP 8

Encouraging Emotion Regulation

MATERIALS

Required materials

Handouts 8.1–8.13 (on *Pathways to Competence for Young Children* CD-ROM accompanying this manual)

Self-Care Activities Handout 1.22

Suggested materials

Pathways to Competence: Encouraging Healthy Social and Emotional Development in Young Children (Landy, 2002)

Three-ring binders with handouts for group leaders and for parents

Overhead projector, blackboard, or flip chart

Tree picture cards to write principles on

Velcro or tape to stick the picture cards on the tree

Self-care boxes for parents

Video clips of parent–child interactions if available

Relaxation or visualization audiotape or video clips

HOMEWORK REVIEW

Ask parents how well the strategy worked that they were using to deal with the behavioral issue they chose. Encourage them to keep trying if the behavior is still proving to be a problem. Check on the success parents had if they chose to make a star chart or to use a time-out with their child. Parents will probably need support implementing the behavioral strategies over the next few weeks. For the self-care activity, was the discussion they had with their partner or friend about discipline helpful?

SETTING THE STAGE

Young children may rapidly cycle through a variety of emotions in any day, and this can, at times, be overwhelming. Until they have fully developed their own coping skills to deal with overwhelming emotions, children sometimes need their caregivers to help them calm down. Most children gradually learn to regulate their emotions during the preschool years. Before that, containment and calming by caregivers is essential and will be needed later as children face situations that are scary and that make them anxious or when other very upsetting emotions are aroused. Some children's temperaments, such as those that are very sensitive or slow to warm up, can mean that the children need extra help to calm down and deal with the stress of unfamiliar situations, changes in life circumstances, or even transitions and changes in routines.

At times, all parents struggle to deal with their child's emotional reactions and the feelings they arouse in them. One of the most difficult things for parents may be trying to keep their "cool" when their child is rude and oppositional or is whiny and demanding.

Have parents discuss what situations they experience with their child that are most likely to be upsetting.

Have parents describe three emotions they frequently feel when they are with their young child and discuss how these emotions can enrich or impede these interactions.

Have parents also discuss what emotions their child probably feels when he or she is interacting with others. If parents do not bring up the emotions of sadness and fear, make sure that they are discussed as well as anger, frustration, and jealousy.

Researchers and others are increasingly recognizing the critical role that emotions play in children's development. As well, there is a growing belief that the majority of behavioral and emotional problems are the result of failures in emotion regulation, or *dysregulation*. For example, some of the major adult mental disorders such as depression, anxiety disorders, bipolar disorder, aggressive conduct disorders, and even schizophrenia have, as a basis, the failure to cope with extreme emotions of different kinds. Clearly, the containment and modulation of extreme emotions that caregivers provide for their children in the early years contribute significantly to their child's capacity to express emotions in socially acceptable ways and to solve conflicts at later ages.

Some researchers have talked about emotional quotient (EQ) and how significant it is for adjusting to life's challenges.

Distribute Handout 8.1: Test Your Emotional Quotient (EQ).

Have parents complete Handout 8.1. Discuss what participants found out about themselves and list some of the characteristics described in the questionnaire, such as calming down and problem solving about a situation, that lead to having a high emotional quotient, or EQ. If parents want to talk about the score they got, let them discuss it but do not push them to reveal it.

Have participants think about and discuss any people they know who are very intelligent but who struggle in many areas of their life or other people they know with average intelligence who do wonderful things.

Highlight that the characteristics being discussed in the Pathways to Competence for Young Children Parenting Program are all qualities that can contribute to a child's EQ.

UNDERSTANDING EMOTION REGULATION

Discussion of Key Terms Related to Emotion Regulation

Everyone can list a number of emotions and identify the facial expressions and body language that accompany those emotions. However, finding a definition for the word *emotion* that can be applied to all emotions is more difficult. Kagan defined emotions as 1) "the acute changes in physiology, cognition, and action that occur in response to novelty, challenge, loss, attack, or frustration," and 2) "longer lasting affect states created by experiences over months or years" (1994, p. 75). (You may want to write out these definitions on a flip chart or create a handout. You may also choose to summarize the concept.) Include this complex definition only if it is appropriate for your group.

Emotions are responses to stimuli (things) that are important to a person. When an emotion is intense, it involves three systems that can be activated in quick succession: physiological arousal, cognition or subjective experience, and action responses.

Have parents imagine a situation in which they are lying in bed and hear unexpected noises in the house as if someone is breaking in. Have them describe what they would be feeling in their body, what they would be thinking, and what they would be doing.

Participants would be likely to describe experiencing some or all of the following reactions that fall into the three systems just described:

- *Physiological arousal of the autonomic nervous system* that causes a rapid increase in heart rate and blood pressure; the activation of blood vessels in the stomach and intestines and in the brain; and hormonal secretions. The panic state that can develop may also result in sweating, flushing, and tightness of muscles and may be so intense that the person is unable to move out of this reaction.

- *Cognition or subjective experience* of the emotional response, which, in this example, could include thinking about an explanation for the noises and deciding how to respond.

- *Action responses* during which people would probably exhibit the facial expression of fear or possibly anger and would initiate motor responses such as going to look for the intruder, hiding, or telephoning 911.

Some emotional states build up over time, and the way we think and feel about these emotions is different from the emotional state described previously. Some of the better known ones that fall into this category are anxiety states, when a person is in a chronic state of generalized anxiety, and depression, in which a person can be overwhelmed with ongoing feelings of sadness, apathy, and hopelessness.

Distribute Handout 8.2: List of Emotions/Affects.

Ask parents if they are surprised at the large number of emotions.

Have parents identify what they think are the eight basic emotions from the list. After this exercise, list what researchers believe to be the eight basic emotions: joy, sadness, fear, anger, disgust, interest, surprise, and love.

Another term that is important to know is *emotion regulation* or *affect regulation,* which refers to the process by which people control or self-regulate internal reactions to emotions as well as their outward expression. As mentioned previously, children, with the help of caregivers, gradually learn to control their own emotional responses. The ways parents can help their children learn to self-regulate are outlined in the section on principles for encouraging emotion regulation.

Development of Emotion Regulation

Distribute Handout 8.3:
Development of Emotions and Emotion Regulation.

Point out that the development of emotion regulation is slow and gradual and goes through various stages. For example, a child goes from an infant with very little ability to control his or her emotions to a 4- or 5-year-old who has far fewer fluctuations in emotions and who will respond with a number of strategies to regulate emotions when necessary.

The process of acquiring self-regulation varies, with some stages more difficult than others. Progress may include plateaus in gaining control of emotions during which few improvements seem to occur and sometimes even periods of regression, if there is an event that is disruptive or upsetting for the child such as moving or the birth of a sibling. See *Pathways to Competence* (2002), pages 426–428, if possible, for a summary of the development of emotion regulation. Some highlights are mentioned here:

Birth to 12 months

From birth to 12 months, infants display various reactions to being uncomfortable such as anger and distress. By 6 weeks of age, an infant usually begins to smile and shows pleasure in being touched and interacting with caregivers. The infant also shows some capacity for self-regulation or calming him- or herself down and may suck on a pacifier, thumb, or toy, or he or she may concentrate on an object, watching it intensely, in order to calm down. Of course, calming by the caregiver is necessary if the baby becomes upset.

Ask parents to discuss if they recall their babies using strategies to calm themselves down when they were upset or needed soothing.

12 to 24 months

At the beginning of the second year of life, a child who has just started walking is often in a state of elation and seems very excited by his or her new view of the world. However, between about 16 to 19 months of age, an increasing wariness develops as the child becomes more aware of the minds and thoughts of others. Increased whining and separation anxiety are common as the child realizes that parents can leave without him or her and not come back. Various new ways to self-soothe appear, such as using a transitional object such as a blanket or stuffed toy and engaging in pretend play or other play with objects. The child also uses social referencing, or looking at the facial expression of caregivers in order to gauge if a new situation should be considered to be exciting and fun or dangerous and upsetting.

24 to 36 months

Typically, the time period between 24 and 36 months is the stage at which a child has temper tantrums most frequently, although these begin to taper off after approximately 30 months. At this age, children only control their emotions about 45% of the time and temper tantrums and tears are common. Shame and embarrassment now occur as self-awareness and self-consciousness develop. Most children are able to use words to describe their feelings and those of others instead of acting them out physically all of the time. They show pride when they can do this, but continue to need the caregiver's help to control their emotions, especially if they are tired, unwell, or stressed.

Have parents think about and discuss when their child's temper tantrums were at their worst and also when the child began to be able to control his or her frustrations more. What capacities or strategies did their child develop to help bring the tantrums under control? What strategies did they use to help with this process?

3 to 6 years

During the period from 3 to 6 years of age, separation anxiety typically subsides. However, new fears often arise over things such as monsters and storms. By 5 or 6 years of age, most children may begin to recognize that they can have two emotions or mixed emotions at the same time. For example, a child might be excited about moving into a new house but sad because he or she will miss a friend. These emotions, once they are under control, also tend to be more socialized and can be faked when necessary. For example, the child may smile and pretend to like a birthday gift that was not the one desired.

The Importance of Emotion Regulation

Have parents discuss ways that a child with emotion regulation difficulties may behave when he or she enters school or begins a new school year.

Make sure the discussion includes the following behaviors:

- Not following the routine
- Being aggressive with other children
- Crying when they are left at child care or school
- Getting upset and crying when they cannot do the work

More recently, a number of writers have pointed out how crucial it is for a child to learn coping strategies to deal with the normal frustrations of life and the intense emotions that are likely to arise in a variety of situations. As mentioned previously, failure to gain the capacity of emotion regulation can result in ongoing disorders. In fact, the incidence in young children of difficulties with emotion regulation is quite significant and, in many studies and surveys, has been estimated to be as high as 15%–25% when the population includes children identified as being hostile-aggressive or anxious or as having attention-deficit/hyperactivity disorder (ADHD). A child who is overwhelmed by or who acts out his or her emotions continually is compromised in many areas of development as well as in interactions with peers, family members, and teachers. Some of the areas that are significantly affected by young children's capacity for emotion regulation are listed below.

Social Relatedness

Children who have good emotion regulation get along better with and are more accepted by their peers. They are generally friendlier, can manage conflicts without becoming overwhelmed, and are able to understand and accept the perspective and point of view of others. They are able to focus away from more upsetting situations by beginning a game, reminding other children about good things coming up, or telling a joke.

Empathy and Caring Behavior

Children with good emotion regulation have the ability to differentiate their own emotions from those of others, which allows them to better understand other children's perspectives. Children who are able to regulate their emotions well are also less likely to become overwhelmed when other people are upset in an emotion-arousing situation. Instead, they have the energy to problem solve about situations and to show caring behavior toward other people who are upset.

Problem Solving and Cognition

Emotion and cognition are clearly related, and children may find it hard to concentrate if they are continually overwhelmed with emotions about stressful situations. These emotions can create difficulties with concentrating, problem solving, and cognitive flexibility. Memory capacity may also be affected. Children with good emotion regulation are less easily distracted and are generally more able to concentrate on the task at hand.

Coping and Resilience

Having a high EQ, discussed previously, has often been related to coping and resilience, even in situations of great adversity. Some of the capacities referred to as EQ include those discussed as part of emotion regulation, such as being aware of one's own emotions and those of others, keeping disruptive impulses and emotions in check, and having empathy and social skills. These abilities can allow a child to be more in control and flexible in adapting to fluctuations and changes in circumstances.

Research Related to Emotion Regulation

Read *Pathways to Competence* (2002), pages 429–434, for an outline of important research findings related to emotion regulation. Select some research findings to talk to parents about that you think they would be interested in. The following are some important research findings that may be interesting to your group:

- The main contributor to emotion regulation in infancy is when the primary caregiver (usually the mother) and the baby are "in sync" or are tuned in to each other. This behavioral and physiological coordination occurs when the primary caregiver adapts to the rhythm of his or her infant and responds sensitively to his or her distress. In fact, research shows that these sensitive responses are related to lower levels of stress hormones, such as cortisol, in the child. Conversely, deprivation that occurs, for example, in certain orphanages is reflected in rising levels of cortisol or stress throughout the day.

- Although basic emotion regulation abilities are present in the first 7 months of life, the "still face" paradigm, during which a usually animated caregiver remains quiet and immobile, has demonstrated that without any reaction from his or her caregiver, an infant soon becomes overwhelmed and his or her behavior becomes dysregulated and disorganized. Researchers studying the reaction of infants using a "visual cliff," a clear flat surface that creates the illusion of a drop or cliff, have been able to show that by the time infants are 10 months of age, they take their cue from their mother's facial expression and will advance over the cliff if they see an encouraging face and hang back in response to a fearful expression. This phenomenon has been called *social referencing*.

- Other shifts occur around 2–3 years of age, when the child becomes able to talk about his or her emotions, to use pretend play as a way to play out difficult situations, and to learn about how to control the emotions that are aroused as a result.

- By approximately age 4, the child's achievement of a theory of mind (i.e., the understanding that others may have separate thoughts and feelings that differ from one's own) enables the child to engage in perspective taking. Also, an increase in the child's ability to attend to things or to pay attention contributes to the development of a number of new emotion regulation strategies. The child is then able to divert attention from a negative situation, to choose social situations that increase positive affect, and to use "self-talk" to talk him- or herself through difficult, frustrating, and anxiety-producing situations. Even with these skills, a young child may have his or her emotions triggered in difficult situations, especially when he or she experiences mixed and confusing emotions.

Ask parents to suggest ways in which family life and early interactions with caregivers can influence children's development of emotion regulation.

Make sure the following are brought up and discussed:

- Parents need to be available to provide calming for a very young child by identifying why the child is upset. Depending on the reason, parents can hold the child, talk in a reassuring way, or spend some time playing with the child.

- A family context that encourages discussion of emotions and models ways to contain them and to deal with conflict is also important.

Have parents discuss ways they help their children deal with emotions.

Discuss how parents affect children's expression of feelings. Ask parents how they think fighting between parents may affect children. Point out to parents that they are inevitably going to have disagreements, but how these disagreements are dealt with is the key to relationships within the family. Ask the group how these can best be dealt with to have the least effect on children.

PARENTING PRINCIPLES AND TECHNIQUES

Distribute Handout 8.4: Principles of Encouraging Emotion Regulation.

Choose video clips of a parent and child in which the parent is calming down a child, acknowledging an emotion, or apologizing for getting upset. Use them while discussing the relevant principles.

PRINCIPLE 1: Structure environments to provide a level of stimulation and soothing that is appropriate for each child's age, frustration tolerance, and reactivity.

Point out that an environment that is fine for one child may be extremely upsetting to another.

Have parents think about aspects of the environment that can be difficult for children who are hypersensitive, such as too much loud noise (e.g., very loud music playing), too much visual stimulation (e.g., a cluttered environment), or too much touching or wearing rough clothing.

Explain that, as discussed in Step 2, some children may be hypersensitive to things such as loud noises; being touched; and being at a shopping mall other environment with a lot of noise, sights, and people. Some children find that they cannot wear certain labels in their clothes. Other children are very shy and get upset when they have to be around adults and children they do not know.

Distribute Handout 8.5: My Child's Characteristics and Emotions.

Have parents fill out Handout 8.5 and discuss if they have noticed any characteristics in their child that seem to contribute to him or her getting upset, the emotions their child has, and how he or she deals with them.

In the discussion that follows, point out that it is very important to expose a child to aspects of the environment that he or she finds difficult very gradually. For example, a shy child will need support initially to play with other children. Also, it may be necessary to make some adaptations to the environment such as eliminating excessive clutter so that the child is not overwhelmed or frustrated by having too many toys or other objects around.

Have parents discuss things that their child gets upset about that do not seem to bother other children.

PRINCIPLE 2: Accept your child's emotions and do not deny, punish, or withdraw from him or her for having the emotions. Communicate this acceptance and coach your child to problem solve to find ways to deal with the emotions.

People tend to be more comfortable with some emotions than with others. Sometimes parents may find it very difficult to show acceptance of a particular emotion.

Distribute Handout 8.6: Strategies for Dealing with the Emotions in My Child that I Find Most Difficult.

Have parents complete this handout. Ask parents to identify which emotions in their child they have the most difficulty dealing with (e.g., anger, jealousy, sadness and whining, fear and anxiety, intense happiness, affection).

During the discussion, have parents volunteer to talk about the situation and emotion they described and how they thought they could deal with it better. The following are some discussion topics to cover:

- Have parents describe a situation in which their child's emotion triggered difficult feelings in them.

- Try and identify what is triggered in them by the emotion.

- Have parents imagine what contributed to their being triggered by the emotion.

- Identify whether they deny or punish their child's emotions.

- Help parents to think of ways to overcome the difficulty.

Point out that continually denying certain emotions that a child has can create a child who is not in touch with his or her real feelings or a child who frequently displays an emotion other than the real one in an effort to remain feeling accepted and connected. This has been called *creating an unreal* or *false self* in the child. For example, a person who always appears nice and tries to smile even when underneath he or she is very angry is exhibiting an unreal or false self.

Ask parents to think about *why* the emotion they described as difficult for them may be hard to deal with. Ask if it might relate to how a certain emotion was dealt with in their family as they were growing up. It may also relate to an emotion that—when expressed—seemed to get out of control.

Have parents in the group think about times when they have been very upset after a difficult day. Ask them what they want from their partners when they tell them that they are tired or upset.

Most participants will say that they would like some understanding of how they are feeling, perhaps the offer of a cup of tea. What they do *not* want is to have their friend or partner tell them to get over it, or to say it is their fault that it happened, or, particularly at that moment, to be told what to do to avoid the situation again. Use this example that parents can relate to themselves to help them appreciate that their child, at times, may need to experience the same level of understanding if he or she is upset. However, a child may not find it as easy to explain what he or she is upset about, and it is possible that at times, the child's emotions may seem to be inappropriate or out of proportion for the situation.

Have parents think about a scenario in which their child has screamed at and hit a younger sibling or another child. This is something that can arouse anger in parents, especially if it occurs frequently, because they probably worry a great deal about the effect this is having on the younger child and the implication that their own child is a bully.

Distribute Handout 8.7: Dealing with Children's Difficult Emotions: Steps of Emotion Coaching.

Explain that Handout 8.7 describes the steps of emotion coaching. This is one of the most important ways to deal with children's emotions. Use the scenario parents described in the previous discussion to review the steps of emotion coaching on Handout 8.7.

Role-play coaching a child who is very upset because his or her sibling broke a favorite toy.

It is important to point out to parents that although they should try to accept their child's feelings, they do not have to and should not accept any hurtful or aggressive behavior.

Helping a child to problem solve in situations in which his or her emotions are aroused can provide the child with strategies to use in similar situations and will encourage the child to develop emotion regulation strategies. When parents use this approach when emotions are less intense, it can provide a very close and intimate time of understanding and connection between parent and child.

PRINCIPLE 3: Teach your child appropriate strategies or outlets to help him or her learn to cope with strong emotions.

Strategies for teaching emotion regulation to infants, toddlers, and preschoolers differ significantly, partly because children's predominant moods differ according to individual temperament styles and also because their cognitive and emotional capacities vary significantly at different ages.

Distribute Handouts 8.8a–e: Strategies to Help Children Deal with Negative Emotions (depending on the ages of the group members' children).

Distribute Handouts 8.8a, b, c, d, or e to parents.

Have parents look at the strategies and discuss whether they use any of them. Ask for other strategies they may have found helpful. Have parents pick some strategies they have not used with their children and discuss how they think these strategies would work with their child.

Point out that at different ages, and as children get older, emotion regulation strategies depend somewhat less on holding and rocking and more on teaching the use of words, pretend play, stories, and pictures. In other words, there is a gradual growth in children's ability to self-regulate and to be able to express their emotions in more socially acceptable ways.

PRINCIPLE 4: Provide your child with frequent experiences that are happy, pleasant, and at times, joyful.

Having fun times with children helps to create warm memories that the child may remember for a lifetime. Also explain that joyful emotions activate the part of the brain (left frontal cortex) that is responsible for speech and language.

Have parents think of fun times they had with one or both of their own parents, and have them think about what was special about those times. Here are some ideas to spur discussion:

- They were able to spend time alone with one parent.

- Their parent seemed to be enjoying the activity as well.

- It was an opportunity to share thoughts and feelings.

- It was time away from the stress and rush of life.

Have parents think of and discuss something fun they could do with their child. Point out that it is important that it is something that they both enjoy, because otherwise the joy will go out of it for both parties. (See *Pathways to Competence* [2002], pages 441–442, for specific suggestions of fun activities and Chapters 2 and 4 for related general information.)

PRINCIPLE 5: If you lose control, talk about the feelings naturally and apologize to your child if your behavior was inappropriate.

All parents lose control at times and scream or yell at their child. Some parents feel that to attempt to repair the relationship at this time by apologizing can cause them to lose face and thus, to lose control of the child. When parents apologize, however, this does not mean that they are saying that the child was right and that they are wrong, but it can help the child to see how important it is to repair interactional missteps and to talk about what happened.

Ask parents to discuss what they believe are acceptable and unacceptable ways to express anger toward children.

Again, see pages 442 and 456–457 of *Pathways to Competence* (2002) for some suggestions of ways for parents to deal with their own strong emotions. Explain that taking a brief "time-out" to calm down is fine as long as the child knows it will be brief and that his or her safety is assured. Point out that these "breaks" or "missteps" in interaction and the relationship are common with all parents and children and that the most important thing is that it is mended and repaired without criticizing, putting the child down, or threatening. This is crucial in order for the child to develop emotion regulation.

PRINCIPLE 6: Provide a context or environment in which emotions are discussed and included when you talk about people and situations.

When families regularly talk about emotions and children have access to a caregiver who is interested in their feelings, they are more likely to understand their feelings and the feelings of others. This quality in the family environment has also been found to relate to children's social sensitivity and the development of empathy and a conscience later.

Distribute Handout 8.9: The Emotional Climate of My Home When I Was Growing Up.

Have parents complete Handout 8.9. Discuss the characteristics they checked and how useful or difficult they were for them. Have parents discuss how they would like things to be the same or different in their current family.

PRINCIPLE 7: Avoid presenting your child with an overwhelming diet of anger, fear, or depression. Seek help if necessary.

Ample evidence supports the fact that children who are constantly exposed to parental depression or severe anxiety or emotional, physical, or sexual abuse are negatively affected. These children are likely to have difficulty developing emotion regulation and may develop depression, anxiety, aggression, or behavior problems as a result. In fact, when infants are exposed to mothers with severe depression, by 3–6 months of age these infants' brain reactions have been found to mirror those of their mothers.

Have parents discuss how ongoing, intense emotions of parents may negatively affect children.

Distribute Handout 8.10: Strategies to Bring Anger Under Control.

Go through the suggested strategies. Explain that these approaches are important because they foster rational thought rather than an angry outburst during which people can become irrational and out of control.

Ask parents to describe a situation that is occurring with their child that is very upsetting for them and role-play it. Use the strategies in Handout 8.10 to demonstrate ways to calm down.

Explain to parents that these methods are helpful in situations when they are angry and in which it is important to gain control, but emphasize that having a chronically depressed, anxious, or fearful parent or having a sibling who is often angry and engages in verbal putdowns can be just as damaging as having a family member who has sporadic episodes of physical anger. If these situations are occurring frequently, it is important for the parent or family to seek professional help.

Introduce an exercise called "Seeing the Grays" (see page 455 of *Pathways to Competence* [2002] for more information). Explain to parents that it can be helpful to use this with their children when emotions become intense.

To do the Seeing the Grays exercise, put words on a blackboard, a flip chart, or a transparency on an overhead projector, placing a word at either end representing the extremes of a concept (e.g., good—bad, sensitive—insensitive, cowardly—brave, ugly–attractive). Then give some examples of these polar opposites; for example, someone who is *cowardly* ignores a person who is in danger of drowning, whereas someone who is *brave* might jump in and save the person or throw a flotation device in the water. Then have the parents think about in-between actions or types. In this example, most people would call for help.

This exercise can decrease black-and-white thinking and help bring intense emotions under control. The strategy can also help individuals to understand that people (children and parents) are a mixture of strengths and weaknesses and to remember positive things about situations when one is emotionally aroused or feeling very sad or angry about it.

This process will help parents realize the "grays" or "in-betweens" of people, their behavior, and their emotional reactions. If applicable to a parent in the group, it may help them to get insight into their own tendency to catastrophize or to ignore the negatives and see only the positives.

PRINCIPLE 8: Adopt strategies to help your child deal with intense negative emotions such as fear, anger, jealousy, and sadness.

In the course of typical development, children display a full range of emotions. Sometimes these emotions can become more extreme and concerning for caregivers. This can occur because a child is facing a stressful situation (e.g., a new sibling, a move to a different child care situation, the death of a grandparent) or because of a new developmental shift.

Strategies to deal with such a radical shift in emotions include trying to figure out what is upsetting the child and why.

Ask parents to discuss whether they have experienced times when their child seemed to be emotionally upset or displayed unusual behaviors and talk about how they worked out what the problem might be and how they dealt with it.

Suggest some ways that may help, such as spending extra time with the child and using emotional moments to get close. If the child does lose control and become aggressive, tell parents to make sure to communicate to the child that "I will not allow you to hurt yourself or anyone else," and use the moment to teach him or her ways to manage the emotion.

Talk about temper tantrums when discussing that emotions can occur for different reasons. Ask parents to suggest reasons for a child to have temper tantrums and put them on a flip chart or overhead projector.

Make sure to add the following reasons if they are not pointed out:

1. The child is tired, not well, or overwhelmed, and genuinely loses control.

2. The child wants something you have said he or she cannot have and he or she is acting out to get you to change your mind.

3. The child is feeling lonely, rejected, or out of control and has "disintegrated" or his or her behavior has become very "disorganized."

Ask parents to suggest what they might do to help in each of the different examples and point out how each situation requires very different strategies.

OTHER DISCUSSION TOPICS

Helping Children with Various Emotions

Distribute Handout 8.11: Common Fears at Various Ages and Handouts 8.12a–e: Some Ways to Deal with Common Emotions: a. Fears, b. Aggression, c. Jealousy and Sibling Rivalry, d. Sadness and Depression, and e. Temper Tantrums.

Handout 8.11 describes different fears that children commonly experience at different ages. The types of strategies listed in Handouts 8.12a–e can be used for dealing with various emotions because they allow the child to begin to get things back in control. As discussed previously, it is also important to put children in touch with their feelings before they get out of control by talking about them, reading stories, encouraging them to play them out using pretend play, and treating them seriously and with understanding.

Most parents at times have issues in dealing with the problems listed in Handouts 8.12a–e with their children and may want to discuss these topics.

Have parents select any of these topics that they would like to discuss. Point out that, although anger and tantrums may be the most obviously problematic to parents, young children also get sad and depressed and can be fearful and anxious about things that are going on at home, with peers, or in the school or child care. Ask parents about what seems to make their child sad, fearful, or anxious.

The message needs to be that helping young children with their emotions can relieve stress and prevent mental health problems. If children's stress becomes chronic, it can affect them psychologically and physiologically for years to come. Explain that research shows that ongoing intense emotions of different kinds, if they are experienced frequently or if they become chronic, can trigger the secretion of a number of stress hormones such as cortisol that can negatively affect brain development and may even suppress a child's immune system, increasing the potential for illnesses. Just as this applies to children, parents can experience ongoing stress reactions, especially if they were previously exposed to abuse of various kinds, neglect, or family violence during childhood.

For parents who are experiencing these kinds of difficulties frequently, suggest that groups that teach mindfulness approaches (e.g., meditation, positive visualization, journaling) may be helpful. Provide the names of local resources such as hospital programs and other support groups, if appropriate. Individual counseling may also be appropriate for certain parents. Group leaders can help them to find that kind of support if they are interested.

Use a relaxation or visualization video- or audiotape. Emphasize to parents that it is important to forgive themselves if they become upset and to concentrate on their breathing if they are trying to calm down.

THE TREE

Have parents write the principles on pieces of cardboard and stick them on the tree under the various parenting roles.

HOMEWORK

Distribute Handout 8.13: Homework.

Describe the homework suggestions. Have parents choose one of the activities and do the self-care activity if the Step is given over only 1 week. If the step is given over 2 weeks, they can do two activities and choose a second self-care activity from Handout 1.22 that would be meaningful to them. Point out that the group will discuss them next week.

1.   Have parents remember a fun time they had with their child and record it. Have parents list times they had fun with their child during the week.

or

2.   Ask parents to apologize to their child if they lose control during the week.

or

3.   If their child is upset during the week, have parents try going through the steps of emotion coaching and note how it worked.

Self-Care Activity

Ask parents to forgive themselves if they get upset and take a few minutes to breathe deeply and think about a place they would find relaxing in order to calm down.

STEP 9

Encouraging Concentration, Planning, and Problem Solving

MATERIALS

Required materials

Handouts 9.1–9.10 (on *Pathways to Competence for Young Children* CD-ROM accompanying this manual)

Self-Care Activities Handout 1.22

Suggested materials

Pathways to Competence: Encouraging Healthy Social and Emotional Development in Young Children (2002)

Three-ring binders with handouts for parents

Tree picture cards to write principles on

Five 4" x 6" or 3" x 5" cards for each parent

Overhead projector, blackboard, or flip chart

Velcro or tape to stick the cards on the tree

Crayons, markers, pencils and/or pens for participants

Paper on which to draw

Markers and erasers for the group leader(s) for discussions

Self-care boxes for parents

Video clips of parent–child interactions if available

HOMEWORK REVIEW

Discuss which homework strategies participants used and how successful they found them either to help contain their own emotions or to help their child with his or hers.

Ask parents about their experience with trying to calm themselves down when their child became upset.

SETTING THE STAGE

Ask parents if they have ever gone into their child's preschool or kindergarten classroom and observed the children playing in the pretend or dress-up corner, building quite elaborate structures with blocks, or completing a craft activity. Did they notice some children being very focused on a particular task or activity while another child was flitting impulsively from one part of the room to another, seemingly unable to concentrate or focus for long enough to complete anything? Have the parents discuss this and write their responses on the overhead projector or flip chart, if appropriate.

As discussed in the previous week, although emotions are critically important determinants of behavior, a child's learning and cognitive abilities are also important. It is important that parents help their child to develop the skills he or she will need to succeed in school; however, it is equally important to make sure that the child's emotional needs are met, although paying attention to both can be challenging for parents. And although the content of what the child learns is important, giving the child the skills to go through the process of learning may be even more so. Researchers and academics are increasingly referring to the skills needed to set the stage for learning new information as **executive functioning** skills. These include the abilities of focusing on the task at hand without being distracted by everything else that is going on around, developing a plan for learning the material, and problem solving in order to find strategies to complete the task. Not only are these abilities crucial for the classroom but also they are essential for later life success.

Finding the Balance

Given the importance of cognitive skills for success in school, some parents have felt a great deal of pressure to stimulate these abilities and to turn their babies and toddlers into "super kids." The message sometimes heard by parents is that the more stimulation young children get, the quicker they will learn. In other words, the more rattles shaken, baby stimulation videos watched, block structures built, and puzzles completed, the smarter the child will be. Also, the message has sometimes been that the **earlier** young children learn their colors, numbers, and letters, the better they will do in school. Some early childhood professionals such as David Elkind, who wrote *The Hurried Child* (2001), have warned that to push or hurry a child by placing too much emphasis on learning and achievement can create a number of negative psychological and emotional consequences. These conflicting messages can all be very confusing for parents because both stimulating children and avoiding placing too much pressure on them have merit.

Distribute Handout 9.1: The Merits of Early Intellectual Stimulation versus Not Pushing Academics Too Early.

Have parents complete Handout 9.1 or generate the ideas in the group. List some of their arguments in favor of both approaches on a flip chart or overhead projector.

Discuss how important it is to acknowledge the positive aspects of both positions and how both concepts make important contributions to our understanding of how best to enhance child development.

Make sure that the following points are brought up in the discussion.

- It is important for children to experience success when they are introduced to cognitive or academic tasks. This will encourage positive self-esteem that in turn fosters good social and emotional development and a desire for learning more. Forcing children to complete tasks for which they are not developmentally ready can lead the children to experience a sense of failure and a reluctance to take risks in learning.

- Research on neuroplasticity has shown that although there are a few areas of development that depend on the child receiving specific stimulation during critical periods, in the majority of developmental areas, adequate stimulation is naturally provided throughout the child's day. As long as the child receives adequate sensitive interaction with parents and other caregivers, develops a secure attachment with his or her parents, has objects to play with and manipulate, and is talked to and read to frequently, he or she will learn the necessary skills to succeed in school. However if they have not already done so, just prior to the child's starting school, parents may want to encourage kindergarten readiness skills such as having the child memorize his or her birthday, hold a pencil, copy a line, and learn basic colors and shapes.

• If a child is significantly delayed or at risk for developmental delay in a certain area, it is important to get help as early as possible so that he or she can receive the appropriate kinds of intervention from parents and professionals that are focused on the difficulty.

• One of the most helpful approaches to encouraging optimal learning is following the child's lead in play, conversation, and interests. This implies that the caregiver is not forcing or pushing the child in a particular direction all of the time but rather, is following the direction of the child's interest and enthusiasm. Early childhood specialists and researchers such as Maria Montessori and Burton White have shown how important this type of "teaching on the fly" or following the child's lead is for developing the child's sense of competence. Many young children like to use a crayon to draw or take pride in learning to write their name. Some may want to learn the names of letters, in which case it is appropriate to follow their lead and to give them the information they are requesting. However, if a child has not yet developed the fine motor coordination or other skills to manage these tasks, being pushed or forced to do them can discourage the child and turn him or her off from future learning, although supporting the child and scaffolding the task may be helpful to get him or her started with the activity.

• As pointed out in Step 1, it is important for parents to remember that finding a balance between the roles of playmate, nurturer, limit setter, and teacher is critical. In other words, while teaching children cognitive skills can be very important, providing loving and sensitive interactions and adequate structure, and having joyful play experiences with your child are also very important.

UNDERSTANDING CONCENTRATION, PLANNING, AND PROBLEM SOLVING

Development of Concentration, Planning and Problem Solving

Ask parents how many of them can relate to the following scene:

Susan is exhausted. She has been up all night tending to baby Joshua, and she has a bad cold coming on. Joshua's older brother, Matthew, almost 3, starts to yell at the top of his lungs just as Susan starts to fall off to sleep at last. "Stop it, Matthew!" she yells. "Don't you understand that Mommy is tired and not feeling well, like I told you?"

Question: Is Matthew being disobedient, or is it that he does not understand or remember what he was told?

Discuss with the group some of the aspects of the situation that Matthew most likely would understand and others that he maybe does not understand just yet. What will he need to learn about in order to behave differently?

During the discussion, explain that at the age of 2 going on 3, Matthew is still struggling with understanding his mother's perspective. He really does not understand that if he yells and Joshua wakes up, Mommy won't get the rest she needs and so it will take her longer to get well. It will only be very gradually over the next 2 years or so that he will become capable of understanding another's perspective and include it in planning and problem solving, especially in this kind of emotional, interpersonal situation. Matthew will be capable of problem solving and creating a plan that can accommodate his mother's needs as his cognitive skills expand between 3 and 5 years of age, however.

Distribute Handout 9.2a: The Steps of Planning and Problem Solving (Sample) and Handout 9.2b: The Steps of Planning and Problem Solving (Blank).

This capacity to respond by taking another person's perspective into account involves more than just being developmentally ready. It involves demonstrating more than one ability and following a sequence of steps. Review Handout 9.2a briefly with the parents and ask them to relate this example to one of their own.

Steps for planning and problem solving	Steps for helping Matthew to plan and problem solve
1. Think about the situation.	1. Ask Matthew, "What is the problem? Do you know why Mommy is upset?"
2. Recognize the problem.	2. Help Matthew to realize that because he yelled, the baby woke up.
3. Reflect on various possible solutions.	3. Gently tell Matthew in a nice voice, "Talk in a whisper, or talk to Mommy later instead of using your big voice."
4. Plan strategies and make a decision about what to do.	4. Help Matthew to come up with the idea: "I need this now, so I will ask for it in a whisper."
5. Take action and evaluate.	5. Encourage Matthew to incorporate this into his actions and see what happens. "I'll whisper to Mommy what I want and see what happens."

By teaching Matthew to follow these steps, he will think first in order to delay reacting impulsively and immediately. Once this capacity develops and becomes an integral part of Matthew's capacities, everyone's life will be a little calmer, feel more rational, and be easier to manage. It will take many explanations from caregivers and negotiations with peers before Matthew will understand and go through the steps outlined previously instead of just yelling without thinking. Sometimes teachers and parents teach these steps to children who are very impulsive and who have difficulty with problem solving and planning.

Have parents think of a time their child behaved impulsively. Using Handout 9.2b, ask them to write the steps they would use to help their child plan and problem solve instead of acting impulsively.

Not only is the ability to delay an impulsive response in order to plan, negotiate, and problem solve crucial for child development but also it is an important life skill. It is used in everything from family life with all of its complex schedules and details to board rooms across the country to international relations!

Discussion of Key Terms Related to Concentration, Planning, and Problem Solving

Although *concentration, planning,* and *problem solving* are familiar words, in this section we will discuss the definitions as they apply to child development.

Concentration and Attention

The term *concentration* and the related term *attention* refer to two major behaviors that entail 1) focusing on a certain piece of information from the wide range of possible sensory input and 2) information processing or considering the information that has been focused on.

It is clear that children who are able to concentrate when other things are going on around them are more likely to be able to problem solve, plan, and complete tasks.

Planning

Planning involves thinking about what to do before acting and deciding on the actions that need to be taken before taking them. Planning is an important part of problem solving but it may take an impulsive toddler some time before he or she is capable of thinking before carrying out an act. This is because planning requires some understanding of past, present, and future. For older preschoolers it may also require thinking about doing something in a different place and/or at another time. For example, "I must remember to get out my shells tonight before I go to bed so I remember to take them for show and tell tomorrow."

Problem Solving

Problem solving is what children do when they have a goal in mind but they encounter obstacles to the goal that require them to come up with strategies to overcome the obstacles in order to achieve the goal. In problem solving, a child needs some understanding of cause and effect, a belief that reaching the goal is possible, skills for generating possible strategies to solve the problem, and the ability to choose a solution from among these strategies.

Executive Functioning

Executive functioning is a somewhat strange phrase to use to describe a capacity in children but is used to describe a set of abilities that are used to obtain a goal. These abilities include focusing on relevant information, tuning out irrelevant information, using working memory (holding information in one's head when solving a problem such as doing mental arithmetic), planning, and thinking about how to do the task. Children use executive functioning to problem solve at home, school, and elsewhere in order to reach goals and to shift responses as needed in order to react appropriately to the environment. Researchers believe these capacities to be located in the prefrontal cortex (PFC), although it is also recognized that other brain regions may play a role.

Development of Concentration, Planning, and Problem Solving

Distribute Handout 9.3: Development of Concentration, Planning, and Problem Solving.

The full capacity for planning and problem solving is not present at birth but develops very gradually over the first 5 or 6 years of life and continues to develop throughout an individual's life. What follows is a brief description of some highlights of the development in these areas. For a more detailed description of the developmental sequence for planning, problem solving, and concentration, see pages 477–481 in *Pathways to Competence* (2002).

When discussing the development of capacities, it is helpful to engage the parents in recollections of their own child's development at each age and stage. For example, you could ask, "Do you remember when your child was a year old and sitting in his high chair and a toy fell off the side of the tray? What did the child do?" (The answer is likely to be that the child looked over the edge for the object in order to try and retrieve it.) This is a problem-solving ability that has developed by 1 year of age. Also have parents check for the section in Step 1 that describes the typical development of a child their child's age and see how their child compares. Ask parents to comment on anything they notice while doing this.

Birth to 6 months

From birth, infants can concentrate for brief periods of time and will turn to things that interest them. Infants start out life with rudimentary problem-solving skills. Even newborns can kick and activate a mobile and then kick again to have the action repeated.

6 to 12 months

By 6 months of age, infants develop what has been called means–ends behavior; for example, a child will pull a string in order to get a toy tied to the end of the string. An infant will also typically use trial and error in order to reach a toy that is hard to reach. By 12 months of age, the infant has a mental picture of an object and will persist in looking for objects that he or she cannot see.

12 to 24 months

Between the ages of 1 and 2, children are keen to do things independently and may persist and concentrate more on tasks. This need for independence gives them a drive to solve the problems that they face. Toddlers now pause and think about their actions, and solutions may be found by thinking them out rather than by always needing to try something out physically, first.

2 to 3 years

During this period, attention span increases dramatically and children spend longer periods of time playing independently or watching an interesting television program. At this age, children begin to use private speech (or self-talk) to help them during problem solving. Play themes expand as well, and children use play to experiment with problem solving.

3 to 4 years

Children are now more aware of other people's points of view. New conceptual abilities appear such as the ability to categorize things into classes. For example, a child of this age understands that dogs, cats, and alligators are types of animals and dresses and pants are types of clothing.

4 to 6 years

At this stage, a child has a "theory of mind" or is able to understand that other people have beliefs and desires that are different from his or her own. He or she can understand and enjoy games with rules and can categorize objects under shape, colors, and size. The child also has more of an idea of the meaning of numbers and understands the concept of quantity.

***Distribute Handout 9.4: My Child and
Concentration, Planning, and Problem Solving.***

Have parents complete Handout 9.4. They can list the skills and activities that their child is able to do in these areas now and what difficulties their child may experience when using these skills. Have parents discuss their lists.

The Importance of Concentration, Problem Solving, and Planning Compared with Other Skills and Qualities

Most people think about a child's acquisition of concentration, problem solving, and planning skills less frequently than they do about other developmental capacities such as language and gross motor skills. In fact, these skills are crucial for the development of intelligence, cognitive ability, and school achievement. Even highly intelligent young children who do not have these abilities may have difficulties with learning relevant material or acquiring basic academic skills, which can compromise their adjustment to school.

Ask parents to think about and discuss a child who lacks these capacities and how this child might behave when he or she first starts school.

Interpersonal Relationships

The abilities of concentration, planning, and problem solving are linked to interpersonal relationships as well as being important for school achievement. This is because the capacity made up of these abilities increases a child's potential for perspective taking and empathy, for waiting for his or her turn and, consequently, for good peer interactions.

Self-Control and Self-Regulation

Children who have adequate executive function skills have longer attention spans and better self-control. They are more able to complete tasks on time, to follow rules, and to meet the requirements of others. They also are more likely to be able to regulate their emotions.

Self-Esteem

Children who can concentrate and plan usually feel in control and good about themselves. This is partly because their behavior brings positive reactions from teachers, parents, and peers that make them feel accepted and competent. Conversely, children with difficulties in these areas often feel confused, out of control, and rejected, which can significantly affect their self-esteem. In some instances, this may result in withdrawal or the development of behavior problems.

Ask parents to discuss whether they had difficulty with concentration and/or solving problems when they were children. How did it affect their experiences with school, friendships, home life, and self-esteem?

Ask parents how much their own parents valued academic achievement as they were growing up and how it may have affected them.

Important Research Findings

Pages 481–486 in *Pathways to Competence* (2002) details findings in these areas; however, some suggestions of findings that might be of interest to parents are listed here.

- Because there have been a number of concerns about the use of infant assessments as predictors of a child's later intelligence, some researchers have considered instead the validity of using tests of concentration and attention as a more accurate estimation of an infant's future intelligence. Much of this research has studied visual attention and selective looking in infants as possible predictors. The results have shown that various aspects of visual processing, such as recognizing and responding to new stimuli and processing information more quickly as infants, do predict better performance on various assessments of cognitive tasks at older ages.

- Children who use trial-and-error exploration at young ages, who enjoy playing, and who use more strategies to problem solve are more likely to have problem-solving success at later ages.

- The ability to seek help from adults when a problem is too difficult to solve has been found to be an important skill. It enables children to remain involved with difficult tasks that enhance opportunities for learning.

- A number of aspects of caregiver interactions have been found to enhance a sense of competence and to encourage concentration, planning, and problem solving in young children. Some of the strategies found to be helpful with young children include the following:

  — *Scaffolding* (i.e., providing a supportive context in which children are able to explore new responses as their mastery expands)

  — Selecting learning tasks that are within a child's *zone of proximal development* (i.e., the level at which the child is capable of doing something with the collaboration of a more competent person but that the child could not do alone)

  — Choosing appropriate tasks, helping the child to stay at the activity, and giving feedback to the child about his or her progress at completing a task. In outcome studies, children who were given this help, achieved greater independence at later tasks.

These and other strategies will be outlined in the next section on the principles and strategies of parenting.

PRINCIPLES OF ENCOURAGING
CONCENTRATION, PLANNING, AND PROBLEM SOLVING

Distribute Handout 9.5: Principles of Encouraging Concentration, Planning, and Problem Solving.

At this point, video clips of parent–child interactions that illustrate the principles may be used. Principles 3 and 4 may be most likely to be more readily demonstrated in these interactions.

PRINCIPLE 1: Show the world to your child and celebrate it with him or her. Allow your child to lead and nurture his or her curiosity and interests.

Research has certainly shown that children who are shown more about the world, with parent(s) who can be excited about its wonder, are more likely to have higher intelligence and to be more creative thinkers. The fun of discovery can be shared in all sorts of situations: on a walk, at the library, in the park, fishing, on the bus or subway (underground transportation), at a museum, and of course, at home or in child care.

Ask parents if they have taken their child on an outing like this and have them describe the interest or curiosity the child demonstrated on the outing. What seemed to fascinate the child?

Busy caregivers find it impossible to give children their attention all of the time; however, when possible, responding to a child when he or she has a question, becomes frustrated with a task, or just wants to share a triumph will encourage the child's love of learning. For example, if the child wonders about butterflies, showing him or her a picture of one or pointing out a real one can support the child's joy of discovery.

A child's enjoyment of discovery can be fostered best in a home that is not too formal and that encourages exploration and play. Obviously, homes need to be safety proofed, and all parents have certain treasures here and there that they do not want broken, but a home that is full of "don't touch" items is certainly not one that encourages a sense of wonder, fun, or curiosity and exploring. Providing play spaces and toys that can accommodate a child's interest, attention span, and intellectual level is also important.

PRINCIPLE 2: Use scaffolding to help your child to learn during problem solving. Encourage your child to concentrate.

As mentioned earlier, scaffolding means providing a supportive context in which children are able to explore new responses as their mastery expands. During scaffolding, caregivers set things up for the activity, simplify tasks for success, and provide structure for the child's attempts. Sometimes a strategy of completing the task together is used.

Provide this example for parents: "At some point you may have helped your child walk by holding his or her hands and providing physical support; however when the child tired of this practice activity, you let him or her go back to crawling to get around. This is an example of scaffolding, when the child was encouraged to acquire this new developmental level of functioning but was allowed to return to his or her current level of functioning when he or she was tired."

Ask parents to think about a time when they supported their child in learning a new skill or activity. Ask them, "How was this experience for you? Was it rewarding or frustrating? What did you notice about your child's reaction?"

Distribute Handout 9.6: Scaffolding Strategies.

Typical scaffolding strategies include the following:

- Be aware of the child's level of functioning and choose an activity that is at a manageable level of difficulty.

- Structure the situation to support the child to solve the problem (e.g., you might put two puzzle pieces close to where they go).

- Structure the situation to fit with the child's motivation and enthusiasm at a particular time.

- Allow the child to take the lead whenever possible but stay close if he or she becomes bored or discouraged and structure the event to meet those needs.

- Encourage the child during problem solving by noticing small successes and commenting on them, such as by saying "Good for you," or "That's great."

- Enable the child to keep trying if he or she sees the problem as being too difficult or it is close to being solved.

If you wish, have two group leaders do this exercise or ask a parent volunteer to do it with you. Role play an example of scaffolding with one leader assuming the role of the parent and the other leader or the parent volunteer taking the role of the child. Choose an example that is appropriate to the age level of the children in the group; for example, put a puzzle together, help a child write his or her name, or put blocks in a container.

Have parents pair up and role play the teaching of a task to their child with their partner. Choose a task that they would like to teach their own child. Have them think of ways that they could support their child in learning that skill.

Children vary in terms of the length of time that they are able to concentrate on an activity. Distractible children seem to be drawn to activities other than the one they are trying to do and do not focus on the task at hand. Children like this typically flit from one task to another and do not settle for any length of time on one task. Consequently, they seldom finish anything and fail to attend to relevant information in order to do so.

Differences in the ability to concentrate are often apparent from early infancy, and distractibility is seen as a temperament characteristic that can persist into adulthood. As a general rule, 2-year-olds should be able to concentrate for at least 7 minutes, 4-year-olds for 12 minutes, and 5-year-olds for 15 minutes. If parents note that children can attend to certain tasks or toys but tend to flit between others that they do not like, explain that this is a common phenomenon and that distractible children have trouble concentrating on tasks that they find more difficult (e.g., academic tasks) but may sit in front of the television or computer for hours concentrating on the picture.

Distribute Handout 9.7: Strategies to Help Children to Concentrate and Focus.

The strategies in Handout 9.7 could be discussed during the group or they could be given to be read at home.

Ask parents to recall the teacher they learned the most from when they were in school. How did that teacher help them to learn new material? What did the teacher do to support his or her students to learn?

Ask parents if they recall their parents teaching them to do things at home. How did their parents help them with their homework? Was home a place where they could concentrate and feel supported in their learning?

PRINCIPLE 3: Encourage the use of self-talk or private speech during problem solving.

Self-talk (private speech) is communication with the self. Preschool-age children use self-talk as a mediating tool during problem solving to guide and direct their activities. It also serves a self-regulating function and can be helpful to encourage young children to keep trying and not to give up. Children, it appears, hear the speech of their caregivers, internalize it, and transform it into private speech. As a consequence, words and phrases that are encouraging and positive can be containing and motivating for children later. Some examples are "You can do it," and "Keep trying." Read the example of Daniel on pages 489–490 in *Pathways to Competence* (2002) for other suggestions and have parents think about the effect of having words in their head internalized from caregivers such as "You can do it," "Good try," "You can manage it," "I know you can," and "You have what it takes to do this," when a problem or a challenge presents itself.

Self-Care Activity

Have parents talk about any messages they have in their heads when trying to do something that is difficult. If these messages tend to be negative, have parents brainstorm about more positive words they could use during self-talk to help them to keep trying so they can get through the task. Write some of their ideas on the overhead projector or flip chart. Encourage parents to remember to use these phrases when they feel themselves becoming discouraged or overwhelmed about something they have to do.

Ask the parents, "Have you heard your child talk to him- or herself to help solve a problem or persist at a task? Have you used words of encouragement to keep your child trying?"

PRINCIPLE 4: Teach your child strategies to solve problems.

Children can be taught problem-solving strategies when they face a real-life situation or a homework task. Review with parents some of the strategies listed there that will help them teach their children problem-solving skills. Some examples are

- Ask questions that can help children consider alternatives to the solution they are trying to find.

- Provide hints on how to do things and stay involved so that the child does not become discouraged. Make suggestions as to how things might work better. Give open-ended responses that are not too intrusive but allow the child to remain focused.

More information on this principle can be found on pages 490–491 in *Pathways to Competence* (2002).

 Provide each participant with five 4″ × 6″ or 3″ × 5″ cards. Dictate the following steps to the parents:

1. Decide what is supposed to be done.

2. Examine ways the task could be done.

3. Focus and concentrate on the task.

4. Find an answer or strategy.

5. Check out the answer.

Have parents choose a situation or task they could help their child with. For each problem-solving step, have parents generate a question that they could ask their child that would help him or her with the step. For example, for step 1, ask "What do you have to do?" Have them write the questions on the five cards and explain that they can use the cards with their child to help him or her go through the steps of problem solving.

Explain to parents that the first few times these strategies are used, they will need to scaffold the task when helping the child by being available, asking questions, and supporting the child to do the task. As the child gets more confident, however, he or she will be able to take over the steps him- or herself. This may be a useful strategy for children who are very impulsive, who do not plan activities, who tend to act in unpredictable ways without thinking about it, and who have little frustration tolerance.

As modeling is an important influence on behavior, it is critically important that families work out ways to solve problems and model these to their children.

Distribute Handout 9.8: How Our Family Solves Problems.

The chart provided as Handout 9.8 will help parents to determine how well their family does in terms of solving problems. Have the parents fill out the chart and discuss their answers with the group as well as some strategies that might help them to solve problems better.

Distribute Handout 9.9: How Problems Were Solved in My Family of Origin.

Ask parents how problems were solved in their families of origin. Point out that the way their parents solved problems in their families when they were growing up may have influenced how they solve difficulties in their own lives. Ask some questions such as

- Did your parents fight physically or scream and yell at one another?

- Did they punish each other by sulking or withdrawing from each other?

- Were problems or conflicts talked about and solutions found?

- Did you learn some ways or develop some ideas about good ways to solve problems and conflicts?

More suggestions for questions are given on page 500 of *Pathways to Competence* (2002). Discuss the parents' responses and how they feel their own parents' problem-solving styles may be influencing the way problems are handled in their current family.

Have a parent identify a conflict that he or she frequently experiences with his or her child or partner. Have the parent play him- or herself while you or another group leader plays the other person. First, demonstrate a negative or conflictual exchange and then contrast that with another that could resolve the conflict.

PRINCIPLE 5: Help your child to learn about the sequences of events and routines. Teach about the past, present, and future.

Teaching about sequencing and time usually comes about naturally as caregivers and children go through the daily routine of the day. Having a relatively consistent structure and routine is the first requirement for introducing a child to the concepts of time and order. It is also important to make children aware of what is going to happen throughout the day; for example, "When you get dressed, we will go out for a walk," and "When you have your bath it will be bed time" are both ways to alert children of what is to come. To help children develop skills in the areas of sequencing and the passage of time, gradually increase the time between discussing the event and when it actually happens. For some children who have difficulty with change during the day, they may need more warnings before a change happens. Sometimes providing a visual reminder of daily sequences of events with pictures can be helpful for children who seem to have a great deal of difficulty with changes or transitions throughout the day.

Ask parents about some strategies they use that encourage their child's understanding of time and the sequencing of events. This might include how they prepare their child for an upcoming event such as a trip, a move, or a birthday party. Write these strategies down on the overhead projector or flip chart. *Pathways to Competence* (2002), pages 491–493, has more ideas to suggest to parents.

PRINCIPLE 6: Encourage perspective taking. Give your child a voice and an opinion about the solution to a problem.

Young children up to the age of about 4 tend to be egocentric, or to believe themselves to be the center of the universe, and see things only from their own point of view. Thus, they lack a theory of mind or understanding of the point of view or opinions of others. In other words, to children of this age, everything is "mine" and "my way." Perspective taking needs to be encouraged by pointing out how other people think and feel about things the child does or events that are happening. Children also learn about others' perspectives through pretend play and in real-life situations when they participate in family discussions about such things as finding solutions to problems or discussing a disagreement that may have come up with a sibling or a parent. What is important about this is that in the process of participating in the discussions, the child will learn that there are different perspectives on most issues and that usually, there is not only one way to do things or one way to feel. The child also will learn that he or she cannot always get his or her own way, although sometimes his or her idea will be appropriate.

Perspective taking can also be encouraged by discussing books, movies, or television shows. The discussions should include talking about how the characters feel, or parents and children can tell stories together, taking turns or taking the part of different characters.

Ask parents for any examples of ways they let their child have a say in what is happening in the family.

Ask parents if they had a say in what happened in their family of origin when they were children. How did that make them feel?

PRINCIPLE 7: Allow your child to experience the consequences of his or her actions, unless to do so would be dangerous. Then explain what happened and why.

Children can only really find out what will happen when they do certain things if we let them experience the consequences of what they have done rather than rescuing them all of the time. Obviously, this does not apply to situations when the child would be placed in danger if the parent does not react, such as running across a road or touching something hot. Tell parents, however, that if their child has been told that he or she will miss dessert or have a toy put away for a week if he or she does not do a certain thing, then the child should have these consequences imposed so that he or she learns, "If I do this, this will happen, or if I don't do something different, this will happen." It is important here that the consequence follows logically from the behavior and is not unrealistic. Consequences that are illogical and unrealistic place both the child and parent in an awkward position. For example, not letting the child watch any television for 2 weeks probably would not work because by the end of that time, the child has probably forgotten the reason for the punishment in the first place, or the parent might have found it difficult to uphold when one of his or her own favorite television programs came on. (See Step 7 for more ideas on natural and logical consequences.) In fact, research suggests that parents who constantly bail their children out and do not allow them to get into trouble when they deserve it from school officials or the police may contribute to the development of delinquency in a child. So in the long run, letting a child suffer the consequences of his or her behavior in many situations may be helpful for the child's long-term development.

Ask parents to think of times they let their child suffer the consequences of his or her actions and describe how it worked out. Did they find this difficult to do, and what kind of feelings did they have about it? Write down their responses for the group.

OTHER DISCUSSION TOPICS

Refer to Chapter 9 in *Pathways to Competence* (2002), pages 494–497, on commonly raised issues on the development of concentration, planning, and problem solving, and discuss any topics in which parents have a particular interest. These topics frequently become important around the time a child starts formal schooling.

Attention-Deficit/Hyperactivity Disorder

Some group participants may want more information on the characteristics of children with **attention-deficit/hyperactivity disorder** (ADHD). As is stated in *Pathways to Competence,* "Children with ADHD have difficulty with short-term memory and with filtering out irrelevant stimulation and instead, attend to extraneous things in the environments" (2002, p. 496). See pages 496–497 in *Pathways to Competence,* if possible, for a lengthier description and strategies for dealing with this disorder. In any discussion or description, it is important to emphasize the following:

- Children who have a great deal of difficulty with concentration, planning, and problem solving are often diagnosed with ADHD. Parents are often confused about the term and wonder if their child meets the diagnosis. Some children with ADHD have hyperactivity as well as attentional problems, whereas others only have one or the other. The proper diagnostic terms for the disorder are ADHD (combined type) when the child has attentional and hyperactivity problems, ADHD (predominantly inattentive type), and ADHD (predominantly hyperactive type).

- It is important to point out that diagnosing ADHD is complex and should be done by a professional, preferably with some specialization in the disorder. It is important that the child is tested, if possible, by a psychologist to identify any cognitive problems such as difficulty with various aspects of executive functioning. It is also important to identify some of the causes of the difficulties, which are usually a combination of genetics, biology, and sometimes interactions in the home or classroom.

- It is sometimes difficult to distinguish between what is a typical behavior for a toddler or preschooler based on the child's temperament and what is a symptom of an actual disorder.

- ADHD is believed to affect 3%–5% of school-age children and is more prevalent in boys than in girls. For children who are accurately diagnosed with ADHD, approximately 66%–70% still have some of the symptoms as an adult.

- One of the primary methods of treatment for ADHD is medication, and much research has been conducted to examine the effectiveness of various medications. However, whether parents, in consultation with professionals, decide to use medication to treat the symptoms of ADHD, it is critical for children to be taught and to learn strategies to help them to improve their concentration, planning, and problem solving to help them manage the symptoms of the disorder. Children who stay on medication *and* learn appropriate strategies usually do better in the long run.

In addition to information in *Pathways to Competence* (2002), parents should be referred to books by Russell Barkley and other books the leaders find helpful on ADHD.

Even if their own child has not been diagnosed with or has symptoms of ADHD, parents often have questions because a child of someone they know has this diagnosis or a friend has been diagnosed with it as an adult, or they may have wondered whether they have it themselves. Discuss questions the parents may have about this disorder.

THE TREE

At the end of the group, before talking about homework, parents are asked to write the principles on a piece of cardboard and to stick them under one of the roles of parenting at the top of the tree.

HOMEWORK

Distribute Handout 9.10: Homework.

Describe the homework activities listed below. Have parents choose one of the activities and do the self-care activity if the Step is given over only 1 week. If the Step is given over 2 weeks, the parents can do both activities and choose a second self-care activity from Handout 1.22 for the second week that would be meaningful to them. Point out that the group will discuss them next week.

1. Ask parents to spend some time helping their child to solve a social difficulty or a problem with completing an activity. Encourage them to try to use some of the strategies discussed for teaching problem solving using the cards that they completed in the group session.

or

2. Have parents teach their child a new skill using the principles of scaffolding and encouraging self-talk.

or

3. Have parents hold a family meeting to plan an outing or upcoming trip or what they might do on the next family holiday. Have them give their young child a chance to make a suggestion about the outing or trip and, if possible, follow through with the child's suggestion. Ask them to make a calendar so that their child can see when the event is coming up.

Self-Care Activity

 Ask parents to identify a problem for which they found a successful solution. Ask them to think about what contributed to their success in solving the problem and make sure that they acknowledge their success to themselves and tell someone else about it, if possible. Ask them to bring the example to the group next week.

STEP

Encouraging Social Competence, Empathy, and Caring Behavior

MATERIALS

Required materials

Handouts 10.1–10.15 (on *Pathways to Competence for Young Children* CD-ROM accompanying this manual)

Self-Care Activities Handout 1.22

Suggested materials

Pathways to Competence: Encouraging Healthy Social and Emotional Development in Young Children (Landy, 2002)

Three-ring binder with handouts: 1 for each group leader(s) and parent

Overhead projector and/or flip chart for recording discussions

Tree picture cards to write principles on

Velcro or tape to stick the cards on the tree

Small file card boxes to use as "self-care" box for parents

Matching blank file cards

Video clips of parent–child interactions if available

Pretend play toys

HOMEWORK REVIEW

For homework review, encourage participants to report on their observations of the homework activities from Step 9, Encouraging Concentration, Planning, and Problem Solving. What did they notice about trying to use some of the strategies for helping their child to problem solve around a social situation or with completing an activity? Did the child seem to find it helpful? Did it seem to calm him or her down? Did it help parents better cope with their child if he or she was frustrated and upset? For parents who used the recommended strategies during scaffolding and teaching self-talk, did the child seem to calm down as a result? Have the parents who had a family meeting describe how it worked for them.

Have each parent tell the group about something he or she did that was successful in solving a problem, and make sure the parent is acknowledged for the success. When appropriate, ensure that there is some discussion of what contributed to the success of the strategy.

SETTING THE STAGE

Every day we are deluged with stories of crime and human cruelty including terrorist attacks, racial brutality, and child abuse.

Ask parents to talk about concerns they may have about society today and about their children as they grow up. Do they have concerns that the world at large is a less caring community, or that the communities in which they live are less supportive?

Discuss with parents that, in spite of this negative picture, examples are plentiful of individuals and groups who display empathy and caring behavior toward others. Have parents think of examples of caring shown toward other people. Some examples that could be given, if they are not brought up by the group, include the following:

- Churches and other organizations that devote themselves to helping the poor and marginalized

- Individuals and families who give enormous amounts of energy and compassion to helping a family member who is ill or who has a physical or developmental disability

- Individuals who contribute time and/or money in the wake of natural disasters in which people are killed, hurt, or made homeless

- Examples of heroism in battle when a soldier has put his or her own life at risk in order to save the lives of others

- Walk-a-thons conducted to raise money for important causes such as fighting diseases (e.g., breast cancer)

Evidence abounds that it is possible for children to develop empathy and helping behavior as they are growing up, and that it is best if caregivers begin nurturing these qualities during children's early years.

UNDERSTANDING SOCIAL COMPETENCE, EMPATHY, AND CARING BEHAVIOR

Discussion of Key Words

Social competence can mean different things in different families and at different ages.

Have parents discuss what social competence means for them and for their child and what type of social abilities they would like their child to develop.

Social Competence

Social competence refers to the skills that a young child develops in order to get along with others, to be liked and accepted, to have friends, and to have rewarding and reciprocal interactions with others. Having social competence results in successful social functioning with peers, teachers, parents, and other family members.

Empathy

Empathy refers to noticing the feeling state of another person and responding with a similar or identical emotion.

Sympathy

Sympathy results from empathy, is other-oriented, and involves feeling concern or sadness for the person and the situation or emotional state that he or she is experiencing.

Have parents discuss the difference between empathy and sympathy and ask if they think their child is capable of displaying one or both of these feelings. Ask them to give examples of when and how their child showed these emotions.

Point out that younger children usually experience empathy rather than sympathy and that if a child is constantly exposed to a caregiver's depression or fear, it may result in personal distress for the child because he or she may not be able to differentiate his or her own emotions from those of the caregiver. In other words, the child may experience the same emotion and, if it happens frequently, become overwhelmed by it.

Have parents think of a situation in which someone they cared about experienced a tragic loss. Have them discuss what they feel would be the most helpful thing to do in that kind of situation.

Make sure the point is made by the group leaders or the participants that simply becoming overwhelmed with the same emotion that a friend is experiencing (i.e., showing empathy by reflecting the same sadness that the friend is feeling) would be less useful than expressing concern, and that helping behaviors such as offering support (e.g., minding the children, making a casserole) may be the most helpful if someone is going through a difficult time. Modeling and suggesting this kind of action can help a child to better understand the importance of giving this kind of support to others. Sometimes supporting the child to take some flowers from the garden or a cookie to a friend at child care who has been sick can be a great way for the child to learn how to show caring to another person.

Prosocial Behavior

Prosocial behavior occurs when someone shows cooperation and caring behavior toward another person such as sharing, helping, or comforting a person who is distressed. This may be experienced positively because the helping person has a sense of being able to actually do something to improve an upsetting situation.

Have parents think of different motivations for people showing prosocial behavior. Reasons may include wanting to be noticed and getting a reward or being really concerned about the welfare of another person or group. In the political arena, individuals appear to have different motivations for their political platforms. Some may seem to be more power oriented, whereas others are more motivated to improve people's lives. You may want to raise this as a point of discussion for the group in order to get them started on thinking what motivates most people to help others.

Altruism

Altruism is another term that is used to describe prosocial behavior that does not involve a reward and is internally motivated. People who engage in prosocial behavior may suffer from guilt and shame if they do not help and may experience feelings of pride and self-esteem if they do. The altruistic person only has others' needs as motivation to help.

The Development of Social Competence, Empathy, and Caring Behavior

 ### Distribute Handout 10.1: Development of Social Competence, Empathy, and Caring Behavior.

Group leaders should highlight some developmental milestones of social competence, empathy, and caring behavior that are relevant for the children being discussed in the group. Choose some from Handout 10.1 or from pages 519–522 in *Pathways to Competence* (2002). For example:

Birth to 12 months

From birth, infants are attracted to other people and like to gaze at the human face, preferring it over other things to look at. They seek out eye-to-eye contact from very early in their lives. As discussed in Step 3 on the development of attachment, infants first smile indiscriminately at everyone who smiles at them, but by 7 months, an attachment is established and the baby will be more likely to save that special smile for his or her attachment figures. The baby may also become upset in the company of others and when the parents leave him or her with someone else. Some infants seem to like to be around other infants and may direct smiles and vocalizations toward them. Early signs of empathy may be shown, and even a newborn may cry if someone else is crying.

12 to 24 months

Signs of empathy continue to occur in a child's second year of life and become more frequent. Toddlers may continue to engage in solitary play, and struggles over the possession of objects are common. Children at this stage generally play side by side (also called *parallel play*) and engage in very little cooperative play. Cooperation only occurs for very brief, fleeting moments. Toddlers still need to feel a sense of security at times when they are playing, and may go up and touch their caregivers or call out to them in order to "refuel" before going off to play again with the other children or to explore things in the world.

2 to 3 years

True cooperative play increases between the ages of 2 and 3, and a child is more likely to initiate interactions with other children. Pretend play is common, and children may try out various social roles in their play. Children also are more able to solve conflicts, especially with help from an adult. They are increasingly capable of understanding the emotions of others without internalizing the emotions themselves, and they may now be able to initiate some helping behavior and try out different ways to comfort another person.

3 to 4 years

Friends become more important to children between the ages of 3 and 4; in fact, they may even become attachment figures. Children of this age may become quite upset if a friend moves away, for example. In this year, children develop a theory of mind that enables them to understand that another person's thoughts and feelings are different from their own. They can also listen and respond to other people's points of view.

4 to 6 years

Children now engage in play with rules and may plan for these games ahead of time. They may identify with a number of people inside and outside the family and want to behave in the same way. Some may pretend to take on other roles, such as a super-hero. They now feel guilty if they hurt the feelings of other people and may respond to another person's sadness by helping and trying to make him or her feel better.

Refer back to Handout 4.9: Toys for Pretend Play in Step 4.

Have available toys for the parents that their own child might play with at home or in child care. Be sure to include some toys that encourage pretend play (e.g., puppets, dress-up props) for the older children. Have parents choose a toy that they have seen their child play with and use it in a way that their child would. Ask parents what feelings they and their child might have during the play.

Encourage parents to put themselves in their child's place and to understand their feelings. Point out that being able to do this can increase their sympathy for what the child may be experiencing and feeling. Ask parents to consider that a child sometimes uses puppets to act out being bullied by an older child, for example. Have parents think about how the child is feeling in such a play sequence.

The Importance of Social Competence, Empathy, and Caring Behavior

Many parents will have identified the quality of *caring* in Step 1 as one of the characteristics that they want their child to have. Ask parents why they feel that having a caring child is so important.

Areas of development previously discussed during the parenting group contribute to the development of various aspects of social competence. These include language and moral development and the ability to engage in pretend play. Social competence skills also contribute to other areas of development such as the following:

Academic Success and School Achievement

Children who are unpopular and who have few friends are less likely to enjoy school. In higher grades, they may have discipline problems, become truant, and eventually drop out before completing school. Difficulties with school are far more common for children who have social problems, although how the link actually occurs is not clear. One reason may be that children who make friends easily and who are popular are more likely to enjoy school and are therefore less likely to drop out.

Self-Esteem

Shyness, aggression, and other socializing difficulties have also been linked with low self-esteem, especially when children enter child care or school.

Emotional Development

The topics presented in *Pathways to Competence* (2002) and during a Pathways to Competence for Young Children Parenting Program group are all geared toward social and emotional development in children. It is clear that social and emotional development are linked. Certainly, children with poor social skills are more likely to have emotional and behavioral disorders. Conversely, socially competent children who have been able to find support from others (both inside and outside the family) tend to be more resilient and are better able to cope at different developmental stages if they encounter loss, trauma, or other difficult situations.

Research Findings Related to Social Competence, Empathy, and Caring Behavior

If possible, refer to pages 523–530 in *Pathways to Competence* (2002) for a more detailed description of research findings in this area. Since the 1970s, research exploring empathy and prosocial behavior has increased significantly, including the study of the development of the capacities and contributors to social competence and prosocial behavior. Some of this seems to have arisen out of concerns about various types of violence in today's society and the lack of caring toward others who are less fortunate. Some of the topics that may be of interest to the group for further discussion are outlined next. Leaders should choose the topics that they feel parents would most like to discuss.

- Researchers have found that there is an increase in the frequency with which children use comforting behaviors from 2 to 3 years of age, but a decline in the preschool years in these behaviors has been noted as well. It has been hypothesized that this shift occurs because children perceive that these behaviors are no longer needed and preschoolers now expect that teachers and parents will assume the role of helping.

Ask parents of children of preschool age or older if they noticed a decline in prosocial behavior at this stage of their child's development.

- Generally, girls have been considered to be more empathetic and to show more prosocial behavior than boys; however, some studies have shown that boys between 2 and 3 years of age actually exhibit more prosocial behavior than girls of the same age. Other studies have found that although boys may show less facial and verbal reactions, their physiological reactions to the upset of others are the same as girls.

- Some researchers have found cultural differences in the expression or amount of prosocial behavior, cooperation, and social responsibility. These societal values are passed down from generation to generation and modeled by parents and taught in school and other group situations.

Parents may be interested in discussing the values of their culture as opposed to the dominant culture in which they are now living.

- Both mothers and fathers have an influence on the development of social competence in their children. Fathers have a particularly important role to play in encouraging its development in their children. Some of the influence may come about because of the father's physical engagement with their children. Although it used to be believed that fathers had the most influence on their sons, recent evidence indicates that they also have a very important influence on their daughters as well.

- Although parents' influence on their children's socialization in the home is obviously crucial, in many families the influence of siblings is often very important. Other influences outside the home such as the modeling of teachers, peers, and friends also affect the development of these capacities significantly.

- Researchers such as Dodge and Frame have demonstrated that the views children have of themselves and the world influence how they perceive ambiguous situations, react to them, and remember them. Children with positive representations of the world and themselves generally make positive appraisals and appropriate responses in social situations, whereas those with more negative images are likely to respond with hostile and even aggressive responses. (See Handouts 3.5a and b). The leader should refer to the steps of social information processing that children may go through when responding to social interactions, found in Step 3 on developing a secure attachment.

Ask parents if they have ever noticed a child who seems to become sad or angry very easily and who attributes negative intent when none was intended. For example, one child may feel that if another child brushes up against him or her when the two are waiting in line at school to go outside that it was a deliberate attempt to hurt him or her, whereas another child might perceive it as the accident that it was.

PARENTING PRINCIPLES AND TECHNIQUES

Distribute Handout 10.2: The Principles for Encouraging Social Competence, Empathy, and Caring Behavior.

If available, choose any of the parent–child video interactions in which a parent comments on the effect of a child's behavior on another person or talks about a conflict and tries to solve it or shows empathy toward the child (Principles 2 and 5).

PRINCIPLE 1: Model caring behavior toward your child and others. Show caring behavior toward the less fortunate. Reinforce and encourage caring behavior.

It is clear from research that modeling caring behavior is one of the best ways to encourage its development in children.

Distribute Handout 10.3: My Caring List.

Have parents list the ways they exhibit concern and empathy toward their children. Some common behaviors are provided on the handout in order to get parents started.

Discuss the behaviors that parents listed as showing caring toward their child.

Not only is modeling caring behavior toward their own child important, but also modeling caring behavior to others outside the family is an important model for children.

Ask parents to discuss ways that they model caring and supporting others. Bringing food to a friend who needs it, minding someone else's children when they go for a job interview, or taking food to the food bank might be good examples. Put some examples on the overhead projector or flip chart.

Ask parents if their own parents modeled caring in their home or community. Ask them, "What did you observe as a child, and did it influence how you care for others now?"

Point out that it is as important for parents to notice spontaneous helping behavior as it is to encourage children's achievements. Parents can let children know how pleasing such behavior is, for example. Young children may show caring behavior by looking after a sibling, comforting a friend, feeding a pet, or sharing a treat with another person.

This principle is about showing caring behavior to others; however, it is important to realize that to parents, self-care is critical as well.

Have parents suggest ways that they can take care of themselves even in the midst of their busy lives; for example, having time to themselves after putting the children to bed at night, reading a novel, or exercising before the children are up in the morning.

PRINCIPLE 2: Help your child to see the effect of his or her behavior on others. Encourage role taking and perspective taking.

Scientists have coined the term *theory of mind* to describe the ability of a person to understand what someone else is thinking and feeling even if it is different from his or her own thoughts and feelings. This ability is not present from birth or in the first few years of life, so a 2-year-old has difficulty understanding that his mother's ideas and feelings are different from his own, for instance. Theory of mind usually develops when the child is approximately 4 years old as a result of caring interactions with parents. This cognitive ability underlies the child's growing capacity for perspective taking.

Experts now know that explaining how another person feels and putting one's self in someone else's place are helpful in building empathy.

Have the group imagine that two children are fighting. One has hurt the other, and the one who is hurt is crying. Ask the group how they might respond in order to help the aggressor understand how the other child feels.

Make sure the participants' responses include that it is important to explain that the crying child is hurt through clear comments such as, "You must not hit other children because you can see how hurt Amy is"; "If Amy hit you, how would you feel?"

Point out that it is important that they make it very clear that they are upset, unhappy, and angry about the child's insensitivity—in other words, that this is a very important issue and should not happen again. Scientists have shown that it is absolutely crucial that children learn about other peoples' perspectives, feelings, and points of view so they can feel for them and have sympathy. This kind of exploration is essential for caring behavior to be learned and internalized for the future.

PRINCIPLE 3: Encourage responsibility by having your child do chores.

An increasing number of families today tend to ignore the need to teach children responsibility. Even young children need to share responsibilities within the family. This can give them good feelings of helping and a sense of their own competence and important place in the family. One way of encouraging responsibility is to have children involved in a small way in the operating of the home by having responsibility for doing certain chores.

Distribute Handout 10.4: Examples of Suitable Chores for Different Ages.

Have parents look at the list and discuss any chores that they might have assigned to their children. Ask them if they have any ideas for additional chores not listed that they could share with the group. Have parents talk about their experiences with assigning chores. Did they go smoothly or were they difficult to implement?

Ask two parents to pair up, then have one assume the role of the parent and the other, the child. Have the "child" refuse to do his or her chore or insist that he or she has done it when it has not in fact been done. Have the parent or group leader insist that the chore is done while encouraging responsibility without shaming the child, and make the child proud for having done the chore.

It is important to promote a balance about feelings of responsibility if children do not follow rules, and to encourage this in children. In other words, responses should lead to a healthy degree of *guilt* (or an internal feeling of having done wrong), not *shame* (a feeling of worthlessness and despair about the act). When a child feels a reasonable amount of guilt, the child knows that he or she did not do the right thing but also knows that there is something he or she can do about the action. The child can make the current situation better or do it better next time. With feelings of shame, the child is left feeling flawed and diminished and that there is nothing he or she can do about it. Shame can be present in a child as young as 2 or 3 years of age, and with constant shaming the child's sense of competence and belief in his or her being lovable and acceptable can be lost.

Distribute Handout 10.5: Encouraging
Feelings of Responsibility without Shame.

Discuss Handout 10.5. Have parents think of alternative ways to give some of the negative messages they may be giving now.

PRINCIPLE 4: Expose your child to contacts with peers and teach him or her social skills and strategies for positive interactions with others.

Most children want to be around peers, but some children have difficulty making friends. It is important for children to have contacts with other children so that they can establish friendships. Children need a number of social skills to interact with others. The ability to enter a group, to join in play with others, and to keep the play going once they have joined the group are important for good peer interactions.

Distribute Handout 10.6: Helping a
Child to Enter a Group and Continue Playing.

Discuss the strategies in this handout with the parents. Point out that all children get rejected at one time or another when interacting with peers, but that children with good social skills are able to find other ways to come back and try another way to make the interactions work. Children with a history of being rejected within the home may quickly become aggressive or withdraw completely from trying to interact with their peers.

Although having their parents constantly organizing and hovering over play is not helpful in the long term, it may be necessary in the beginning to help a child who lacks social skills to experience some success in entering a group so he or she can begin to feel more positive about the experience and begin to build his or her belief in being able to have a friend.

Distribute Handout 10.7: Various Social Skills Young Children Need to Develop, and Handout 10.8: Encouraging Children's Cooperation and Sharing.

Discuss whether parents have tried any of the strategies in Handout 10.8 and how they worked for them.

For preschool children, learning to share is a difficult process and one that does not happen without a lot of coaching. This is because young children have an egocentric view of the world and often equate sharing with giving something away completely. Moreover, they cannot see that if they share a toy now, someone will share with them later.

Ask parents to discuss some of the things they do to encourage cooperation and sharing in their children.

PRINCIPLE 5: Teach conflict resolution and interpersonal negotiation skills to your child.

Being able to solve conflicts effectively is a critically important skill for family functioning. Parents can understand quite a bit about the way they deal with conflict by looking at how their own parents handled conflict when they were growing up.

Distribute Handout 10.9: How Conflict Was Solved in My Family as I Was Growing Up.

Have parents complete Handout 10.9. Discuss the strategies that were described and ask parents how they deal with conflicts in their own family now.

Conflicts occur all of the time when toddlers and preschoolers play together. Most of the time, children are able to settle the conflicts by themselves, with one child submitting to or cooperating with the other. Nevertheless, it is important for adults to teach young children conflict resolution skills. This is best done when a conflict occurs such as a fight between peers over a toy or a battle between siblings. The skills are best taught on the spot while the conflict is occurring and before the children get too worked up. Learning to resolve conflicts can involve two major strategies in which parents help children to learn 1) to process and interpret the social cues or reactions of the other child, and 2) actual conflict resolution skills.

As pointed out previously, some children continually misinterpret what other children are doing or saying as rejection or aggression. Some conflicts can be prevented or diffused by explaining to a child what another child may have actually meant. However, when a conflict cannot be avoided, some of the strategies outlined in Handout 10.10 may be helpful.

Distribute Handout 10.10: The Steps of Conflict Resolution.

Go through the steps in Handout 10.10 and describe them. Many parents will be surprised to hear how well these techniques can work with children even as young as 3 years of age.

Have two parents assume the roles of two children who are arguing or fighting over something (e.g., what channel they want to watch on television, who will get to play with a toy). Then have a group leader assume the role of the "parent" and demonstrate the steps of conflict resolution with the "children." Have a group participant play the role of parent in a different scenario if someone is willing to volunteer to do this.

OTHER DISCUSSION TOPICS

Parents may wish to discuss a number of other topics related to social competence, empathy, and caring behavior. These may include

- The effect of watching television and videotapes on empathy and caring behavior
- How to keep children safe in an unpredictable world
- What to do about bullying
- How to overcome grandiosity and self-centered behavior
- Autism spectrum disorders

These are described in more detail next.

Distribute Handout 10.11: Making the Impact of Television Positive.

The effects of television on play have already been discussed in Step 4; however, some parents in the group may wish to discuss its possible effects on their children's social interactions and capacity for caring. Research has shown that frequent watching of violent television and video games can have a causal effect by increasing aggression in children. Moreover, certain television shows that depict violence can produce a dulling effect so that cruelty or another person's pain is no longer upsetting or significant. Thus, it is important to emphasize the following to parents:

1. Television, when used appropriately, can be a useful teaching tool and can have suitable entertainment value. It can also provide good role models for children.

2. Supervision of the child's use of television and computers is critical to make sure that he or she is not bombarded with shows that depict scenes of sexuality or violence.

3. Television should not be used to replace warm social interactions and play with toys that will enhance emotional development.

Ask parents which television shows/videos/DVDs they think have a positive effect on their children and which shows have a negative effect. Discuss how the more positive shows or films might be used to teach perspective taking and empathy and caring behavior.

Keeping Children Safe in an Unpredictable World

Because a significant number of crimes are reported every day in newspapers and on television, it is clearly important to develop strategies in order to keep children safe. However, young children must learn to trust and to feel safe in the world in order to develop an inner sense of security and competence and a belief in their own ability to solve problems and manage the world. Read the following vignette, which appears with other vignettes on page 540 of *Pathway to Competence* (2002), and discuss how the mother dealt with safety issues but still allowed the child to enjoy himself in the world and other people.

> *Mary had moved with her husband from a small town where she knew everyone to a large city. At first, she felt overwhelmed and lonely, especially after her baby was born and she was home on maternity leave. At this point she decided to make a conscious effort to get to know people in the community and to make sure her son, Thomas, had other children to play with. When Thomas was a preschooler, Mary told him about and showed him many exciting things that he could do in the city. Although she taught him about how strangers could be dangerous, she also made sure he knew that not all people are bad, and that there are people close to home who can help him if he needs it.*

Protecting young children is the parents' responsibility, and expecting a child to assume that responsibility or overwhelming him or her with information about terrifying occurrences like rapes, robberies, or murders is likely to cause emotional damage. It is also important to remember that news programs can be very upsetting for children when they show scenes of terrorist attacks or natural disasters such as earthquakes, because the realism may be even more upsetting.

Distribute Handout 10.12: Keeping Children Safe.

Have parents discuss the rules for keeping children safe. Ask parents if it would be difficult for them to implement these rules in their community.

What to Do About Bullying

Bullying is not a new issue, and some of the parents may have been recipients of bullying themselves. However, recent research has indicated that bullying can have devastating effects on children and it has also provided information on the causes and interventions for dealing with bullying in schools. Researchers have identified two types of victimized children. One group is composed of children who are provoking and aggressive and a second group is made of up children who are passive and insecure. Children in the first group may act as both bullies and victims.

Distribute Handout 10.13: Helping Children Who Are Being Bullied.

If parents in the group have children who are being victimized by bullies, discuss how the suggestions in Handout 10.13 could be used to help the victimized children.

Some parents may have been bullied as children. What did their parents say or do when this happened?

Overcoming Grandiosity and Self-Centered Behavior

Some children after the age of 4 continue to show types of behavior that are typical of much younger children. They have a very self-centered view of the world and have little interest in the perspective of others. They may also have a sense of grandiosity that is quite fragile and easily deflated if things do not go as expected. This can occur whenever they find that they cannot control others or are unable to achieve a skill they wish to perform. These children antagonize both children and adults alike, often becoming very isolated, unpopular, and lonely children. Have parents discuss why this may occur.

In the discussion, make sure that it is brought up that parents need to be in control and to provide adequate limits. On the one hand, children who are never given limits or taught to respect others will continue to believe that they are all powerful and can do anything. On the other hand, although limits are essential, a child should not be made to lose all of the battles and should be given the sense that he or she is cared about and noticed for efforts toward showing concern and caring behavior. Encourage the child to have perspective taking and to understand the thoughts and feelings of others.

Distribute Handout 10.14: Strategies for Helping Children to Overcome Grandiosity and Self-Centered Behavior.

Discuss the suggestions in Handout 10.14 with the parents.

Autism Spectrum Disorders

Parents who are very concerned about their child's lack of social competence and caring behavior may fear that their child has an autism spectrum disorder. More information on autism spectrum disorder is given in *Pathways to Competence* (2002), pages 543–544. Unless parents have a particular interest in this spectrum, a brief description of it would be all that is necessary given the scope of this program. An explanation that there is a broad range of characteristics on this spectrum is important because the term is alarming for parents who have only seen people depicted in the media, usually falling on the most extreme end of the spectrum. Many children—even those who are eventually diagnosed as falling on this spectrum—who receive appropriate interventions can learn to socialize to some degree, attend general education classes, and live relatively normal lives.

THE TREE

As you near the end of this Step, ask parents to write the principles on a piece of cardboard and to stick them on the tree under one of the roles of parenting at the bottom of the tree. It may be helpful to review how the principles fall under the different roles of parenting. Have parents discuss their success with using the various principles and if they have found that their comfort level with the four roles of parenting has shifted in any way.

HOMEWORK

Distribute Handout 10.15: Homework.

If this is the last week, homework should not be assigned, although parents may wish to try one of the activities on their own. If Step 10 takes 2 weeks, homework can be given after the first week. Distribute Handout 10.15 and describe the homework activities. Have parents choose one of the activities and do the self-care activity.

1. Assign your child a chore this week. Use the chart in Handout 10.4 to make sure that it is an age-appropriate task. Report next week on how this went. Did your child enjoy helping you? Did you need to give him or her extra support to complete the task?

or

2. Support your child to try hard when he or she is learning something. Let the child know that several attempts may be necessary to get something right.

or

3. Sit with your child on one or two occasions during the week while he or she watches television. Use the suggestions in Handout 10.11. Help describe the perspectives and feelings of the characters in the show to your child. Emphasize the prosocial messages and teach about self-control.

Self-Care Activity

Have parents draw the name of another parent in the group. Ask them to bring a small gift next week for the parent whose name they drew. This could be something from a dollar store that would be meaningful for the person or a homemade item (e.g., a baked good, a craft). Alternatively, instead of buying or making something, ask parents to try writing something they have appreciated about the person during the group on a card and give it to him or her the following week. If parents have a self-care box, be sure they take it home this week and use the materials to help them continue to relieve the stresses of parenting and in other areas of their lives into the future.

EVALUATION

Congratulations! You have now completed the program. Congratulate the parents as well, and hand out copies of the Parent Satisfaction Form found in Section III: Supplemental Materials. Be sure to answer parents' questions about how the evaluation results will be used. Have each parent fill the form out and return it to you.

Other topics that parents may wish to discuss include

*   Follow-up meetings

*   Possible referrals for further services for their child and themselves

*   Questions about any of the earlier topics

*   Further resources such as books, videos, and DVDs about parenting

Certificate of Completion

Parents like to receive something that shows they have completed the program. If you wish, you can copy and distribute a certificate such as the one provided in the Supplemental Materials or you can make your own. Be sure to thank all of the parents for attending and allow them time to exchange telephone and e-mail addresses, if they wish.

SECTION III

SUPPLEMENTAL MATERIALS

CONTENTS

Pathways to Competence for Young Children Parenting Program

Join a Parenting Group

for Parents of

Young Children with

_____
(e.g., aggression, noncompliance, emotional)

Problems

Learn Strategies for Improving
Your Child's Behavior

Presented by _____ (Agency)

The facts about aggression and noncompliance in young children

- Approximately 25% of parents of young children report that their children act aggressively.
- A similar percentage of teachers report that children entering school have problems with aggression that can make these children's behavior difficult to manage.
- Almost half of all young children with aggression will continue to have problems as they get older.
- Intervening early can help avoid later problems.
- Although the reasons behind aggression and noncompliance in children are numerous, there are ways to intervene that make a difference.

Who should attend this Pathways to Competence for Young Children Parenting Program?

Parents and other caregivers of young children experiencing problems with aggression and noncompliance, including but not limited to the following behaviors:

- Hitting, biting, scratching, and throwing things when frustrated or disciplined
- Refusing to follow requests
- Being cruel to others and lacking empathy for the needs and concerns of others
- Hurting animals for no particular reason
- Answering back or swearing
- Destroying toys or other property
- Deliberately annoying people

Description of the groups

The groups will follow the format of an established program, the Pathways to Competence for Young Children Parenting program. The program has proved to be successful in improving child behavior. You will

- Learn about early child development and the capacities your child needs to develop in order to overcome difficulties and foster positive behavior and self-esteem.
- Discover the reasons children act in these ways.
- Gain an understanding of your child that can help you decide on optimal ways to react to him or her.
- Find out about practical parenting ideas you can use to help improve your child's behavior.
- Have the opportunity to meet with parents whose children are having similar difficulties.

Group meetings

The groups will meet for a total of _____ weeks beginning on _____.

They will be held on _____ evenings at _____ p.m.

The sessions will last for approximately 2 hours each.

Staff involved

The meetings will be led by the staff of _____.

Costs

The program is free and materials will be provided.

Enrollment

Space is limited, so register early.

Refreshments

Refreshments will be provided during the parenting group sessions.

Child care

Child care will be made available for parents registered in the parenting program at no extra cost.

Location

The parenting sessions will be held at _____

Address: _____

Our philosophy

Each weekly session builds on the prior session. We would appreciate your commitment for the _____ week session should you choose to register.

How to register

Please complete the enclosed registration form. Submit the form to
_____

If you would like more information about the Pathways to Competence for Young Children Parenting Program, please leave a message at: _____ (telephone number)

You will be contacted by the parenting group leaders regarding availability before the first session.

Pathways to Competence for Young Children Parenting Program

Dates: _____

Number of sessions: _____

Day of the week: _____

Parents will have the opportunity to:

- Learn about child development
- Develop parenting skills for interacting with their infants and young children
- Learn ways to encourage positive behavior and self-esteem in their children and to overcome any behavioral difficulties their children may be experiencing
- Meet and share joys and concerns with other parents with young children

The course and child care are free.

Space is limited.

For more information or to register, call_____

Pathways to Competence for Young Children
Parenting Program

Registration Form

Today's date (day/month/year): _____

Parent's/caregiver's last name: _____

Parent's/caregiver's first name: _____

Relationship to child: _____

Child's last name: _____

Child's first name: _____

Child's date of birth (day/month/year): _____

Child's sex: _____ M _____ F

Child's address: Parent's address (if different):

_____   _____

_____   _____

_____   _____

Postal/ZIP code: _____   Postal/ZIP code: _____

Home telephone number: _____

Cell (mobile) telephone number: _____

Work telephone number: _____

Family doctor: _____

Telephone number: _____

Parent Consent for Child Care

Name of child: _____ Child's age: _____

Please check each item:

_____ I need child care in order to participate.

_____ I understand that child care is not a treatment program.

_____ I understand that during the sessions, children will participate in fun activities.

_____ I understand that if my child is having any difficulties, I will be called in.

_____ I understand that there is no cost to me for this child care.

Parent/caregiver signature: _____

Relationship to child: _____

Date: _____

Parent Consent for Child Care

Name of child: _____ Child's age: _____

Please check each item:

_____ I need child care in order to participate.

_____ I understand that child care is not a treatment program.

_____ I understand that during the sessions, children will participate in fun activities.

_____ I understand that if my child is having any difficulties, I will be called in.

_____ I understand that there is no cost to me for this child care.

Parent/caregiver signature: _____

Relationship to child: _____

Date: _____

Child Care Questionnaire for Parents

Name of child: _____ Date of birth: _____

For the following questions, circle yes or no for each:

Do you give permission for a name tag to be placed on your child's back?   Yes   No

Does your child have any allergies that we should be aware of?   Yes   No

    If Yes, explain: _____

_____

Does your child have any diet restrictions?   Yes   No

    If Yes, explain: _____

_____

Can we give him or her snacks such as crackers and juice?   Yes   No

If your child needs diapering, do you prefer that we (circle one):

    Come get you

    Wait for the break

    Change him or her ourselves (if so, please provide diapers)

Are there any special ways to keep your child happy if he or she becomes upset?

_____

_____

_____

_____

Weeks your child will be attending (circle those that apply):

1	2	3	4	5	6	7	8	9	10
11	12	13	14	15	16	17	18	19	20

Pathways to Competence for Young Children: A Parenting Program, by Sarah Landy and Elizabeth Thompson. Copyright © 2006 by Paul H. Brookes Publishing Co., Inc. All rights reserved.

Attendance Sheet

Write each group participant's name in the left-hand column. Enter dates of the sessions for the group across the top row. Each week, check off each participant's attendance and enter the totals at the bottom.

Parent/caregiver name	Dates																			
Total attended																				

{The Tree (blank model)}

The Tree

| Body control and positive body image | Secure attachment | Play and imagination | Language and communication | Positive self-esteem | Self-regulation, morality, and a sense of conscience | Emotion regulation | Concentration, planning, and problem solving | Social competence, empathy, and caring behavior |

In the United States, "trees" can be found at most teacher supply stores. In Canada, these trees are available at Scholar's Choice Retail Stores. Of course it is possible to create your own tree if your artistic skills permit, or you may use this one. Feel free to photocopy it and enlarge or reduce it and the accompanying labels to suit your needs. If you draw your own model, you may need to draw a large-enough version of the tree to accommodate the size and number of labels you will need to place on it. Laminate the tree, principles, roles, and other labels for ease of use and reuse.

[The Tree (sample)]

The Tree

Nurturer	Playmate	Limit Setter	Teacher
(Principle)	(Principle)	(Principle)	(Principle)

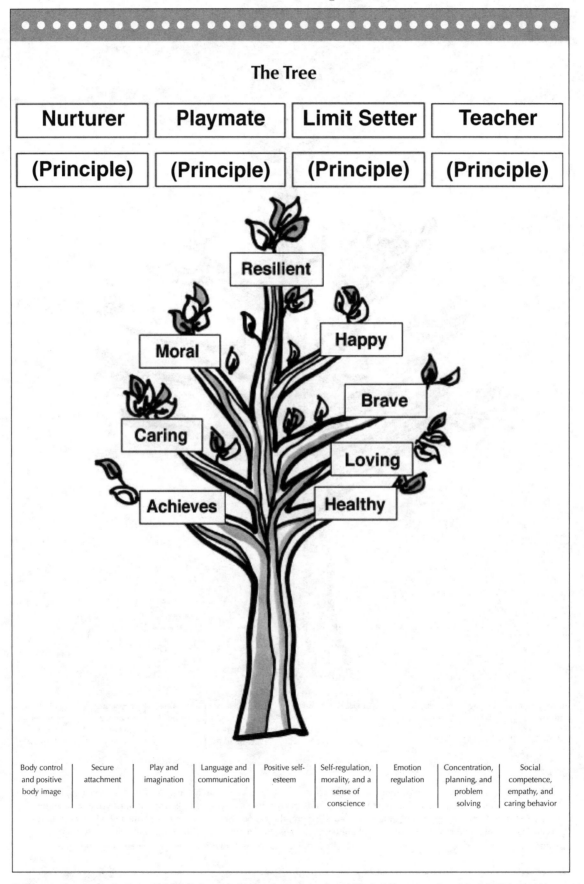

Resilient

Moral

Happy

Brave

Caring

Loving

Achieves

Healthy

Body control and positive body image	Secure attachment	Play and imagination	Language and communication	Positive self-esteem	Self-regulation, morality, and a sense of conscience	Emotion regulation	Concentration, planning, and problem solving	Social competence, empathy, and caring behavior

Cards for Parenting Roles

Laminate and use the following cards (enlarging or reducing as needed) when asked to discuss parental roles. They can be applied to the tree as needed.

Teacher

Nurturer

Playmate

Limit Setter

Parent Satisfaction Form

Which parts of the group did you find most useful? Check all that apply.

_____ Talking about how I was parented as I was growing up

_____ Group exercises

_____ Self-care exercises

_____ Principles of parenting

_____ Information on my child's development

_____ Discussion with other parents

_____ Support provided by group leaders

_____ Gaining better understanding of how my child thinks and why he or she does certain things

_____ Increasing my sense of competence as a parent

_____ Learning strategies to use with my child to encourage his or her development

_____ Learning strategies to use with my child to deal with negative behavior

_____ Homework activities

_____ Other (please specify) _____

_____

_____

Please rate in order of preference from 1 to 10.

The steps I found the most useful were

_____ Step 1: Introduction and Understanding Development and Temperament

_____ Step 2: Developing Body Control and a Positive Body Image

_____ Step 3: Developing a Secure Attachment

_____ Step 4: Encouraging Play and Imagination

_____ Step 5: Encouraging Language and Communication

_____ Step 6: Laying a Foundation for Positive Self-Esteem

_____ Step 7: Encouraging Self-Regulation, Morality, and a Sense of Conscience

_____ Step 8: Encouraging Emotion Regulation

_____ Step 9: Encouraging Concentration, Planning, and Problem Solving

_____ Step 10: Encouraging Social Competence, Empathy, and Caring Behavior

Please check the answer that most closely represents your opinion of the following:

How did you find the length of the group?

Number of sessions

_____ Too many   _____ Not enough   _____ Just right

Length of sessions

_____ Too long   _____ Too short   _____ Just right

Would you recommend the group to a friend?

_____ Yes   _____ No

What suggestions do you have to improve the groups?

_____

_____

_____

Certificate of Completion

This is to certify that

_____

has successfully completed a

Pathways to Competence for Young Children
Parenting Program

_____
(Instructor)

_____
(Date)